W9-CDA-812

THE ROMANOVS

The Romanovs

*Three Centuries of
an ill-fated Dynasty*

E. M. ALMEDINGEN

Holt, Rinehart and Winston

NEW YORK   CHICAGO   SAN FRANCISCO

80350-0116

Printed in the United States of America

CONTENTS

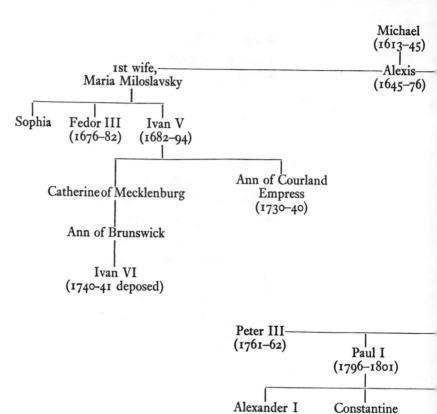

Michael
(1613–45)

Alexis—
(1645–76)

1st wife,————————————
Maria Miloslavsky

Sophia   Fedor III   Ivan V
          (1676–82)   (1682–94)

Catherine of Mecklenburg   Ann of Courland
                                Empress
                                (1730–40)

Ann of Brunswick

Ivan VI
(1740-41 deposed)

Peter III—————————
(1761–62)   Paul I
                 (1796–1801)

Alexander I   Constantine
(1801–25)   Tsarevich
                 (Viceroy of Poland)

DYNASTY

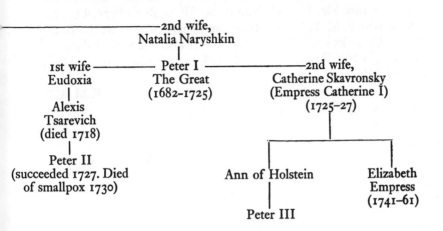

```
                                    ─2nd wife,
                                  Natalia Naryshkin
                                        │
      1st wife ──────────── Peter I ───────────────2nd wife,
       Eudoxia                The Great          Catherine Skavronsky
         │                   (1682-1725)         (Empress Catherine I)
       Alexis                                        (1725-27)
      Tsarevich                                          │
      (died 1718)                         ┌──────────────┴──────────┐
         │                                │                         │
      Peter II                       Ann of Holstein          Elizabeth
(succeeded 1727. Died                     │                    Empress
 of smallpox 1730)                    Peter III               (1741-61)
```

─Catherine the Great
  Empress (1762–96)


```
        │
     Nicholas I
     (1825-55)
        │
    Alexander II
     (1855-81
    assassinated)
        │
    Alexander III
     (1881-94)
        │
     Nicholas II
    (1894-1917)
   (forced to abdicate,
  and later assassinated
   with all his family)
        │
      Alexis
     Tsarevich
```

ACKNOWLEDGMENTS

I gratefully acknowledge all the help given me during many months of research by Mr. J. S. G. Simmons, All Souls College, Oxford, and by Miss F. M. Pilkington to whom in particular I owe the Index and the Genealogical Table. My thanks are also due to the Librarian, Public Library, Wells, Somerset, and to the Librarian, R.U.C., Central Library, London.

E. M. A.

To
Miss A. Pickles
with much gratitude

PREFACE

IT WAS said by Gregorovius that no true history of the Western Church could ever be written since neither Catholic nor Protestant authors could achieve impartiality when presenting the landscape as they saw it. Such a statement may be sweeping when regarded in its entirety. None the less, some of its aspects may well be applied to other branches of History.

Adam Olearius was certainly not an ecclesiastical historian, but his experience in Muscovy must have made it plain to him that it was a country where the best-trained observant faculty could not always succeed in reaching the heart of the matter. The true *res Muscovita* was not allowed to become *res publica* to its own people, and how could a casual foreign visitor hope to learn of the secret? Many rooms of the national house were not only curtained but padlocked against the least stir of outside curiosity, however legitimate the impulse. The gigantic devastation, which preceded the beginnings of the Romanov dynasty, was mourned for more than reasons of national economy. Those chaotic years might be likened to so many predatory hands which tore one veil after another off the nation's cherished mysteries and enabled the detested foreigner to wander at will through the nation's sanctuaries. Their truths were supposed to be safely hidden from all alien comprehension. None the less, the foreigners' mere presence could not but violate the immemorial purity and brush against the mystery which even true-bred Muscovites dared not meddle with. The world entered by the first Romanov sovereign was a world of sharp disillusionment, darkly coloured by the necessity of having to re-clothe ancient values into new and unfamiliar dress. It was also a world where shame, anger and a sense of lostness were neighboured by a stupendous challenge.

The sources dealing with that period are largely based on ideas which must be re-interpreted today not so much because of factual inaccuracies as because of a biased approach and a certain adroitness in jettisoning details not quite in accord with the national honour. There was much unwarranted intrusion of the alien. Equally, there was much treason from within and, as will be seen later, Michael Romanov's father suggests a Muscovy-bred Vicar of Bray.

Be it said at once that a certain aspect of historiography was not allowed to run an unhampered course before the October Constitution of 1905 or even before 1917. Censors watched jealously over the handling of dynastic matters. Bilbassov's monumental work on Catherine the Great could neither be published in Russia nor kept in Russian libraries. Schilder was compelled to repeat the fable about the Emperor Paul I dying of a stroke. Alexander II's long liaison with Catherine Dolgoruka might never have existed for all the mention it gets in the nineteenth-century sources. On a certain day in December 1916, the *Novoye Vremia*, when reporting a session of the Duma, referred to 'a bombshell of a report which electrified' the whole assembly, the only permissible reference to Rasputin's killing. The ancient Muscovite tenet that the Tsar and all his doings, being sacrosanct, must stand above the least criticism did not really die out until March 1917. The comparative liberty afforded to the printed word by the 1905 Constitution was a bird with badly clipped wings.

But old Russia, however closely involved with the fortunes of its dynasty, was immeasurably more than a dynasty, and Russian historians of the past were not debarred from accepting the primary law of history as defined by Cicero: '*Quis nescit, primam esse historiae legem, nequid falsi dicere audeat? deinde nequid vere non audeat? . . .*' and also by Pliny the Younger '*nam nec historia debet egredi veritatem, et honeste factis veritas sufficit*'.

Imperial censorship concerned itself with the suppression of facts likely to prejudice the honour of the monarchy. It did not go much further. It certainly did not impose distortions of proved facts, or force a particular point of view upon the scholar. And even in dynastic matters, it allowed a certain latitude for reasons of pure chronology. If, in 1900, you could not be frank about Alexander II's love affairs, you were at perfect liberty to deal with the decidedly shady origins of Catherine I, Peter the Great's second wife, who died in 1727. Above all, away from the glitter of the throne, it was possible to tell the story of men and women and of the society they lived in. Whatever the limitations imposed by the imperial censorship, History, as a discipline, moved and breathed, attained shape and colour, and historians never forgot the living quality of the material they used. Karamzin's deductions are certainly archaic today. Karamzin's people, however odd the clothing he gave them, remain men and women and not so many colourless dots scattered up and down an immense sociological map.

The late George Orwell has certainly been proved right in one particular. To judge by the educational methods, the textbooks, and books for the use of an advanced scholar, history in USSR seems to have sunk to the level of a handmaiden of the Marxist '*Diktat*'. That anything concerning the vanished dynasty should be subjected to most rigorous censorship is but a detail – which, ironically enough, echoes the old Imperial policy. But the present day censorship is not satisfied with the suppression of facts. Those must be altered – sometimes out of all recognition – so that yesterday's political drift vanishes completely under the layer of today's reappraisal of facts which at times are too simple to admit of such interpretation. Two out of the three Kremlin 'tsars' having fallen from grace, the story of Stalin's and Khrushchev's reigns must now be rewritten from end to end. Students of the future will certainly be faced with a dilemma affording no easy solution. '*Quid est veritas?*' asked Pilate, and heard no answer. '*Quid est Historia apud Russos?*' we may well ask, and a reply would not be long in coming: 'A tool in an ideologist's hands.'

The late Professor's Pokrovsky's *History of Russia from the earliest Times* can be taken to illustrate the point. It is a work of immense and honest erudition, however marred towards the end by the insertion of unsubstantiated stories about the private lives of the last Romanovs, so many crude vignettes of backstairs gossip, most painfully out of place in a work of indubitable scholarship.

None the less, erudition apart, is Pokrovsky's work truly historical? Pliny the Younger's words still stand today – '*nam nec historia debet egredi veritatem . . .*' Pokrovsky's book is brilliantly written, and style does count for much in the writing of history. We can still spare some time for Macaulay and Froude. Their judgments sometimes provoke a smile. Their mastery of English still weaves its spell.

Oddly enough, Pokrovsky's impeccable style carries no such redeeming chrism. He is Marxist before he is historian, and he seldom misses an opportunity to remind us of his allegiance. His work deals with masses and masses alone. Taken in its entirety, it suggests a gigantic landscape of lines curving up and down, a most painstakingly executed graph, the very excellence of its execution as chilly as a slab of marble. Pokrovsky's masses are serried so closely that it is difficult to tell face from face. No room is left for untrammelled movement or individual expansion, no opportunity to pause and assess the value of strictly individual accomplishment – divorced from its probable 'sociological' merit. The shades of the landscape vary from pale grey to dark grey, all telling colours being sternly excluded. A group wanders about, decides to settle down, finds occupation, chooses its social pattern, abides by it, revolts against it, and chooses another, the choice being invariably communal, never individual. Man is wholly absorbed by the group, its hungers, necessities and ambitions. Man's identity is entombed within the pattern adopted by the group, and the latter is a model in little of the state to come into being some day. The state would betray itself if it spared the least effort to reckon with an individual apart from the mass.

The image evoked by Pokrovsky is by no means devoid of a strangely persuasive compulsion, its root lying in the undoubted advantage of dumb assent over vocal dissent. Assent on some such scale certainly ensures a measure of comfort. Even more than that: assent promises that truly diabolical freedom from responsibility which is accorded by patterned herdishness, a freedom which no individual dare accept without running the risk of an ultimate betrayal of soul and mind.

Pokrovsky's image is not static. The landscape shifts continually from one social change to another, from one imperative to another. But it is always the masses held together, responding to communal needs and communal desires, and controlled by a communal imperative. Every stage of the development is floodlit, as it were. There is no room for either mystery or wonder, still less for the sustaining warmth of dreams. The least detail of the development is explained by the iron stresses of a sociology which, deeply and honestly concerned with the well-being and the progress of a group, does not care a tattered shoelace for an individual. In the final reckoning, for all the compulsion it carries, it remains a false image glaringly out of alignment not only with a sanely balanced interpretation of facts but with the facts themselves. To cite but one particular example: from Pokrovsky's point of view, the Stenka Razin rebellion during the reign of Alexis, the second Romanov Tsar, in the seventeenth century, and the Pougachev Mutiny under Catherine the Great are no more and no less than twin expressions of the masses' awakening hunger for liberty and recognition. There is no need to be an advocate of the Romanov cause to prove the very opposite reason behind both outbreaks. Stenka Razin and Emelian Pougachev were adventurers. Neither of them had anything to lose and both were carried away by the prospect of ultimate personal grandeur to fall to their lot if they were victorious. Pougachev for one, clung to his pseudo-imperial origins up to the very moment of his capture. If they promised freedom and the easing of burdens to the masses in their wake, that was done from no other motive than the wish of winning more and more adherents to a purely personal cause. The hordes which followed Razin and Pougachev were a faceless mob, plundering and killing its main and immediate objective, not the remote prospect of civic liberties.

The idea that at certain moments the stresses of history are at one with great poetry would have been dismissed as heresy by Pokrovsky. The influence of creative thought, divorced from the demands of a sociological covenant, is made to appear in the light of a futile daydream. The moral value of Alexander Nevsky's victory over the Swedes in the thirteenth century, Dimitry Donskoy's mood on the eve of the Kulikovo battle in 1380, a mood so richly interpreted by Blok, Alexander I's link with the entire nation in 1812, all those and many more get no mention at all in Pokrovsky's *History*. The omission is understandable. A nation's finest moments are born of an element not to be found in the Marxist gospel: the element of the spirit.

In some such way the diamond-bright style fails to redeem the grandiose conception. All unplanned striving, wild hope, desire, anguish and achievement are here reduced to the unalive terms of a strictly patterned sociological development. What can any historian make of an interpretation of the past where the individual *esse* is engulfed in the mass? And more. It is never enough to read a source. It is imperative to listen to it and to allow it the liberty of speaking in its own accents. However dry the latter, they never close the door on the healthy interpretative urge. The livingness of history depends not on herd-like movements of a group but on man, his shame and glory together, his futility and achievement and, finally, on his frequently uncharted quest for truths not to be proved by sociologists and statisticians but guessed at by musicians and mathematicians. Certainly, ideologies should be given their place in the great tapestry since their development and duration are part of history. But to make the latter subservient to any ideological creed is as unnatural as to expect walnuts to grow on an apple-tree. History ceases to exist and ideology becomes a butt for mockery.

I

The World They Entered

IN THE present book, an endeavour has been made to tell the story of one of the most tragic dynasties in the European record. Its sins were many and grievous, and its mistakes all too frequently bordered on absurdity. Both the sins and the mistakes are almost greedily remembered today, and some of them have been exaggerated. Its virtues, today almost wholly forgotten, were not as few as has been imagined. All in all, beginning with Michael Romanov in 1613 and ending with Nicholas II in 1917, the House of the Romanovs was neither wholly angelic nor wholly diabolical. They had an immense country to rule, and they were convinced of the divine bestowal of their autocracy because of their anointment. The idea that the coronation *fitted* the sovereign for the throne has now been discarded in most countries. In the past it was accepted all over Europe. The Russian form of the service suggested first and foremost a solemn threshold which – once crossed – enabled the participant to carry both the honour and the burden of the high office. All through the long service, God, the Tsar and the nation stood, as it were, shoulder to shoulder. The Tsar's power came from God and to God alone he was responsible for its use or misuse. Millions of Russians, whatever their indifference to the basic monarchist idea or to the person of the sovereign, knew well the meaning of the coronation.

The Romanovs were not all lazy, cruel, or immoral. Few among them went to their graves without having left some trace of their care for the millions committed to their care, and that care was plinthed in their regard for the individual soul.

For all their frequent moral lapses, their faith in God forbade them to forget that soul. However archaic the expression of that faith may seem to us, to them it mirrored the truth. The early Tsars were almost continually in attendance on the heavenly hierarchy and the business of governing was interwoven with the business of the Church. They ordered their year in strict accordance with the memorials left by the Lord, the Lord's Mother and the company of saints. The Tsars' work and leisure, their clothes and food, even their gait and demeanour were all patterned in conformity to what they believed to be God's will for them. Their wives never shared their board, and could share their bed only on such nights as were sanctioned by the church ordinance. The season of Lent and of all the lesser fasts enjoined continence. So did all the great feasts since their honour would have been polluted by sexual intercourse. The rigour practised in the seventeenth century had not altogether vanished in the twentieth. Within the author's memory, pious Orthodox people were apt to frown on anyone's birthday falling upon Christmas Day since it implied conception on the feast of Annunciation.

The eighteenth century saw the disappearance of many among those outward forms, and their going was as inevitable as the passing of seasons. Yet all those forms had a deep inner content and the compulsion behind the complicated and often incomprehensible ritual was not born of the flesh. The outward mould came to be shaped by custom and tradition together, and custom in particular could date the mould, distort its original purpose, deaden its colours and, finally, commit it to a fate of indifference, cynicism and total rejection. But the compulsion behind the outward form retained its hold. It was a breath and a challenge, not an attitude of the mind or a mechanical allegiance to custom, but a living thing and a continuous response to a reality never comprehended by the senses. It certainly carried no atonement for many misdeeds. If anything, it deepened them and left them naked to a judgment far more severe than it would have been in the case of a materialist's transgression.

It is within some such framework that the chronicle of the Romanov dynasty is here to be unfolded, a colourful, compelling and frequently violent story of eighteen men and women who all bore the sovereign title, though two among them, Ivan VI and Peter III, never came to their crowning. The chronicle will also include the story of a remarkable woman, Tsarevna Sophia, Tsar Alexis's daughter and half-sister of Peter the Great, for whom she acted as regent during his long minority. Sophia's ethical standards were not particularly high, but her statesmanship deserved well of her country. It came to be eclipsed – most unjustly – by her brother's place in history and legend.

More will be said later on about the origins of the Romanov family. Their sovereignty starts in 1613. Michael, aged sixteen, came to the throne in the wake of a tempest which had ravaged the country for several years before his election. That tempest, its causes far more complicated than any dynastic tangle, might well have changed the face of Eastern Europe if it had ended in any other way.

The period is known as '*Smútnoe Vrémia*', i.e. 'The Troubled Time' but the word '*smútnoe*' carries more meanings than one. It is something of a fog-born word and it suggests a fog-bound landscape, though the comparison answers in part only. The milky-grey curtain grows thin here and there so that several details of the chaos stand out with a shattering clarity – red-stippled battlefields, devastated towns, burnt-down villages and plundered manors, with alien hordes plunging deeper and deeper into the heart of the country. The landscape is peopled by thousands upon thousands of dispossessed and unanchored men, women and children too, the last flicker of mental and physical direction gone out of them. There is nothing except thickly wooded spaces to offer protection. There is no fire on the broken hearth, no roof to shield from snow or rain, no corn in the barn, no bolt to the door to keep the enemy out.

Most of those wanderers, driven this way and that way by panic and hunger, had no idea whether there was a Tsar in Moscow or not. The fear of the supernatural, a legacy from a heathen past, never wholly eradicated by Christianity, kept adding to the day's burdens. The people, unaware of any trespass by them committed, were none the less conscious of the gods' anger falling upon them, and the consciousness increased the sense of lostness to the un-regarded masses of common folk, for whom rivers, fields and woods were still peopled by gods and goddesses, a few among them sup-posed to be kindly, but the majority known to take pleasure in active malevolence. Behind it all was the fear that the alien had not come merely to pillage and to destroy but to stay, to force his hate-ful otherness on the national faith, custom and preference.

In loose terms, '*smútnoe vrémia*' of one kind or another is seldom absent from the scrolls of Russian history. More narrowly and much more violently, the ferment thickened during the second half of the reign of Ivan the Terrible. The Tsar's specially chosen bodyguard, the infamous *oprýchniki*, ruled the land under him. All those men were upstarts, with no roots of their own, and they did not shrink from any brutal tasks commanded by Ivan. One by one, members of the ancient aristocracy fell victim to the stake and the gibbet. Having ordered their execution, the Tsar entered their names into a special 'memorial' book and prayed for their souls. Ivan feared treason far more than he feared his Maker, and he was persuaded that the *oprýchniki* alone could protect him against a sword thrust or a cup of poisoned wine. Genuine and fabled conspiracies hung thick in the air. Certainly, Ivan had good cause to mistrust the old nobility. He little knew what the formation of a new aristocracy, who had neither roots nor tradition nor yet conscience to sustain their rapid advancement, would mean to the country one day.

The terror created by Ivan killed many people; it also served to quicken many dormant energies. Prince Andrey Kurbsky was but one of a great company to seek shelter under an enemy aegis. Little by little, cells of discontent were being formed, dispossession and persecution of the Tsar's *oprýchniki* serving for so many paving-stones along the way. During the reign of Fedor, Ivan's son and the last ruler of the Rurik dynasty, such cells took to growing most alarmingly to the south and the west of Moscow. The *oprýchniki* were gone with the death of their founder but the climate they had created did not vanish. Discontent and more than discontent brooded over the country.

And all of it was formless. Even at the death of Tsar Fedor in 1598 there was no organized protest against the ghastly conditions of life in the country. There were waves of sporadic discontent, occasionally breaking out in violence here and there, outbreaks by peasants, by the turbulent Cossacks along the banks of the Don and the Dnieper, and by those who had fled the country from the wrath of Ivan the Terrible.

Conditions in the interior of Muscovy were virtually unknown in the West, always with the exception of Poland, Russia's immemorial enemy and at the time the most powerful Slav country. Allied to the West by cultural links and by a common faith, Poland considered Muscovy a barbarian country. Towards the end of the sixteenth century, Polish statesmen began nursing the idea of a Slav union – with Muscovy as a cowed and voiceless satellite of Poland. But the Poles waited for a propitious moment; their ambassadors to Western powers kept their counsel and their residents in Moscow kept most prudently taciturn about the matter. But Polish money and Polish promises of a millennium were already beginning to penetrate the ranks of the Muscovite malcontents along the south-western borders of the country.

Meanwhile, the terrible Tsar having gone to his judgment, his son Fedor succeeded him. The fourteen years of Fedor's reign would have been so many pallid streaks in the country's history if it had not been for the Tsar's closest and most trusted counsellor and brother-in-law, Boris Godunov, who governed Moscow in the Tsar's name. Boris puzzled and irritated his contemporaries and angered posterity. In the final reckoning, all his contradictions considered, he remains somewhat enigmatic to this day.

Born about 1551, Boris was of Tartar stock. A fortunate chance carried him into the neighbourhood of Ivan's court. The Tsar recognized the young man's ability, but Ivan, though extending many favours, remained cautious, and not until Fedor's accession in 1584 was Boris able to prove himself in the Council chamber. For all the persecutions of the terrible Tsar, there were still some remnants of the ancient nobility in the Boyar Duma, and they would have none of Ivan's favourites at the Kremlin. None the less, Boris succeeded in keeping his foothold. And far more than that: he began proving the brilliance of his gifts until the most conservative among the Boyars were compelled to admit that 'the Tartar upstart' possessed prudence and foresight in no common measure. Boris's policy towards Sweden and the Crimean Tartars came to be fully justified by Muscovy's successes on both fronts. It was the policy of a diplomat rather than that of a war leader. 'We wish you no harm,' he said to the King of Sweden and to the Crimean Khan, 'and we threaten nobody, yet if you threaten us, you might come to your hurt. Peace is far more profitable than war – so we think.' All of it was said in the august name of Tsar Fedor, his innumerable titles affixed to every document, the same Tsar Fedor, who, piously following the Vespers for the feast of Our Lady of Riazan, would not have greatly cared if a Swedish army or a Tartar horde were to appear at the gates of Moscow. Fedor could not govern; the Boyar

Duma, the hierarchy, the military and, in fact, the entire populace of
Moscow knew it. But under Boris's guidance a semblance of peace
stole over the tired country. A great many magnates, earlier exiled
by Ivan the Terrible, came back to the capital, and hoped for a
chance to mend their broken fortunes. Tsar Fedor received them
kindly enough, but his graciousness did not fill the empty purses.
The returned exiles waited upon the Tsar's brother-in-law, whose
manner neither heartened nor discouraged them. 'I follow the Tsar's
majesty in all things,' was his reply. Almost inevitably factions
began forming in Moscow, and the uncertainty of succession lent
sharpness to the day's climate. The sickly Tsar was the last Ruri-
kovich living, and his Tsarina, Boris's sister, had not borne a single
son. Voices were raised that it was time for the Tsar to put Tsarina
Irina into a nunnery, marry another girl, and beget sons. It is doubtful if any of those voices ever reached Tsar Fedor.

Boris kept aloof from all court intrigues. The language of descent
said nothing to him. He performed the Tsar's business for him but
he never wearied Fedor with trivial complaints about slights and
insults he, Boris, received at the hands of ancient nobility. All those
were such small-meshed intrigues in his eyes, and none of them
damaged his standing at the Kremlin.

Arrogant, sometimes contemptuous in his dealings with old aristocracy, whose pedigrees stretched back for some seven centuries,
Boris looked for and found support elsewhere – among the military,
the merchantry and the humble urban fry. To them all the Tsar
remained beyond access by custom and tradition, but Boris was no
Tsar—only the chief counsellor, wielding an authority all the
mightier for the absence of any formal definitions. He could afford
to move freely among the people, and he did so. The Boyars
accused Boris of diabolical pride, but the common folk came to see
him as '*láskovy*', 'an amiable man'. Into a world pillared on the
twin foundations of theocracy and autocracy, Boris Godunov seems
to have brought the very first democratic breaths.

In 1597 Tsar Fedor's health worsened sharply. Intrigues about
succession became the order of the day. There were four main
factions. Nikita Romanov, Ivan the Terrible's brother-in-law,
headed a movement which stood for a closer rapprochement with
the West, and Nikita's adherents toyed with the name of a Romanov
as a successor to Fedor. But Nikita Romanov, though connected

with the old dynasty by marriage, was not of Rurik descent. The ancient rights and all they implied were championed by Prince Ivan Shouysky and Prince Ivan Miloslavsky, their respective pedigrees going back to the ninth century. The two men should have worked together for a common end, but jealousy dug a deep gulf between them. A third faction was led by Prince Bielsky, a creature of Ivan the Terrible, who had succeeded in winning the confidence of civil servants. Finally, as was to be expected, there was Boris's own party – but he did not head it. It very much looked as though a minor war for the Monomach cap would be declared on Fedor's death.

One day in February 1598, all the belfries in Moscow began tolling, and unease bit deep into the people. For some time Fedor had been beyond forming decisions and he had died, his successor unnamed. The throne became vacant at one of the most critical moments of the century. Threats of an imminent invasion from Sweden and Poland were in the air. Boris had had to send troops to the west to fortify Smolensk against the Polish attack and to Pskov in the north when the Swedish menace could no longer be ignored. The military formed the core of Boris's supporters and he could ill spare so many regiments away from Moscow, but there was no choice for him.

The end of the dynasty which had ruled for seven hundred and thirty-six years inevitably meant the end of an epoch. To the Muscovite mind it also stood for a sign of God's anger. Not for nothing, said the common folk, had the Almighty God denied male children to Tsar Fedor. Itinerant soothsayers were busier than ever, and the bitter flavour of apocalyptic matters became blended with more or less overt treasonable prophecies. The hierarchy and the Boyar Duma, having buried the last Rurik Tsar with the traditional splendour, began their deliberations about his successor.

They sat in one of the great halls at the Kremlin, the hierarchy in black and white mantles, gleaming crosses on their breast and jewelled croziers in the left hand, and the nobility in their tall fur hats, their wide velvet gowns sweeping down to the ground. Deliberations went on unhurriedly, all haste being alien to the Muscovite mind. As weeks slipped by, however, not the Kremlin but the city of Moscow broke into a turmoil. The hierarchy and the Boyars were wasting their time – small merchants, artisans, people from the suburbs and above all the military had already reached a decision. Boris's name rang from end to end in Moscow. At last it was heard at the Kremlin, and the assembly tried to ignore it. One by one, names of proven ancient lineage were put forward by the aged chairman and shouted down by the assembly. 'A Dolgoruki for your Tsar?' 'No.' 'A Golytzin?' 'No.' 'A Miloslavsky?' 'No.' 'A Bielsky?' A deafening 'no'.

In the end Boris's adherents at the Kremlin and the vast crowds in the Red Square forced the electoral issue. They wanted none but Boris for their Tsar. Iona, Metropolitan of Moscow, yielded in all sincerity since he hoped for a stable government under Boris. The majority of the Boyars gave in largely from fear of the common folk's anger.

But the newly-elected sovereign could not be found at the palace. His sister, the widowed Tsarina Irina, had retired to the Novodevich Abbey immediately on her husband's death, and Boris had joined her there. When at last the Metropolitan of Moscow, together with some representatives of the assembly, was able to see him, Boris, passionately desiring the crown, refused it in such a way that even his most intimate adherents despaired of the outcome. Day after day, the exquisite and futile comedy continued, most adroit persuasion meeting with stony refusals. Boris played his part so convincingly that everybody's nerves were frayed to a thread. At precisely the right moment Boris consented to be Tsar, 'in deep humility, with great reluctance, his heart heavy within him,' as was recorded by a contemporary devotee.

They crowned him in May 1598, the first and the last Tsar of mean descent. Boris did not come to the throne as a novice. Having learned statesmanship under Ivan the Terrible, he had exercised sovereignty in all but name during Fedor's reign, and he had no misgivings about his ability to rule. He knew that prosperity would keep away from the country's gates so long as the Treasury resources were stretched to the utmost by demands of war, and he kept declaring his peaceful intentions to all the foreign emissaries arriving in Moscow.

The election might have brought great benefits to Moscow. It did not. An anointed Tsar though he was, Boris remained an alien and a commoner. His piety stood beyond doubt. Not so his roots and even less so his intentions. Insecurity haunted him from the very day of his election, and it is precisely the sense of insecurity which explains some of the mistakes committed by Boris. He hated and feared the ancient nobility, but his persecution of them was far more harmful to him than to them: he exiled them to the south-western borders of Muscovy where their plotting against him was greatly encouraged by the Polish and Lithuanian nobles. Boris professed to care for the common man – and yet he increased his hardships by ordering measures to combat the dearth of labour in the country-side. He legalized serfdom by making it an offence for serfs to change their masters. Merchants had carried him to the throne, and Boris certainly encouraged trade. He invited French, German and Dutch traders to sail across the White Sea where he founded a port 'in honour of St Michael the Archangel', but Boris's readiness to lavish privileges on foreign merchants did not increase his popularity at home. There were murmurs at Novgorod and Pskov that the Tsar lowered the import dues only to raise indirect taxation at home.

Zealous for the heightened honour of the national church, Boris had the Metropolitan of Moscow raised to the rank of a patriarch, but the distinction did not lead to the enthusiasm he had hoped for. Anxious to establish firm links with the West, Boris had his only daughter, Xenia, betrothed to Prince Johan of Denmark – to the undisguised anger of the people to whom the mere idea of an Orthodox Tsarevna being given in marriage to a Lutheran suggested sulphur and brimstone. The Prince arrived in Moscow but died of a fever just before the wedding – to the relief of the common folk, who asserted that the young man's fatal illness had come as an obvious sign of God's displeasure. Boris sent numbers of young men abroad to study commerce in Germany and the Low Countries, and not one of them returned to Moscow. It was at once alleged that the young people had been 'sold to the devil overseas'. As the Tsar's closest counsellor, Boris had commanded the affection and loyalty of unnumbered thousands among the common people. Within a bare two years after his coronation, he could count on no other support than that of the military, and one conspiracy after another was being shaped in Moscow. One such was traced to the Romanov family. Its head, Fedor, was forcibly turned into a monk under the name of Philaret and kept a virtual prisoner. His wife was also compelled to enter the cloister. Their infant son, Michael, was not considered important enough to be persecuted.

And early in 1600 a skeleton in the Russian cupboard crept into broad daylight. At the very beginning, at least, it need not have been a very dangerous skeleton since its existence started with a rumour and rumours do not flourish if they are persistently and firmly ignored. But neither Boris not the Boyar Duma nor yet the hierarchy could ignore that particular rumour which, however fantastic its ramifications, was based on facts. At the death of Ivan the Terrible in 1584, two of his sons were living, Fedor, who succeeded him, and Dimitry, a baby, born of Ivan's seventh wife, Maria Nagaya. By his father's will, Dimitry inherited certain towns and manors at some distance from Moscow, and Boris persuaded Fedor to have the infant prince and his mother sent to one of those towns, Uglich. There was certainly one good reason for it: the presence of the widowed Tsarina at the Kremlin was a thorn in everybody's flesh. Maria Nagaya may have felt affection for her little son, but she loved herself much more. Outbursts of self-pity, endless trivial quarrels with the other ladies at the Terem, and a well-proved proneness to mischief made her removal desirable, and nobody missed her in Moscow.

In the spring of 1591 Dimitry was reported to be dead 'of a mischance', the people of Uglich asserting that he had been murdered. With the Tsar's approval, Boris sent Prince Vassily Shouysky to preside at an official inquiry at Uglich. Shouysky returned to Moscow and reported that the little prince, known to have been subject to epileptic fits, had inadvertently, fallen on a knife, and Moscow thought no more of the matter. But Boris's enemies never forgot the allegations made by the people of Uglich. The very first unpopular measure, ordered by Boris as Tsar, helped to bring Dimitry's ghost into the national consciousness. Boris's enemies – at home and abroad – began spreading the story that Boris and none other had instigated 'the murder' in 1591. Men of obscure origin, who had never been to Uglich in their lives, succumbed to bribes a little too readily and claimed to have been eye-witnesses of 'the infamous crime'. Some among them alleged that the murderers, overpowered by the crowd, had confessed themselves to be Boris Godunov's hirelings. People remembered that Prince Vassily Shouysky had always stood high in Boris's favour, and Shouysky's report about the Uglich matter was now held to be spurious. The widowed Tsarina Maria Nagaya, now a nun at a Moscow convent, bided

her time and prudently abstained from the least involvement.
Little by little, the first variant came to be replaced by another.
Boris had indeed meant to have Dimitry killed, but the child had
been rescued, and was still living, his identity kept secret all down
the years. The story caught at the people's imagination. If Dimitry
were really alive, he alone was the rightful Tsar and he must certainly come into his own at the right hour.

It is impossible to tell at what stage such stories reached Boris.
As it was, he had much to contend against over and above his
enemies' intrigues. He had not been on the throne three years when
the country was scourged by the worst famine of the century. Its
ravages which unpeopled numberless villages and several lesser
towns were at once explained by the divine displeasure at the nation's
choice of a Tsar. Boris spared neither himself nor money to ease the
people's sufferings. He fought all speculation in corn and other
staples, lowered taxation, organized free distribution of bread, fish
and meat at special centres up and down the country, but not one
of those measures restored the people's confidence in him. The
military alone remained loyal enough but not all the regiments could
be kept in Moscow. There were mutinies far to the south of the
capital, there were thickening threats in the north from Sweden and
in the west from Poland and Lithuania. Home-bred brigandage was
on the increase, and soldiers were needed to safeguard foreign
merchants and their goods particularly on the way from the Polish
frontier to Moscow.

Meanwhile, at the Kremlin, the anointed commoner sat in the
Council hall, aware that nearly every nobleman present wished him
ill. He appeared at all the solemn church functions and wondered
how many among the clergy shared the dark suspicions of the
populace. Presently a courier arrived and was received in very secret
audience. He came from the western frontier and reported a most
disquieting rumour. A young man, living under the protection
of a Lithuanian magnate, had declared himself to be Dimitry, the
youngest son of Ivan the Terrible. The courier added that so far the
claim was regarded rather sceptically by the Poles and the Lithuanians, but such a postscript meant thin comfort for Boris. Presently
there were more messengers and more reports. In his efforts to sift
fact from fable, Boris began striking even at the semblances of conspiracies in Moscow. The decree of exile was replaced by the block

and the gibbet, and unmasked terror took to creeping up and down the streets of the city. Soon Boris's secret agents left Moscow for the countryside and dealt with any 'evidences' of treason as they saw fit.

To darken the landscape still more deeply, the famine years had left one unhappy legacy: hordes of dispossessed and desperate men and women wandered about, plundering and killing wherever they went.

The final blow fell in the autumn of 1603 when all wild rumours vanished in facts. The Pretender appeared in the south, crowds of Cossacks and some few Poles openly supporting his claim to be Ivan's son. All the available troops at once left Moscow, but for a time it looked as though Boris's men would have nothing to do: the Pretender moved northwards, and every town along the way opened its gates to him and every belfry pealed in honour of 'Tsar Dimitry'.

At last Boris's army met the enemy outside Sevsk, and the Pretender's forces were routed. Eighteen months of racking uncertainty seemed to be resolved in Boris's favour, but his commanders wasted the fruits of the victory by quarrelling among themselves. 'Tsar Dimitry', given an unlooked-for opportunity to restore his shattered strength, used the chance to the very utmost. When he struck again in the spring of 1605, some among Boris's troops decided to acknowledge 'Tsar Dimitry' and others were routed. His further progress unimpeded, the Pretender moved nearer and nearer to Moscow. When in April 1605 the news reached the Kremlin, Boris had a fatal seizure.

He had trained his only son to succeed him, but Muscovy had had enough of the Godunov stock. Prince Vassily Shouysky was dragged into the middle of the Red Square and forced to make a public repudiation of his Uglich report. 'Yes, Orthodox people,' he shouted to the crowds, 'Boris meant to have the child murdered, but good Christian folk rescued the prince, and a priest's little son was killed instead.' The mob applauded because they heard what they had come to hear. The Polish heralds, sent by the Pretender, were received with singular honours, and on the same day Boris's widow, son and daughter were strangled at the orders of the Boyar Duma. During an urgently summoned session, the Boyars decided that it would be to everybody's advantage to acknowledge the Pretender as their lawful sovereign.

More than three centuries were to pass before Boris Godunov received fair treatment at the hands of historians and men of letters. His contemporaries having adjudged him to be an arrogant, cunning and cruel criminal, the judgment was echoed from one generation to another, and the Uglich incident was firmly grafted into Boris's record. The cruelties of Ivan the Terrible were said to be revived by him, and even his ambition came to be painted in the ignoble colours a common adventurer would have chosen for his own. Pushkin's Boris, haunted by blood-stippled phantoms, was far easier to believe in than the real Boris. The deeply rooted vanity of the nation had to be satisfied in condemning an alien parvenu so mistakenly and disastrously crowned Tsar at the Assumption Cathedral.

The responsibility for the crime at Uglich remains something of an enigma to this day because of many contradictions in the records. But what facts are known about Dimitry's infancy go a long way to prove that there was little likelihood of the child threatening to wreck Boris's chances of the crown. Dimitry, an epileptic from birth, showed scant promise of ever reaching his teens.

It goes without saying that ambition was the lodestar of Boris's life. Yet, to judge by the seven years of his rule, that ambition could never have been cradled in self, to the exclusion of all other motives. First and foremost, Boris was a statesman shrewd enough to realize that the continued isolation of Muscovy would wreck the nation's health and its chances of prosperity.

What ultimately defeated him was not the lack of troops or of money, or even the disloyalty of his commanders. Boris was vanquished by one of his own many selves – the self of a coward. He well knew that popular rumour held him guilty of Dimitry's death, and he allowed a ghost to make pitiful dust of the strength, common sense and courage that his other selves possessed in no mean measure. By all accounts, 'the fatal seizure' happened immediately after dinner. Was he poisoned? Did he poison himself? We shall never know.

'Smuta' gripped the country in grim earnest that spring of 1605. For more than seven years after the death of Boris, Muscovy resembled a battered ship tossed here and there on the breast of a storm. Her people were no longer able to disentangle one issue from another, nor would they have cared to do so. The true national signature was all but wiped off Muscovy. Swedes, Poles, Lithuanians, with the turbulent Cossacks very much to the forefront, all pressed the claims of no fewer than four candidates for the Cap of Monomach. There was no government. Members of the Boyar Duma still sat in a hall at the Kremlin, but they did not govern. They drifted down one current after another.

The Pretender's origins are obscure. Even the name bestowed on him by posterity, Gregory Otrepiev, may not have been legally his. He was supposed to be the son of one Youri Otrepiev, a petty landowner of Galitz. Nothing is known of 'Dimitry's' earlier years or the place of his birth. His boyhood was spent in the household of Nikita Romanov in Moscow. Aged about fourteen, 'Dimitry', known for his piety, entered a monastery as a novice. There follows a gap in the chronicle until we hear of the young man in Lithuania and his claim to be the son of Ivan the Terrible. As is well known, the claim was not at first admitted either by the Poles or the Lithuanians. Those in Russia who believed it to be true alleged that 'Dimitry' had been sent to Lithuania for reasons of safety, but the argument becomes rather thin when we remember the efficiency of Boris's secret agents. Had there been the least rumour of the boy's supposed identity during Fedor's reign, Boris would certainly have taken prompt and ruthless measures to deal with it. On the other hand, it is only fair to add that the Romanov family may well have had very good reasons for giving sanctuary to a possible rival of the man they detested. Which is no proof that 'Dimitry' was Ivan's son.

   Was he indeed? There exists at least one sound reason against it – the ease with which the Pretender entered the Roman Church in order to pave the way to his marriage with Marina Mnishek and – much more importantly – to secure the financial assistance of King Sigismund of Poland. A son of Tsar Ivan, reared in the strictest Orthodox principles and steeped in the climate of an Orthodox cloister, would hardly have taken such a step. A penniless adventurer, whatever his origins, might well have done so. There is also another reason against accepting the Pretender's claim. Members of the House of Rurik could be bestially cruel, mean, immoral and treacherous, but at least one negative quality is absent from their record: they were never vulgar. 'Dimitry's' vulgarity was obvious even to those who accepted his claim to be Ivan's son. Certainly he had charm, and Marina Mnishek, related to some of the noblest Polish families, was carried away by it, but Marina had neither experience nor common sense to tell a gentleman from a parvenu.

The Pretender's claim duly made public, neither Poland nor Lithuania was in a hurry to sponsor his cause. The King of Poland made many promises and kept none of them with the exception of certain sums of money. But 'Dimitry' needed men under his banner, and the Poles were slow in coming forward. His future father-in-law, Mnishek, succeeded in recruiting about two thousand men, but even 'Dimitry's' total lack of experience did not prevent him from realizing that a host of two thousand men would never win Moscow for him. Delay followed delay until the story about 'the rightful Tsar' seeped into the south-western reaches of Muscovy. It was the Cossacks and the vast hordes of malcontents exiled to the south who paved the way to the capital. After the first victories, both Poland and Lithuania recognized the Pretender, but by that time he had no need to rely on foreign hirelings, town after town having opened their gates to him.

When in late spring of 1605 he rode into Moscow, the widowed Tsarina Maria left her cloister and publicly recognized him as her 'son'. The Boyar Duma had no alternative but to accept the claim, and the Pretender was crowned as Tsar Dimitry at the Assumption Cathedral.

It proved a disastrously expensive business for the country. Within about a year, 'Tsar Dimitry' squandered the wealth amassed by several generations. His attitude to the old nobility was tinged with obvious contempt and the crowd of Polish gentlemen who had followed him to Moscow had no respect for national feelings. 'Dimitry' talked far too much about his 'father', occasionally plunging into personal memories, and that plumbed the very depths of absurdity when people remembered that Ivan's youngest son was a few months old at the time of his father's death in 1584. The arrival of his wife, Marina Mnishek, hastened the crisis. She came surrounded by priests, monks and friars of her own faith, and the people's murmurs rose higher and higher. 'We have been sold to the Latins. . . .' 'Dimitry', dividing his time between love-making and plans for a campaign against the Crimean Tartars, seems never to have given a thought to his own insecurity. With lightning speed a conspiracy was formed. In about a fortnight after Marina Mnishek's arrival, the widowed Tsarina Maria tearfully acknowledged her mistake in 'recognizing' 'Dimitry' as her son. Conspirators surrounded the Kremlin and the Pretender was killed. Marina escaped her husband's fate and fled to Yaroslavl and then further south where in due course she gave birth to a son.

Once again Muscovy was without a Tsar. In June 1606 the Boyar Duma elected Prince Vassily Shouysky. His most memorable act was a humiliating public confession of perjury: Tsar Ivan's little son had indeed been murdered at Uglich. Presently Shouysky suborned the hierarchy to canonize the child as a martyr. His body was brought to Moscow and sumptuously enshrined at the Assumption Cathedral, and there followed a fearfully solemn ceremony which condemned the Pretender to everlasting flames.

Vassily Shouysky inherited an empty Treasury, a divided Boyar Duma, and a country torn by turmoils. One mutiny after another kept breaking out along the banks of the Volga as far as Astrakhan. There were ugly outbreaks at Viatka and Perm. Tver refused to acknowledge Vassily as Tsar and clamoured for the National Assembly to be summoned. The people of Pskov on hearing that Vassily had been elected by the Boyar Duma massacred great numbers of gentlefolk and rich merchants. To the south-west, Polish agents were hard at work to persuade the masses that 'Tsar Dimitry' was really alive but in hiding. Troops sent from Moscow were dealing vigorously with the peasant rebellions along the western border when the King of Poland decided to interfere and his army began marching towards the frontier of Muscovy.

By the autumn of 1607 the old capital was beleaguered. A second pretender, recognized by Poland and a great many Russians as 'Tsar Dimitry', set up his camp at no great distance from Moscow, at a place called Tushino. That second pretender, his origins wholly unknown, went down in history as '*Tushinsky vor*', i.e. 'the Brigand of Tushino'. During his brief 'reign', Tushino became a capital in little, with its own court, government, and Patriarch, who was none other than Philaret Romanov.

In the end Vassily turned to Sweden for help. When King Sigismund heard of that move, he promptly laid siege to Smolensk. The Swedish mercenaries reached Moscow, but Vassily could not pay them, and in the end they joined the enemy ranks.

It was one chaos within another. Vassily was still Tsar but the last shreds of sovereignty were wrenched away from him. At a sitting of the Boyar Duma in February 1610 it was decided to offer the crown to Prince Wladislas, King Sigismund's son. By the end of that turbulent year 'the Brigand of Tushino' was killed in a skirmish and Vassily, the most pallid creature to occupy the Russian throne, was forcibly turned into a monk. In Moscow, the party in the ascendant pursued but one objective – that of bringing Muscovy and Poland together with Wladislas for Tsar. Such a union, it was argued, would at once cripple the enmity of Sweden, lessen the aggressiveness of the Crimean Tartars, and increase Western respect for the Slav race.

Those specious arguments were framed by men who had no clear idea about the conditions in the heart of their own country and who believed that they could ignore the temper of the people. The decision to bring an alien to the Kremlin made the Cossacks declare that Marina Mnishek's infant son was the rightful sovereign, and they swore allegiance to him.

The Boyar Duma issued one feeble directive after another, and all were disobeyed. There was no government in Russia. There was just an assembly of mostly elderly, frightened men who sat wasting time on deliberations of no moment. Clause by verbose clause, they drew up a document setting forth all the limitations of Prince Wladislas's authority. They prefaced the paper by declaring that their offer to the crown was conditional on the Prince's entry into the Greek Church, and it never occurred to any among them that to have a Pole for Tsar meant the cession of Russian sovereignty to Russia's immemorial foe.

Whilst the Duma was engaged in snail-like progress from one point to another, the Cossacks and others blockaded Moscow from the south, and the threat of famine in the city grew more and more immediate. The Swedes were settling down in Novgorod and Pskov and, to crown all the infirmities of the national course, King Sigismund's army entered Moscow not as allies but as masters. Members of ancient princely houses were turned into errand-boys and lackeys, compelled to remain at the beck and call of any captain or serjeant from Cracow or Wilno. The Polish commanders at once introduced curfew and martial law. Plundering, arson and murder became so many details of daily life for the Muscovites.

In the end, the Duma, its authority in the dust, was allowed to dispatch an embassy to Cracow to ask the King's formal consent for his son to become Tsar. To increase the ironic cruelty of the moment, the embassy was headed by none other than Philaret Romanov. The people of Moscow, however cowed they were, did not hesitate to give free vent to their bewilderment. Philaret's rôle in the whole business was indeed an unpleasantly tangled skein of many threads. The first pretender had been brought up in his kinsman's house, 'the Brigand of Tushino' had had him as Patriarch at his 'court', and now Philaret was using all his eloquence to persuade his peers in the Church and the Duma that their country's salvation depended on the union with Poland. They must all have known that Prince Wladislas, most carefully brought up by the Jesuits, would never relinquish his faith, and it was more than strange to see an Orthodox Metropolitan set forth on a journey to invite that alien princeling to rule over an Orthodox nation. None of it made sense, but by the end of 1610 what few men of sense still remained in Russia did not dare to break into articulacy.

That odd embassy reached Cracow, was received by King Sigismund, and immediately imprisoned by him. The King had no intention of allowing his son to accept a crown which he desired for himself. All the members of the embassy were honourably lodged and treated, but they were not at liberty to communicate with one another or with any of their countrymen in Moscow where the Duma still awaited their return. Instead, the King's messengers arrived to demand that the oath of allegiance be made to Sigismund. Crowds collected in the Red Square, shouting a deafening refusal. The suburbs rose to protest against any alien put on the throne. The Poles set fire to all the poorer quarters of the capital and every mutinous breath was answered at the point of the sword. By the spring of 1611 the whole country from the shores of the White Sea to the Caspian was held in the twin clutch of lawlessness and famine until the Crimean Khan wondered about a possible return to the days of the Golden Horde.

But, having conquered Moscow, the Poles found themselves trapped there. The Cossacks, having pillaged all the towns along the Volga, rode northwards and took the capital by storm. The Poles barricaded themselves behind the Kremlin walls. But the savagery of the Cossacks hardly fitted them for the rôle of saviours. They plundered and killed even more energetically than the Poles. In an underground cell of Chudov Abbey at the Kremlin the Poles kept one of their most important prisoners, Patriarch Hermogen. So old and frail was he that his jailers did not consider it necessary to exercise much vigilance. The Patriarch was allowed to keep one of his chaplains and two secretaries, and there must have been a few loyal friends outside since writing materials in plenty reached that underground cell. Soon fierily worded appeals went from Chudov Abbey. They urged the people of Russia to muster together, chase the alien out of the country, call a national assembly and choose a lawful sovereign of their own blood and faith. Those messages were carried north and south, east and west. We cannot tell how many of them reached the hands of men capable of responding to the Patriarch's call. In the end, the old man was betrayed by a guard. Hermogen's sole reply to the charge was to call on his Maker to save his country. The Poles starved him to death.

In the autumn of 1611 one of Hermogen's appeals reached Nijny-Novgorod and came into the hands of a wealthy butcher, one Kuzma Minin. He summoned a public meeting, and the town rose as one man. Prince Pozharsky was chosen commander. The new army had noblemen, clergy, civil servants, merchants and peasants all welded together. Prevalent conditions considered, the very process of that welding should have been slow and difficult. It proved almost too rapid for Pozharsky and Minin. The people of Nijny and the surrounding country saw all too clearly what their task would involve. They were not even certain if the rest of the country would answer the Patriarch's challenge in the same way. None of it dismayed them. A new and invigorating sense of unity was being born, and a prince's jewelled sword carried the same significance as a serf's blunted hatchet. A couple of jealously hoarded coppers sacrificed by an artisan had the same moral value as a pearl and ruby necklace brought by a nobleman's wife. The formation of Pozharsky's host carried the imprint of the miraculous, every man in it awakened to the consciousness that he could be greater than he was.

The march on Moscow started in February 1612. By the following autumn the ancient capital once again belonged to itself. Within less than two months, representatives from every town reached Moscow to hold the *Sobor*, i.e. the National Assembly, its main purpose being the election of the sovereign. By the will of the people the choice fell on the 16-year-old boy, Michael, only son of Philaret Romanov then still a prisoner in Polish hands. It should be noted that the boy's whereabouts were unknown at the time.

From one point of view, the choice was certainly odd. The Romanovs could not claim their descent from Rurik in the ninth century. They were not great landowners. They were certainly connected with the old dynasty by the marriage of one of their women to Ivan the Terrible, but the connection did not raise the family to any dizzy heights. Michael, to whom the crown was to be offered, was wholly unknown to the nation. The few who had met him knew him to be upright, pious and rather delicate. But the Tsar-elect's father, Philaret, had not only served 'the Brigand of Tushino' but had openly favoured the union with Poland and had headed that hapless embassy to Cracow.

Here and there we come on intimations that Michael's election was neither spontaneous nor unanimous. Many other names were put forward, and there exists a vague story that a few members of the *Sobor* toyed with the idea of choosing Prince Philip of Sweden on condition of his accepting the Orthodox faith. The story, however, is barely credible: no alien candidate would then have been acceptable to the people. Another variant has it that Prince Pozharsky cherished the ambition of ascending the throne, and the upholders of the theory argued that it explained why the prince did not come to occupy any high administrative post under Tsar Michael. But in the first place Pozharsky certainly served in Michael's government. Secondly, the prince, wounded in an earlier campaign, had not spared himself during the march to Moscow and his health did not permit of any further exertions.

Considered from a different angle, the choice of the *Sobor* loses its apparent strangeness. In 1612 the country hungered and thirsted for a unifying symbol, for an aegis to lead her back to sanity, for a salve to quieten her wounds. A Romanov was neither a Golytzin, not a Dolgoruki, nor yet a Miloslavsky, whose election would have paved the way to rivalries and created uncomfortable factions. Michael was chosen as an affirmation of the sacrosanct principle of monarchy and not as a person.

The leaders of the *Sobor* exercised all their ingenuity in slurring over Philaret's earlier record and the purpose of that embassy to Cracow. In all contemporary sources, with one exception, and for many generations later, Michael's father was painted in a martyr's colours, the years of his imprisonment being proof of his great service to his country. The background considered, such an attitude of the *Sobor* need not be condemned out of hand.

II

Father and Son

Michael, born 1597, elected 1613, died 1645.
Alexis, his son, born 1629, succeeded 1645,
died 1676

IT HAS been said that the *Sobor*'s decision was an expression of the national need for a symbol. In the light of later events, that decision evokes the image of a great bird, its wings now black, now brushed with crimsoned silver. The bird started its flight over the vast country, and it seemed as though the savagely scarred landscape and the bird shared a secret beyond man's channels of communication. The bird continued its flight for more than three centuries, a singular Phoenix, its body immune from flames, the colour of the great wings changing so rapidly that none could tell where one shade merged into another. Only towards the end of the flight did all the pride of colour vanish. The wings were black from tip to tip, and the bird no longer flew high overhead but hovered closer and closer over the land once again gripped by anarchy where condition, circumstance, need and identity were coiled together with no apparent pattern or aim. At the appointed moment, its great wings outspread for a skyward flight, the bird vanished, and the last beat of the great wings bore the signature of the christening more than three centuries ago.

The name of the bird was Fate.

Not until March 1613 did the embassy sent from Moscow find the Tsar-elect and his mother, Marfa the nun, at Ipatiev Abbey near Kostroma. A weakling would have blessed his God for the incredible fortune fallen to his lot, for the ending of penury, uncertainty and all manner of peril.

But Michael's first reaction was a firm rejection of the offer. 'He refused the crown most angrily,' recorded a contemporary. He refused it again and yet again, and his manner left very little room for hope in the delegates' hearts. Argument followed argument, one persuasive onslaught came on the heels of another until after some hours of solitude and prayer Marfa the nun came to see that her own vehement protests against her son's acceptance of the crown ran counter to God's will for him and for the nation. Michael's own 'I will' stood for more than consent: it was the promise of a life-long dedication.

It took the embassy nearly two months to reach Moscow, the boy Tsar-elect being guarded day and night. The capital was indeed clear of the enemy – but there was little, if any, peace in the country. War was still carried on from village to village, from forest to forest, one band of marauders grappling with another, neither aware of the cause of the struggle between them. Such were the grim evidences of that warfare that at some point along the journey Michael exercised his sovereign will for the first time by refusing to ride any further unless some immediate measures were taken to stop the senseless bloodshed, bury the corpses, and give some care to the wounded.

When at last Moscow was reached, Michael found no other welcome than the shouting of crowds and the pealing of bells. At the Kremlin there was absolutely nothing for creaturely comfort. The palace walls were bare, the windows smashed, the roof torn here and there. There was literally not a chair for Michael to sit on, or a platter for his dinner to be served on. The Pretender's mad extravagances had depleted the Treasury and the Polish occupation had ended in an orgy of destructiveness. Bedding and kitchen equipment had to be borrowed from the nearest monastery which had rather miraculously escaped most of the depredations of the troubled years. There was neither timber, nor labour, nor money. Immediate needs were answered by rich merchants, particularly the Strogonovs. The young Tsar and his mother had to make shift in one of the old parts of the Kremlin where Ivan the Terrible used to live at the beginning of his reign.

The *Sobor* was engaged with large and admittedly important issues, but surely someone might have thought about a fowl for the Tsar's dinner and a counterpane to cover his body at night. Nothing

except the liberality of the Strogonovs and others, who had succeeded in safeguarding their fortunes, enabled the government to
start on the building of a wooden palace, to replenish the young
Tsar's wardrobe, to stock his larders and, finally, to clean the
Assumption Cathedral in time for the coronation in July, 1613.

If the domestic economy was in sad tatters, the outside situation
offered little for comfort. Pozharsky's army had recaptured Moscow
and the *Sobor* had elected a ruler. But the alien hordes were not
yet chased out of the country and the young Tsar's dominions were
torn to pieces. The Swedes sat at Novgorod and their threat to
Pskov grew more and more alarming. The Poles were entrenched
in Michael's western provinces, and quite a number of Russian
noblemen had not changed their mind about Wladislas's candidature. For all the solemn oaths of allegiance received by him, Michael
had but a thin trickle of loyalty to depend on. The Cossacks, their
whimsical policy making them run with the hare and hunt with the
hounds, could not be trusted. There was no army to pursue the
hordes of brigands. It almost looked as though the great initial
response made to the call of Minin and Pozharsky had sapped the
very last shreds of national energy.

So it seemed. But, little by little, the brigand menace was cleared
off the horizon. New huts were built and ploughs and harrows were
again seen in the fields. Laughter, song and dancing returned to the
villages together with much lusty swearing, casual immorality and
unbridled drunkenness. Landlords were back at their manors.
Trade began stirring out of stagnation. Many new taxes were
imposed and the treasury chests began to be refilled. The *Sobor*
still sat in Moscow, and the Saltykovs, the Tsar's kin on his mother's
side, helped Prince Trubetzkoy and others with the business of
governing.

As for the Tsar, he found himself at school. The alphabet of
statesmanship had to be learned in a hard way, and he made rather
clumsy mistakes at the beginning. Such was his choice of an uncouth and ill-tempered gentleman, one Oushakov, as an ambassador
to Europe on his accession. Oushakov succeeded in controlling himself in England, and James I sent one John Merrick to mediate in
the Russo-Swedish dispute. But Oushakov's self-control deserted
him when he crossed over to the continent. From the Low Countries
down to the states of Italy, unsavoury stories of drunkenness,

arrogance, lust and brawls in public places blazed the trail of Michael's ambassador. 'A savage Tartar,' said Europe, 'what could the young Tsar have been about to send such a creature abroad?'

The young Tsar was deep in work – learning how to be Tsar. He could not be said to have governed through those first years, but he had able counsellors and he learned to listen. He was not an autocrat and the very term '*samoderzhietz*' was omitted from the long list of his titles. Michael ruled together with the Boyar Duma and the *Sobor*. He had no other rewards for his servants except grants of land and even those had to be sanctioned by the Duma, but there reigned amity and concord at the Kremlin. The bitter chaos of the Troubled Years had killed, however temporarily, the sour atmosphere of intrigues. And from the beginning Michael seems to have realized the importance of outward demeanour. Foreign ambassadors, received in audience, spoke of the boy's dignity, courtesy and his awareness of the high office he bore. At the very least, the young dynasty did not start with an unmannerly boor.

Little by little, Russian statesmanship stirred out of the ashes. In 1617 a truce was concluded with Sweden at Stolbovo. The treaty brought few advantages to Russia: she had to cede her very last foothold on the Baltic coast so that Archangel, founded by Tsar Boris, now remained her only port. Still, Stolbovo assured the safety of Novgorod and Pskov and proved a valuable respite. It went otherwise where Poland was concerned. At the end of 1617 Wladislas decided to claim the Russian crown. He set out with a great army, laid siege to and captured Viazma. In October 1618 he attacked Moscow, but the old capital was ready for him, and the Poles were repulsed. The brief campaign ended in the Truce of Deulino – once again scarcely favourable for Michael since he lost Smolensk and Poland persisted in her refusal to recognize him as Tsar. None the less, the treaty led to an exchange of prisoners, and Philaret, the Tsar's father, was released from captivity in the summer of 1619.

It was an open secret that Philaret had hoped to win the crown for himself. Tsar Boris had forced him into the cloister, but the statesman had never died in the monk. He knew far more than the bare rudiments of national economy. The fourteen years of Philaret's fiscal policy would prove hard going for nobleman, merchant and peasant, but the policy bore good fruit in the end. Philaret's dignity was acknowledged by Michael's offer to share the sovereignty with his father, and the diarchy continued until the old man's death in 1633. A hard and unforgiving man, he succeeded in removing all his likely rivals and enemies from the neighbourhood of the throne. For fear of banishment, crippling fines and worse penalties, people hastened to forget much of Philaret's past, his dalliance with the Poles, his services to the Brigand of Tushino, and his approval of the union between Russia and Poland. Philaret's long captivity had been spent in honour and in comfort, but his contemporaries' imagination insisted on manacles, short commons and dungeons. None the less, the diarchy served its purpose and measures introduced by Philaret went a long way towards establishing some semblance of order throughout the country.

With enemies at no great distance from his gates, it was imperative for Michael to have a strong army, but the ancient regiments were sorrily disorganized and the volunteers' host, mustered by Pozharsky, had more or less melted away. During the very first year of his reign, the young Tsar, greatly influenced by his kinsman, Nikita Romanov, invited foreign military experts to come and train his people. Conscription as such did not exist, but landowners were ordered to send a specified number of their peasants into towns, there to receive training under English, Irish, Scots and German officers.

Soldiers were needed not only for garrison and battlefield but for Michael's palace. By far the worst legacy of the Troubled Years was fear. Its tentacles having spread all over the country, it did not spare the Kremlin where every gateway and staircase must be guarded day and night. The maddeningly complicated protocol which surrounded every audience, whether private or public, was explained by the awful dignity of the Tsar's office. In reality, every detail of the lengthy and tiring ceremonial was born of fear lest 'anything untoward' should happen to the Tsar's person. None of his subjects, however exalted, might drive up to the porch of the palace. Strangers on foot found loitering in the neighbourhood ran the risk of summary arrest and torture to make them confess to a non-existent conspiracy.

The north regained its quiet and Poland kept to the terms of the Deulino Treaty. But the Cossacks and the Crimean Tartars remained a danger, the former changing their policy as it pleased them and the latter constantly marauding in the south. The Tartar depredations in particular engaged the Tsar's armies to such an extent that in 1632 Poland was emboldened to break the Deulino Treaty. Few Russian troops could be spared to ward off the Polish attack. The war lasted two years and though in the end Poland recognized Michael as Tsar, enormous tracts of land on both banks of the Dnieper remained under Polish suzerainty.

Yet not every corner of the Tsar's dominions was thus imperilled. Siberia had been partially conquered under Ivan the Terrible. In 1623, the last remnants of Khan Ishim's forces were shattered and Russian explorers and trappers reached the banks of the Lena and beyond. The value of an ever-increasing fur trade meant much to the exchequer, and Michael encouraged the Siberian enterprise because it did not involve his government in any unpleasantness with other powers. But he was learning prudence year by year. When in the early thirties the Don Cossacks got a foothold on the shores of the Black Sea and captured Azov, the Tsar at once ordered them to withdraw: Turkey's displeasure would have been a calamity Russia could not afford to face.

One by one, breaths of a new climate were changing Muscovy into Russia, but at the Kremlin the court life still followed the rhythm mistakenly believed to have come from Byzantium. In reality, it owed much to the days of the Tartar yoke when absolute segregation of women was accepted by the Slavs. It fell to the first Romanov Tsar to introduce a new note into the old rhythm.

He had no brothers; there were several male cousins, but it was acknowledged that a successor to a sovereign elected by the will of the nation must be begotten by him. To the undisguised horror of the adherents of ancient traditions and the pleasure of all 'Westerners', Michael began considering matrimony out of all accord with tradition. He would have a foreigner to wife. An embassy was dispatched first to Copenhagen and then to Stockholm, and was met with a contemptuous rebuff in Denmark and in Sweden. No Scandinavian princess could possibly marry a Muscovite.

In the end, the Tsar was compelled to follow the old custom and choose a bride from among his own nobility. The first Tsarina,

Maria Dolgoruk, died in labour within the first year, leaving neither son nor daughter to her husband. In 1626 Michael married Eudoxia Streshneva, by whom he had ten children, six of them dying in infancy, but the male succession was assured. Both marriages were strictly contractual affairs.

Meanwhile, Western influences went from strength to strength in Moscow. The Tsar's cousin, Nikita Romanov, and a few other noblemen took to wearing clothes of 'a German cut', though they would not have dared to wear them at court. Anything foreign – from a book to a cunningly contrived clock – attracted the Tsar, but even his interest in 'foreignness' was not allowed to leave the faintest impress on his immediate surroundings. His domestic life was all but monastic; every day must be spent in rigid accord with the calendar of the Church. Michael's only public appearances were at ecclesiastical functions whenever his delicate health allowed him to leave the palace. All foreign ambassadors remarked on his unfailing graciousness but he was never seen to smile or heard to laugh in public. The grave young Tsar, his brocade robes gleaming with jewels, seated on the gold throne in the audience hall, does not suggest the least affinity with a young man who loved music and singing above all other entertainments, who could listen to story-tellers by the hour, and clapped his hands for the pleasure of having a lion sent him by the Shah and some rare brocades brought by an envoy from Venice to embellish the walls of the new stone palace built by John Taylor.

That gravity of Michael's was a mask. His love of merry-making is evidenced by descriptions of his leisure hours, the lists of his private possessions, and the documents relating to his household with their inclusion of sixteen dwarfs and fools, all of them dressed in sky-blue and crimson. He loved listening to folk-songs, laughed over amusing riddles, and chose his children's toys with great care. Colour delighted him. He liked 'good smells', and had perfumes sent from India and Turkey. His apothecaries made a soap for his sole use; oil of cinnamon, rose water and cloves went into its making. Himself abstemious in the matter of food and drink, he loved pro-viding sumptuous good cheer for his guests. Once his exchequer had recovered, the young Tsar developed something of a passion for surprising his intimates with costly and amusing presents.

But all those simple and happy details were not known to the masses or to the foreigners visiting the Kremlin. Simplicity and merriment were never allowed to leave the private rooms of the palace for the public square or the audience hall. The Tsar's office was sacrosanct, and none except a few intimates might see the Tsar and his office divorced from each other.

And there was something else. Adherence to tradition prevented him from wholly belonging to himself. Michael had no normal family life. He could not sleep with his wife except at such times as the Canon Law permitted. The Tsarina and the children, particularly the daughters, lived in most rigid seclusion in a part of the palace called the Terem. The Tsar visited the Terem daily. His family never appeared in his apartments, nor did the people ever see them. In 1644, Michael's heir, Alexis, was solemnly 'announced' to the nation, which meant that crowds in the Red Square saw the boy carried shoulder-high to a lofty dais and proclaimed his father's successor. This was the first occasion when anyone, the household apart, was permitted to see Alexis.

Michael's first-born, Tsarevna Irina, was supposed to be a great beauty, and her name came to be linked with a surprising decision made by her father. Tsar Michael was known to delve deep into the history of his country and it seems that those studies of his led him to shape his daughter's future. Before the Tartar invasion in the thirteenth century, Russian princesses would often go as brides abroad to Norway and Sweden, to Poland and Hungary, to Germany and France. The Tartar yoke ended all communication with the West. The Muscovite Rus, having shaken off the Tartar, retained some of the customs he had left. Tsars' daughters could not marry their fathers' subjects. Therefore they never married at all. In history, those women are no more than names appearing in the household records together with the details of their maintenance, their clothes, jewellery and various materials they needed for their needlework. They were taught their letters, but their libraries consisted of the New Testament and the church service books. For amusement, there were fools and dwarfs to divert the royal ladies with crude antics, sham fights and the like drollery. If they accompanied their mother to a church in Moscow or went on a pilgrimage to some shrine in the neighbourhood of the capital, they were heavily veiled and rode in closed carriages, every window curtained. Some of those ladies ended by entering a convent, but the majority stayed at the palace from cradle to coffin, none but the members of the household allowed access to them.

Tsar Michael wanted something different for his daughter. He decided to find a foreign husband for her. His choice fell on Prince Waldemar of Denmark. His father, the King, agreed, to the surprise of every Muscovite. Irina was thirteen at the time and Waldemar about twenty. In January 1644 the Danish prince was officially betrothed to a girl he had not yet met, and Michael had a stone palace built for him in Moscow. The nobility liked him. Still, there remained the hierarchy to be reckoned with. Waldemar pledged himself not to interfere with Irina's faith and he promised that any children of the marriage would be brought up in strict Orthodoxy. But the promises did not satisfy the Patriarch and the bishops who began insisting that Waldemar himself should embrace the Greek faith before his marriage. Not only did he refuse but he broke the engagement with a princess he had not met. The Duma's indignation knew no bounds. Michael found himself in a quandary: he did not wish to offend Denmark and he knew he could not quarrel with the hierarchy. He took refuge in delaying tactics, and futile theological arguments continued, with Prince Waldemar being held in honourable custody, until Michael's successor sent him home in 1645. Tsarevna Irina remained a spinster. Public opinion insisted that the disappointment about the Danish affair caused Michael's death in his late forties.

His successor came to be known as '*tishaishy*', i.e. 'the most peaceful', but Michael seems to deserve it more than Alexis. Carried to the throne in the arms of a storm, the first Romanov was never of it. He lived within the traditional enclosure, and his own self suggested an enclosed garden. Neither of his two marriages had touched his heart, but there is enough evidence of the tranquil devotion and affection he had for his children. He preferred music and singing to politics but he never absented himself from the sittings of the Boyar Duma even when the business bored him. He was not clever and, with the exception of his matrimonial plans for Irina, left little imprint of originality, but he remained true to the purpose underlying his election to the throne: he was the unifying symbol the country needed for its health.

A portrait, painted by some unknown artist soon after Michael's coronation, used to be kept at the Kremlin. The Tsar is shown wearing the Cap of Monomach surmounted by a cross and edged with fur, and another cross hangs on his breast. He wears an empearled and bejewelled '*dalmàtik*', its grotesquely wide sleeves heightening the thinness of the wrists. The globe, carrying yet another cross, is held in the left hand and the sceptre in the right. Under the fur-edged cap is a beautiful grave face with a softly moulded mouth and large dreamy eyes. The three crosses seem to reaffirm the symbol Michael stood for.

In 1613 the embassy from Moscow found Michael at Ipatiev Abbey near Kostroma. Three hundred and five years later a ghastly massacre in the basement of Ipatiev House at Ekaterinburg in Siberia marked the end of the dynasty.

Alexis was born in 1629. By that time life beat to a normal enough rhythm in Moscow. The Kremlin palaces were rebuilt, the treasury replenished, and commerce was expanding year by year. All the activities going on in Moscow and far beyond came to be known at the Terem at a remove, as it were. Activity as such belonged to a world the Terem might never know, and until 1634 the Tsar's little son had never been away from those low-ceilinged rooms, fragrant with musk and incense and hung all over with ikons, a small world where the boy lived with his mother, Tsarina Eudoxia, and her female kin, with his sisters, and a whole regiment of women including the midwife who, having brought Alexis into the world, was retained for her knowledge of herbs and simples. No man, the Tsar and his retinue excepted, dared cross that threshold. Conversely, no inhabitant of the Terem ever appeared in the Tsar's apartments. The Terem was a separate cloister. It had its own chapel, exchequer, offices, kitchens and cellars. Both entry and exit were subjected to severe scrutiny and hedged about with formalities. No fewer than fifteen officials would be concerned when 'an artificer's' services were needed to re-glaze a broken window or to mend a door jamb.

Fear of 'mischance' haunted that doorstep – and that even in greater measure than elsewhere. Thunder, lightning and moonlight, a stranger's 'evil eye', some malefactor's attempt at the sacrosanct lives of the Tsar's children – all those and many more must be reckoned with and guarded against. To the population of Moscow the Tsar's family were no more than names. When the children left the Terem for a church within the walls of the Kremlin, they walked surrounded not only by guards but by tall screens which were carried right into the church. When, on rarely spaced occasions, they went to make their devotions at some shrine in the neighbourhood of the city, they rode in hermetically closed carriages, a company of mounted guards threatening the people with whips and musket butts at the least attempt to get too close to the carriages.

At the age of five Alexis left the Terem for the stone palace built for him by Michael. Now the boy had his own household, 20 playmates of his own age, and his tutors, headed by Boris Morozov. Alexis learned to read, write, do sums on an ivory abacus, and sing the church chants. The new palace was furnished with incredible luxury, gold, brocades and semi-precious stones being used in abundance. The Tsarevich's treasure coffers were filled with pearls, uncut emeralds, rubies and sapphires. The clothes he wore were bejewelled from collar to hem.

But his board was as frugal as that of a commoner's son. Porridge and stews, boiled meat or fish, with sweet turnips, nuts and apples for dessert, such were the two daily meals. No intricate spiced subtleties were ever sent from his kitchens. Most of Alexis's toys were equally simple: little brass bells, sheep, horses and cows carved of wood. There were some exceptions, however, asking for much space in the household inventory: a suit of armour, made by a Dutch 'artificer' living in Moscow, and a banner woven of scarlet and yellow silk. There was also a rocking-horse of 'very cunning' German workmanship, the mane and tail of real horsehair, the harness made of gleaming copper and the saddle of crimson velvet. As the boy grew older, outdoor sports and military games engaged him more and more, and his tutor-in-chief seems to have spared him too early lessons in statecraft. Alexis knew that he would be Tsar some day, but that lay in a future there was no need for him to trouble himself about. Boris Morozov, an enlightened man for his generation, developed in his pupil a taste for falconry, geography and 'foreign contrivances'. Himself a careful and keen landlord, he taught Alexis much about agriculture, gardening and climatic imperatives. Yet, commendable as all those studies were, they could hardly be said to prepare the boy for the throne.

His father's subjects knew that the Tsar had a male heir and no more. Alexis's intimates knew him for a boy of sharply bladed curiosity, rare generosity and dislike of idleness. From his earliest childhood he had outbreaks of terrible temper, sometimes merging into cruelty. Such moods alternated with surprisingly gentle spells.

Neither by his character nor by his education was Alexis prepared for the task fallen on him in 1645 when within a few months his father and mother were gone. Alexis could not govern, and Morozov did not mean him to govern, and for about three years the tutor-in-chief stood at the helm. The young Tsar preferred the leafy freedom of Izmailovskoye to the shadowy halls of the Kremlin. For dynastic reasons he married early, his bride being Maria Miloslavskaya, by whom he would have sixteen children, seven dying in infancy.

In 1648 public feeling began hardening against 'the dictator'. A mutiny broke out in the environs of Moscow, and some of Morozov's underlings were killed in broad daylight. The mob rushed to Kolomenskoe, a country manor where the young Tsar happened to be staying at the time, and shouted that they had come to fetch Morozov away and deal with him as he deserved. The people certainly had legitimate grievances: the favourite's underlings were busily feathering their own nests at the expense of the tax-payers.

The young Tsar faced the mob and refused to deliver Morozov to his death. A hurriedly summoned regiment quelled the mutiny. Morozov, removed from the Tsar's council, was sent into exile, and Alexis's own voice began to be heard in the Council hall.

There followed a curious development in Alexis's life which came to affect the entire country. It might be a little rash to assert that the mutinies in Moscow and elsewhere were wholly responsible for the change in the Tsar. There were other reasons for his apparently unreasonable action. To the forefront of all was his sudden consciousness of responsibilities he had no right to delegate. And what follows might well be described as the sunset of ancient Muscovy.

Some time in the sixteenth century, one Sylvester, a priest at Novgorod, wrote a book entitled *Domostróy*, literally 'the Foundation of a Home'. The work was not conspicuous for its originality. Many of its ideas were borrowed from early Greek patristics and later Byzantine theologians, but that groundwork was liberally leavened with Sylvester's own approach to life, his dread of Satan, his hatred of women, 'by whom evil entered the world', and his horror of all manner of gaiety. He set out to prove that the most innocuous pleasure came from a satanic bourne. In brief, *Domostróy* out-puritan'd the Puritans. The theme answering the Muscovite mood of the time, Sylvester's verbose monstrosity became a household book in a great many families. Still the work had to wait for Alexis Romanov to acquire a tragi-comic national importance.

Not even the hundred and sixty odd years of the Tartar yoke could destroy the hunger for merry-making in the Russian people. They were illiterate and their landscape stretched no farther than a handful of neighbouring villages. The rigours of climate and the several hardihoods of field labour were theirs for life. But every village throughout the length and breadth of Muscovy succeeded in snatching opportunities to brighten the bleakness of their sky. Dancing, singing and fairy-story telling were necessities. So was the pleasure afforded by the occasional visit of a pedlar with his teasing accounts of a fair at some town they would never see. So was their passion for colour. A peasant might possess but one platter under his leaking roof but that platter would be painted red. His women might never see a single copper piece in their lives, but they waited for spring and summer and then adorned themselves with necklaces and coronals woven of forget-me-nots, red-hearted daisies, and any other flower that answered their fancy. At weddings and on all great feasts they must have dancing, the rhythm going back to a pagan past none of them knew anything about. They liked swinging on gaily painted see-saws and they laughed like children.

So very little leisure fell to the peasants' lot, and they used it to the uttermost in the lusty and rough manner of those whose whole lives are companioned by nature. According to the grim teaching of *Domostróy*, all those people were on the way to nethermost hell.

Now in 1648 a very stern old man was Patriarch of Moscow, and he wielded great influence at the Kremlin. During the reign of Michael, for all the prevalent piety, much fun went on in the Tsar's private apartments and national amusements were never interfered with. But Alexis was very much of a boy. The Patriarch prudently bided his time. With Morozov removed from the Tsar's world, old Joseph began arguing that all the troubles fallen upon the country together with the recent mutinies were so many direct consequences of sinful and unrestrained merry-making. The aged Patriarch had something of a case – merry-making certainly ended in drunkenness and often led to worse lapses. Yet the churchman's mind could never admit that the hardships endured by all the commoners in the country demanded an occasional plunge into those waters where the day's many bitternesses could be washed out by wine, dancing and laughter.

Alexis greatly venerated the old Patriarch. Within a few months the Tsar's decrees were sent to governors of all the towns in his dominions. All manner of merry-making was prohibited, even the harmless see-saw falling under the ban. Musical instruments, fancy-dress and masks were to be burned immediately, and the officials were commanded not to spare even the humble recorders. The decrees carried a long catalogue of penalties for the least infringement of the new laws – fines, prison and mutilation. At the Tsar's own wedding, the guests were entertained by the chanting of psalms and canticles, and Patriarch Joseph rejoiced at such a marked return to the days of ancient piety.

But the Tsar's 'conversion' would hardly have pleased Sylvester, whose book carried many a fulmination against all field sports. No mention of them crept into the list of forbidden pastimes. Alexis and many of his subjects still devoted their summer days to falconry, and much time during autumn and winter was spent in hunting bear, wolf and fox. In yet another particular, the Tsar's 'conversion' lacked completeness. All foreigners were 'children of Lucifer, wallowing in their Lutheran mud and despising the pure waters of Christ's Gospel'. In spite of the hierarchy's anxiety and criticism, 'the children of Lucifer' were received more and more frequently by the Tsar.

Alexis never knew the economic impasses and discomforts experienced by his father. By mid-seventeenth century the barbaric splendour of the Tsar's court dazzled many a foreigner. All the Kremlin palaces were built of stone and embellished by the finest craftsmen in Alexis's service. Gold and silver plate, goblets studded with gems, wash-basins edged with semi-precious stones, gowns and caps trimmed with costly furs and all but covered by pearls, priceless fabrics covering tables and benches, walls and floors inlaid with mosaic, all of it suggested wealth beyond all common reckoning. And yet, considering the national expenditure, Alexis's Russia was far

from wealthy. Since no Russian government produced a budget until
the second half of the nineteenth century, we cannot be certain of
all the details of either income or expenditure. At the time of Alexis,
the vast natural resources were barely being tapped. In large terms
the national income was derived from taxes, import dues, fines
imposed by the courts, large-scale confiscations of land, and the
varied produce of Crown manors. Alexis's personal resources were
enormous chiefly because his cousin Nikita Romanov, reckoned to
be the greatest landowner in the country, died childless, naming the
Tsar his sole heir. From the fiscal point of view, Russia lived from
hand to mouth as was evidenced by the frequent 'occasional taxes'
levied whenever the government was facing an emergency, but the
several splendours of the glittering façade in the capital screened off
the general economic insecurity and the actual penury in the heart
of the country.

Alexis's day was spent in rigid accord with the Church demands·
Summer and winter alike, he rose at four in the morning. Dressing
and ablutions completed, he went to the little private oratory for
lengthy prayers read by his confessor. The first duty of piety done,
the Tsar sent a messenger to the Terem to inquire after the Tsarina's
health and immediately after met her in the hall leading to the
entrance of the Terem. Husband and wife heard matins together in
the palace church. On return to his own apartments, the Tsar began
the day's work, one official after another bringing state papers into
'*kómnata*', i.e. Alexis's private study. At nine o'clock he was back
in church to hear mass which lasted two hours but, the most sacred
moments apart, his ministers were free to approach him if the
urgency of their business required it. Between noon and one o'clock,
the Tsar broke his fast with a ceremoniously served dinner. Except
for important occasions, he fed alone in his private rooms.

Unlike most members of his household, his subjects and some of
his guests, Alexis neither ate nor drank to excess. Seventy courses
might be served at his meals, but every dish, once 'shown' to the
Tsar, was sent away as a present to a relative or a friend, sometimes
to prisons and almshouses. His own tastes were as simple as any
commoner's: a little gruel, a little meat or fish, rye bread, apples, and
a cup of oatmeal beer. In Lent and during other fasts the Tsar dined

three times a week. Every dish and cup were tasted by three different persons before reaching his hands. The meal finished, he slept until Vespers. After church he would spend some time at the Terem with his wife and children. About ten a frugal supper was brought into his private rooms. After lengthy evening prayers recited by one of the chaplains, the Tsar went to bed. His apartments were rigorously guarded, and four members of the household slept on the floor between the Tsar's bed and the door.

Such was his ordinary day in Moscow, but the routine was often broken by solemn audiences to ambassadors and by banquets lasting five and sometimes six hours when the incredible profusion of food and drink confirmed the Western idea of Russian gluttony. Banqueting tables were laid in a rather curious manner: cloths, napkins and cruets, one for every four guests, summed up the appointments. There were neither plates nor knives nor yet forks. Spoons were brought in for sauces and filled-up goblets were carried about by cupbearers. Joints and poultry were carved by butlers in a room adjoining the hall, and portions were brought in on silver dishes, one for every two guests. Foreign palates rebelled against the very sharp flavourings used by the Tsar's cooks, and ambassadorial fastidiousness received rude shocks at the evidences of barbarian table manners – dirty fingers dipped into the dishes, much spitting and belching and, finally, drunkenness. Hardly a Boyar could leave the table unless he were assisted by servants. All the more were the foreigners surprised at the Tsar's abstemiousness. A sip or two of wine to toast his guests seemed enough for him.

On certain great feasts, such as Epiphany, Easter Day, Trinity Sunday and other occasions, there were ecclesiastical functions when Alexis's subjects could see their Tsar at a distance, making his way to some monastery outside the Kremlin walls. He wore robes so heavily studded with jewels that two courtiers held him up by the arms. On those occasions the whole military strength of the city came out on duty, and the Tsar was closely guarded on his right hand and on his left. An embroidered handkerchief, a cushioned chair, a rug for his feet, and a huge umbrella to protect him from the vagaries of the weather, all those were carried behind him by courtiers, whose duties lay light upon them. Far more onerous were the tasks of the Tsar's secretaries, who walked within earshot, laden with paper, inkhorns and quills. 'To the governor of Tver, write,'

Alexis might say, barely turning his head, and the secretary 'on immediate duty' prayed to the entire heavenly hierarchy that he might acquit himself of the task without too many mistakes.

On all the great feasts of the year, the Tsar would get up long before daybreak. Dressed in 'sober clothes' and accompanied by a few friends and some musketeers, he visited all the prisons and alms-houses in the city, his retinue distributing food, drink, money and clothes. 'Don't forget that Christ is risen for all of us,' he would say to prisoners on Easter Day. On such occasions, all the gorgeous trappings cast aside, the Tsar moved as a man among men. Tsar Michael, elected by the will of the nation, had never wielded absolute power, but Alexis had mounted the throne by the right of succession. By the early fifties, the title of '*samoderzhitz*', i.e. 'autocrat', found its way into the charters. The title was preceded by the words '*Bózheiu milóstiu*', i.e. 'by God's favour'. Alexis's assurance of the divine provenance of his sovereignty was as real to him as the skies over his head or the shoes on his feet.

But even the reality of that power as it was envisaged by him never helped to sustain a climate of security. Every moment of the Tsar's day was hemmed about by most painstaking precautions against 'mischance'. Some of the best minds in the country laboured over the reform of the law, but the '*Oulózhenie*', when finally approved by the Tsar, carried fearful and inhuman penalties even against those who, being innocent of genuine treason, had the misfortune to fall under the suspicion of the authorities. The Moscow mutiny which preceded Morozov's fall was followed by many others. The sense of insecurity grew into a frightening likelihood of peril round the corner. Penalties were increased and precautions heightened. Foreign diplomats were known to remark in surprise at the Chinese wall erected by protocol. Before being admitted into the august presence everyone was submitted to careful and repeated scrutiny. The Boyars gave a two-fold reason for the exhausting ceremonial: first the Tsar's own dignity demanded it and next the honour of the foreign sovereign must be paid its due. The explanation carried little conviction.

The sense of insecurity deepened most alarmingly when, in late spring of 1649, Alexis learned about the fate of Charles I. His wrath against Parliament outmatched his sorrow for the king. Cromwell and others were solemnly anathematized. All the English merchants were banished from the capital. The Tsar would have liked to order a total embargo on all imports from England, but his counsellors dissuaded him from a measure which might have damaged the trade of his own country. So Alexis agreed to keep Archangel open for English shipping, but import dues were raised, the population of Archangel forbidden to hold any intercourse with 'the wicked infidels', and no Englishman was allowed to leave Archangel for the interior. Alexis recalled his representative in London and there were no diplomatic dealings with England until the Restoration. He also announced that his purse and friendship were at the service of the Royalists, but that intention seems to have gone no further than a promise of help.

Alexis was twenty at the time. He heard the story of that cold January morning in London so many times that its details came to be graven in his memory. He would have been at a loss to find his way in among the complicated causes leading to the cleft between the King and Parliament. Anyhow, all of it would never have been of much concern to the Tsar. There was just one central enormity: an anointed sovereign being beheaded by his own subjects who had sworn allegiance to him. From Alexis's point of view, regicide was tantamount to a sin against the Holy Ghost, and it troubled him to realize that all the plagues of Egypt had apparently not fallen upon England.

❊

There could be no question of a permanent peace between Russia and Poland, and the thirteen years' war which broke out in 1653 was more or less inevitable. Ostensibly, it wore the noble air of a crusade. In bald reality, it was a Russian attempt not only to safeguard but to enlarge her Western borders.

The Ukraine and the provinces of Podolia and Volyn were then in Polish hands. The beginning of the trouble lay in the policy of King Sigismund who, using the Ukrainian Cossacks as a buffer against the Crimean Tartars, ended by reducing the Cossacks to the level of serfs. In 1653, Bogdan Khmelnitzky, the Cossack hetman, started a revolt and sent a messenger to Moscow to ask for the Tsar's help in the struggle. Khmelnitzky laid a particular stress on the Polish persecution of the Orthodox population in their power. Alexis's mind was divided. He had no love for the Poles. He had no confidence in the Cossacks. He consulted his closest intimate at the time, Athanasius Ordyn-Natchokin, who suggested that the Tsar could not do better than lay the matter before the Boyar Duma. The reaction of that assembly was unanimous: help must be given to Khmelnitzky. With the aid of the Cossacks, urged the Boyars, the might of Poland would be crushed for ever. 'If this is the great outcome you expect,' said Alexis, unaware that his irony would be lost on the assembly, 'I had better lead the army myself'. He expected heated protests. None came. The Boyars bowed their heads to the Tsar's will. In due course Alexis left Moscow at the head of his army.

The campaign started well for the Russians. The Cossacks did not waver in their allegiance to the hetman. Presently the entire Ukraine and most of Galicia fell to the Russians. Ordyn-Natchokin urged an immediate truce, but the Tsar argued that the business was by no means finished. At one of the most critical moments Swedish intervention altered the course of the war. Charles X marched into Lithuania, proclaimed King Jan-Kazimir of Poland an usurper, and claimed the Polish crown for himself. Ordyn-Natchokin knew well that the Western powers were looking askance at the prospect of a Swedish hegemony in the north. He did his best to persuade the the Tsar that the long-drawn-out quarrel with Poland on behalf of the turbulent and unreliable Cossacks would bring no lasting benefit to Russia. It was far more advantageous to open hostilities against Sweden and to wrest back all that had been lost by Russia at the beginning of the century. A foothold on the Baltic coast was far more valuable than any number of Polish towns, said Alexis's chancellor. The Tsar agreed rather half-heartedly but he refused to consider any truce negotiations with Poland. In the end, the war against Sweden brought nothing but the humiliating terms of the Kardis treaty which confirmed the Stolbova agreement of 1617. Russia had failed to regain her foothold on the Baltic coast.

Meanwhile the war with Poland dragged on, its fortunes definitely against the Russians. It would have ended disastrously for Alexis if the Turkish attack on Poland had not compelled Jan-Kazimir to send some of his forces to the south. In 1667 the Treaty of Andrussovo ended the carnage. Its terms were rather surprisingly favourable for Russia who regained Smolensk and Kiev. But the Baltic problem, so clearly envisaged by Ordyn-Natchokin, was left unsolved.

The Tsar had great hopes for the first-born, also called Alexis. In 1659, at the age of five, the boy left the Terem for his own palace, the great scholar, Simeon Polotzky, Rtitchev, one of the most enlightened Muscovites of the day, and Ordyn-Natchokin being his tutors. 'I wish the Tsarevich to be prepared for the future,' said the Tsar.

The boy showed little love for sports and open-air games. Books and lessons meant everything to him. To please him, the Tsar had foreign journals sent to Moscow and translated into Russian. Soon enough Polotzky knew that the boy's intelligence was far above the average. By the time he was ten, young Alexis had learned Greek, Latin, German and Italian. History and geography delighted him. He begged to be taught philosophy and the time came when he would not be parted from his Aristotle. With the Tsar's permission, Russian ambassadors returning from abroad were received by young Alexis and they were amazed at the questions put to them by the boy. Not all of them were easy to answer.

In 1667, although he was only thirteen, the Tsarevich was 'announced' to the people. Everybody remarked that he looked much older than his age.

He made very few public appearances. He kept studying harder and harder. At Christmas 1669 his absence at church services was explained by 'chest trouble'. In the middle of January 1670 the boy was dead. The Tsar, barely forty-one at the time, looked an old man. All his hopes had been fixed on his first-born whose lovable nature and great attainments had promised so much. There was – at that time – comparative peace along Russian borders, and her trade grew from year to year together with an ever deepening consciousness that the days of her cloistral isolation were numbered. Alexis the Younger had received an education which, together with his natural gifts, would certainly have enabled him to steer his country towards an ever widening acceptance of Western culture. The Tsar had certainly been justified in feeling that the goodly heritage he hoped to leave would come into hands capable of holding it.

Deep winter lay all over Russia and deep winter lay in the Tsar's heart. He still had two sons living, but Fedor, the elder, was even more delicate than his grandfather, Tsar Michael, had been, and Ivan had 'a sad head' to quote the contemporary euphemism for near-idiocy. In the Terem lived a very clever and brilliantly educated daughter, Sophia, then aged thirteen, but to Alexis she was just one of his many daughters destined for the grey path of secluded spinsterhood.

Troubling breaths of mutinies which kept breaking out till the very end of the reign, wars, the schism in the national Church and the subsequent defection of Patriarch Nikon, at one time the Tsar's most intimate friend and counsellor, occasional tumults in the streets of Moscow and even at the sittings of the Boyar Duma, and always the invigorating influence of such staunch 'Westerners' as Ordyn-Natchokin, Rtitchev, Artamon Matveev and Prince Ivan Golytzin – the years' tapestry had far too many living elements for the persuasion of *Domostróy* not to begin slipping into its grave. The end of 1671 saw the return of music and singing at the Kremlin with the Tsar's second marriage to Natalia Naryshkina, a beautiful, vivacious but not very intelligent girl of seventeen, who, having been brought up by the Matveevs, had imbibed many 'Western' ideas from her foster-father's Scottish wife. The first theatre was built at the Kremlin, with plays, based on biblical themes, written by Simeon Polotzky. The grim decree to ban all manner of merry-making throughout the country had long since been in polite abeyance.

The Tsar's travels during the long Polish war had extended far more than his geographical horizons. He would make careful notes of different clothes, manners, furniture, trees and plants seen during his absence from Russia. Back at home, he began visiting the crown estates, and himself wrote detailed instructions to bailiffs about timber, cattle and corn. At Izmailovo, his favourite country palace about three miles out of Moscow, the Tsar created gardens which moved foreign visitors to admiration. Great Muscovite landowners of the past had seldom, if ever, been interested in horticulture. Alexis delighted in it. Gooseberry bushes, being a novelty, seemed as worthwhile as roses and lilacs. There was a zealously cared for vineyard and a small grove of mulberry trees. Alexis ordered plants and seeds from all over the world and his herb gardens were in the charge of German experts. The Tsar introduced agricultural implements from England and had cattle imported from the Low Countries.

But all those were individual ventures into the realm of the unusual. The countryside at large was never affected by them. The peasantry continued working in their fields after the ancestral fashion, and horticulture would never reach the village. Again the Tsar's exertions towards the establishment of more and more industries had no other end than that of replenishing the treasury. He organized expeditions to Siberia in search of silver ore and he would choose foreign experts to stand at the head of all these enterprises, such was his confidence in the technical supremacy of the foreigner. On one occasion he wrote to his agents in Prussia that they were 'to search for enlightened men able to make roads under rivers and lakes and through mountains.' He certainly desired prosperity for the country he governed, but it does not seem that any of the measures by him begun were directed at the amelioration of the conditions under which nearly three-quarters of his subjects were living.

Alexis kept most zealously all the pious practices commanded by the Church, but even those were not allowed to interfere with his work. Secretaries always followed him to church and important letters were dictated during the less solemn moments of a service. Tsar Alexis had a finely-developed sense of logic: he was God's anointed and his business was entrusted to him by his Maker, and it followed that there was no reason against his pursuing that business in God's house.

In one way, the busy Tsar was a forerunner of Catherine the Great. In all the instructions sent to his ambassadors abroad he emphasized the importance of presenting the Russian matter from the sunniest possible angle. To Catherine, the terrible Pougachev mutiny was no more than 'a spot of trouble in the south'. Alexis depicted his country's prosperity and peaceful intentions at a time when his armies were engaged north and south, east and west, and when a succession of poor harvests had brought Russia to the very threshold of famine. It was neither boastfulness nor vainglory but rather the constantly deepening consciousness that, no foreigner having ever written the truth about Muscovy, it was time for the Muscovites themselves to present their own case as their eyes saw it.

Alexis's private account books make pleasant reading today. He had small use for personal extravagances. All the dazzling luxury at his court, the jewels he wore on public occasions, and the fabulous presents he gave were in answer to the demands his high office made on him. Those private books strike warm and homely notes, a record left by a wealthy man able and happy to help his kind and anxious that such help should not appear in any official records. Not a single name follows any sum given by him – so much for a wedding, a dowry, a christening, a funeral, for fire damage, 'for great patience in captivity', 'to pay off the debts', 'to build a house', 'to buy medicines' and, finally, a sum given to a coachman 'for coat and boots'.

In 1652, at the age of twenty-three, the Tsar wrote to the Patriarch, 'Now they listen to me and things get done without dissension and argument.' He fully understood the meaning of autocracy. He could not be said always to understand the responsibilities it carried. He blundered badly in the matter of the future Russo–Swedish relations and left an uncomfortable legacy to one of his sons. He had not enough means to tackle one of the most difficult problems his successors would have to face – the continuous unrest in the deep south together with a clarified policy towards Turkey. He had a great new world opened before him, and of sheer necessity he had to make his way by slow and careful inches. His vision certainly might have been clearer in what concerned Poland, whose supremacy over Slav countries was definitely on the wane towards the end of his reign.

The extent of his private generosity certainly argues a kindly nature. Alexis's temper was terrifying, his repentances swift and genuine. But was he a humanist in the true sense of the word? Hardly. To take but one point, there was his attitude towards the peasantry. Whenever details of injustice or brutality in an individual case came to Alexis's notice, he at once atoned for the injustice and softened the consequences of brutality. But in a larger sense his point of view was wholly different. He had no feeling for the peasant masses as men and women and no improvement of their hard lot found its way into the reformed laws. Every stratum of society as he found it on his accession had its duties and rights. The Tsar's responsibility lay in safeguarding the rights and in exacting the duties of each stratum. To lighten the burdens borne by the peasants would have meant interfering with the rights of another social stratum. Not the heart but reason alone guided the Tsar's policy.

A son was born to him in May 1672, a child whose sturdy physique certainly pleased Alexis. But by that time the climate at the Kremlin was vitiated by the rivalry between the Miloslavsky family, kin of Alexis's first wife, and the Naryshkin clan. The Tsar's temper soured in the last years of his life. The Razin revolt deepened his fears of further conspiracies much nearer home than the Caspian. His public appearances grew rarer and rarer. No mention was made of the nature of his illness when he died in January 1676 in his forty-seventh year. His death was said to be 'peaceful'.

The sun had never set upon his anger; he had never betrayed a friend, or harboured ignoble grudges against a defeated enemy. Almost all the happenings of his reign suggest how much more he might have done if he had not been yoked to a lichen-covered tradition.

III
A Woman at the Kremlin

Sophia, third daughter of Tsar Alexis, born 1657,
died 1704. Regent, 1682–89

SHE WAS the fourth child and the third daughter of Tsar Alexis, and her arrival could not be said to give much joy to her parents. A traditionally solemn christening, generous alms to the city beggars, and a banquet at the Kremlin were so many necessities linked with the birth of a sovereign's child. But once the shouting was over, Moscow forgot Sophia, and it is doubtful if the rest of the country had even learned her name.

Nothing at all is known of her early years except that for once life at the Terem did not follow the normal pattern. Sophia's mother, Tsarina Maria Miloslavskaya, should have had precedence there, but frequent illnesses and pregnancies compelled Maria to stay in the background. The matriarch's place was taken by Princess Irina, Sophia's aunt, a sour-thoughted spinster, whose broken betrothal to a Danish prince had left her firmly committed to the isolationist ways of ancient Muscovy. Irina's grip was iron. She did not trouble even to look for a velvet glove. A younger sister, Anna, followed her slavishly, but there was another, the gentle and surprisingly learned Princess Tatiana, never popular in the Terem, whose kindliness and even temper somewhat softened the stoniness of Irina's government.

The harsh and unpromising background of tedious compulsory prayers and services, fasts appointed as punishments, heavily pious conversation and frequent whippings may well – for all we know – have contained hints that Tsar Alexis's third daughter would not be content to remain a thin submissive shadow gliding along a darkly painted wall. Yet there is neither rumour nor legend to throw the least light upon the narrow tunnel of her childhood spent within the walls of the Terem.

Obscurity breaks down after Sophia had passed her tenth birthday, and the first evidences go far to prove that in spite of Princess Irina's grimly reactionary tutelage, the child had been nourished on breaths alien to the common life of the Terem, and that the influences that moulded her had not been wholly feminine, contracted into the narrow grooves of piety, gossip, needlework and the excitement of a novel 'subtlety' for dinner. It is equally obvious that the ordinary Terem diversions, such as the edifying narratives of 'God's fools' and pilgrims and the antics of court dwarfs, had not deeply engaged Sophia's attention. Finally, it was evident that she, though early enough taught to use her needle, was much more at her ease with a book, and that she liked to listen to conversations between the Tsar, his heir and their intimates. Therefore, Irina's rule could not have been that of an autocrat and Tatiana's healthy influence must have made itself felt at an early date.

By the time Sophia was ten, she knew her brother's tutor, the enlightened humanist Rtitchev, to whose energies and generosity Moscow owed her first hospitals and almshouses. She had also met Ordyn-Natchokin and had something of an idea about the pattern of the world outside Moscow. She knew her father's English doctor, Collins, who talked to her about Parliament in England. She was deeply attached to her uncle, Prince Ivan Miloslavsky who, though a prodigiously indolent man, kept telling her that work alone lay at the root of man's happiness.

Little girls in the Terem were fortunate indeed if an opportunity to listen came their way. But they dared not open their own mouths unless asked a question by their elders – which did not happen very often. Sophia did not talk, but she must have listened creatively. Her hunger for larger horizons than those allowed by the Terem compelled her to absorb every detail. The Andrussovo Treaty delighted her. Ordyn-Natchokin's inauguration of a postal service between Russia, Courland, Poland and Sweden seemed to her little short of a miracle. Alexis the Younger was deeply in her confidence, and it was he who suggested to the Tsar that Simeon Polotzky should become Sophia's tutor.

Simeon Polotzky entered Sophia's life when the Tsar, back from his travels in Poland, felt more than ever drawn to Western thought and custom. It was a propitious moment for Moscow and it proved a landmark for Sophia. Polotzky, for all he was an Orthodox cleric, belonged to the West. A consummate Latinist and proficient in other languages, with the exception of Greek, at home in European political drifts, Polotzky was not slow to realize that in Sophia he had a pupil whose intelligence and thirst for knowledge compelled him to give of his best, and Polotzky's best was good indeed. From the start, his lessons illumined many dark corners for Sophia. Maps and books from the Tsar's library were brought into the Terem, and she pored over them. Polotzky taught her Latin, French and Polish. What was much more immediate and important, he gave her the day's political landscape, and his lessons set Sophia on fire. She understood that a permanent peace with Poland was a *sine qua non* for her country, to lessen the threat from Sweden. Her recorded criticism of France and Denmark for the support they gave to the Dutch against England proves that even in her early teens Sophia was able to read the political map of Western Europe. Under the brilliant tuition of Polotzky, history became a well of living water to her. Collins, her father's English physician, began giving her regular lessons in English history, and Sophia came to understand why her father had refused to acknowledge the Commonwealth. When she heard about Charles II's love affairs, she said they did not matter. 'A king can do what he likes in his palace and in the country.' 'But not in England,' replied Collins, 'because of Parliament.' Sophia paused to reflect. 'Your Parliament,' she said to her father's doctor, 'is a real puzzle. One beheaded the King's father. Another recalled the King. So political institutions can be either vicious or virtuous. But your kind of Parliament would never do for my country.'

After a history lesson with Polotzky, Sophia asked abruptly: 'Am I right that the greatest danger to sovereignty lies in treason?'

'Yes,' said Polotzky, 'but sovereignty is a great responsibility to be accounted for before God.'

'Ah,' replied the thirteen-year-old girl, brought up in the most narrow surroundings imaginable, 'that is far harder than being accountable to man.'

Sophia condemned the Thirty Years' War as a wicked futility since, as she saw it, the mailed fist and the matter of the altar should have nothing to do with each other, but the spiritual accents of the

Reformation spoke a somewhat familiar language to her, for all the numberless differences of scope and environment. Patriarch Nikon's reforms in the Russian Church were followed by a schism, the so-called '*Raskól*'. It was officially proscribed, but its adherents were many and some of them found their way into the Terem. They were known as the Old Believers and held God's truth to be contained in age-hallowed gestures, such as, for instance, that two fingers and not three must be used to make the sign of the Cross, and in ancient service books, though they were full of scribes' omissions and mistakes. The Muscovite schism seemed a small enough matter by comparison with the Western upheaval, but Sophia knew that it troubled her father.

Month by month, year by year, Polotzky continued moulding Sophia's mind, and more and more she felt drawn to the West, its achievements, freedoms and promises. More and more clearly did she begin to understand that her own country could not afford to continue in its isolation. Her studies in Russian history ended by convincing Sophia that the circumstances which had led to the creation of barriers between Muscovy and the West belonged to the past, and that there was every reason to develop a rapprochement with the West by means of gradually and prudently introduced reforms. Her tutor, himself a convinced Westerner, made it clear to his pupil that there was a contribution the Russian mind could make during the process of assimilating the Western content. It was a daringly novel idea for those times, and Sophia seized it eagerly. It certainly answered her national pride. It also accorded with her own ambition.

❋

Yet all those were so many glimpses into a future, its promise hard to foretell. The landscape of the present hour carried few pleasant colours. Tsar Alexis's reform of the law had eased the lot of some of his subjects but it had hardened that of many more, particularly the peasants.

Up to the mid-seventeenth century a peasant's servitude had not been complete; he used to be tied to the land but not to the owner of the land. A peasant enjoyed many civic rights; he could make a will and engage labour, and he was at liberty to sell the surplus of the yearly yield. By paying a certain sum to the landowner, the peasant could redeem himself 'from the land tie' and turn from agriculture to trade. His condition was in no way to be compared with that of real serfs, the so-called '*kholópy*', who belonged absolutely to the owners of the land they tilled.

But Tsar Alexis's '*Oulózhenie*' laid it down that a peasant must be bound to the landowner's person, and little by little the enjoyment of civic rights came to be whittled down until there was no difference between the peasant stratum and that of the serfs. In other words, Sophia's father had begun what Catherine the Great would complete – the absolute servitude of the peasantry. In Sophia's own day, that measure was taken as a juridical precaution since vagabondage among peasants constituted a serious menace to law-abiding people and led to grievous dereliction of the land forsaken by the labourer for more than one season. Enlarged rights over the labour force added to the landowners' responsibility and the cumbrous government machinery was relieved of at least one of its burdens. None the less, a harsh measure considered necessary in view of the slow-to-heal ravages of the Troubled Years proved to be the foundation stone of the worst evil in Russian history.

Such problems, however, were still too complicated for Sophia to grasp. She had never been out of Moscow but she knew quite enough about national distresses, and the frequent mutinies could not but occupy her thoughts. She knew well they were caused by penury, famine and graft. The very vastness of her father's dominions, lack of regular communication partly owing to the climate but mostly to the scarcity of roads, the sheer physical impossibility to keep a check on numberless administrative lapses from justice, all of it together turned the business of governing into a life-long dedicated activity – which demanded ceaseless efforts of mind and will. The map of her father's possessions soon teased Sophia's latent ambition. That colossus of a country stretched from Archangel in the north to Astrakhan in the south. To the west lay the temporarily quietened boundary with Poland. Far to the east was Siberia where the unceasing, occasionally clumsy Russian penetration had already begun troubling Peking. And Muscovy's trade was expanding year by year, reaching out to Bokhara, Persia and India.

But to Sophia the key to further expansion, greater prosperity and a less imperfect administrative efficiency did not lie in the east. She considered the Crimean Peninsula as a gateway to a European recognition. She traced the course through the Black Sea and the

Straits into the heart of the Mediterranean world, the cradle of European culture. She was intensely practical but her realism was not of the wooden kind to forbid her cherishing visions. Polotzky had early taught her to distinguish the civilizing march of the mind from a severely technical progress.

Her studies kept being enlarged. She perfected her Latin, and her knowledge of French enabled her to translate some plays of Molière. She knew whole passages from Caesar and Tacitus by heart, and tried to imitate Horace and Catullus in her own admittedly home-spun verses.

But, the growing volume of her enlightenment notwithstanding, Sophia still remained a virtual prisoner in the Terem, subject to the deadly monotony of the daily run and the numberless pious ordinances. It is a matter for wonder how and where the girl found time to pursue her private studies, and so inobtrusively, too, that none, her tutor excepted, took the least notice of the Tsar's third daughter, known to be passably good with her needle and fairly assiduous at her devotions. Her aunts Irina and Anna saw to that. Her aunt Tatiana must have known the truth and was wise enough not to mention it to others.

Sophia was thirteen and considered 'grown-up', not for her mental attainments but for a physical reason, when the early death of Alexis the Younger made Fedor the heir to the crown. He was a gentle eight-year-old, subject to frequent illnesses and so frail that he could hardly wear the heavy ceremonial robes of a Tsarevich. He was known to love books, to hate all manner of open-air sport, and to fear war. There was no other male Romanov except for Sophia's still younger brother Ivan, the 'sad-headed child'.

Tsarina Maria having been dead for some time, Tsar Alexis's second marriage in 1670 flung the Kremlin into a turmoil. Natalia Naryshkina was a beautiful social nobody. Her foster-father, one Artamon Matveev, for all that he enjoyed the Tsar's friendship, could boast of no ancient descent. The Miloslavsky family were horrified. Natalia was eighteen, incredibly lovely and as incredibly feather-brained. Inordinately fond of music, singing and sweets, she could not have been a menace to the Miloslavsky had she not possessed a crowd of male relations.

The Miloslavsky found themselves ousted from their place of honour, and the Terem became a battlefield in little. Sophia, a mere four years younger than her unwelcome and silly stepmother, stood wholly committed to the Miloslavsky party, but such was her prudence that she never permitted herself to take sides in any of the frequent imbroglios in the Terem rooms. None but her Aunt Tatiana knew her mind. It must have been galling for Sophia to watch a chit of a Tsarina, of unimportant origins and brought up on charity, take precedence over her aunts, sisters and herself. To make matters even more difficult for the Terem ladies, Natalia's health left nothing to be desired. Unlike her predecessor, she did not vanish into her bedroom with a headache or some other ailment, and remain there for days. Kneeling, as custom demanded, morning and evening to kiss the young Tsarina's hand, Sophia hoped that the unwanted stepmother might give birth to a succession of daughters.

Meanwhile, the Naryshkin men, inebriated by their kinswoman's elevation, became wholly at home at the Kremlin. The Tsar's apartments, the banqueting hall and the council chamber were all open to them. They lacked education, manners and political acumen. They certainly did not lack arrogance. They visited the Terem often enough, privileged as they were because of their relationship to the young Tsarina. From her corner Sophia watched them, and kept reminding herself that there still remained her brother, Fedor. However frail, he would certainly reach his manhood, marry, and beget sons to follow him. And Sophia thought of such things all the harder when Natalia's pregnancy became known at the Teren.

A crisis broke on 30th May 1672 when the young Tsarina gave birth to a son christened Peter. The Naryshkin star became a constellation overnight. The Terem rang with many sourly-worded exchanges, Natalia's own ladies insisting that the newborn baby was unlike any other in health, strength and intelligence, and the Miloslavsky princesses exerted themselves in singing the praises of their nephews and brothers. Sophia listened to it all and remained aloof. The situation grew somewhat calmer when someone remembered that the Tsar was still in his forties and blessed with remarkably good health.

And, still in his forties, Alexis died in 1676, and Fedor was Tsar at fourteen. His bodily frame was frail. His will was firm. He disliked all quarrelling. He showed courtesy to his widowed step-mother, her foster-father Matveev remained at court, and none of the Naryshkin men fell from favour. But the Miloslavsky clan began girding up their loins, and it pleased them to watch the deep friendship between the boy-Tsar and Sophia. It was not long before her uncles and cousins realized that she had not been Polotzky's pupil for nothing.

Sophia's discretion was incredible. She heard much malevolent gossip in the Terem and repeated none of it. Compelled to be present at many family arguments and even quarrels, she neither took sides nor lost her temper. She forced herself to follow Fedor's example and showed great courtesy to Natalia, whose only concern now was for her son, Peter, remarkably precocious for his four years and already absorbed in military games.

Sophia was nineteen, her horizons enlarged, her ambition fully matured. Carefully and unerringly she took to intrigue. Tsarina Natalia was insignificant enough. Not so, however, her foster-father, Artamon Matveev, who was the honorary head of Apothecaries' Hall, and there lay an opportunity not to be ignored. Sophia made no move that could be traced to her, but in the presence of some cousins she dropped a hint or two about the doubtful efficacy of medicines sent from the Hall since the young Tsar's health did not seem to improve. She said no more. By 1678 Fedor's condition worsened, and Prince Ivan Miloslavsky spoke rather anxiously about some mixtures alleged to have been prepared at Matveev's orders. Sophia did not hesitate to repeat her uncle's words to the Tsar though she would not admit that she believed in the story. But Fedor did. There followed a hurried and rather clumsy inquiry. No guilt could be laid at Matveev's door, but the suspicion was enough to deprive him of all his court offices and to exile him to the north. Tsarina Natalia, her little son and daughter left the Kremlin for Kolomenskoye Palace in the neighbourhood of Moscow, and the Naryshkin leaven vanished from the court.

Sophia had won the first round of a difficult and dangerous game. To make things even more pleasant for her, the death of Princess Irina made Tatiana the head of the Terem, or nominally so. In reality, the reins were in Sophia's hands, and soon enough she decided that the moment had come to enlarge her personal liberty of movement and behaviour.

That meant an unprecedented challenge to tradition. It was an unheard-of thing for a woman, even if she were the Tsar's sister, to visit the Tsar's private apartments, to listen to his ministers' discussions, and even to confront those ministers with pithily relevant questions about the Crimea, Turkey, Sweden and Poland, about trade, import dues, taxation and the development of home industries, about finance and the administration of justice. With the exception of the Miloslavsky clan, all the Boyars were taken aback, but the Tsar's presence forbade the least expression of bewilderment, surprise and, most understandably, anger that a woman, be she a Tsar's daughter ten times over, should permit herself to open her lips in the presence of men – and one of those men the Tsar, her sovereign and brother. The Boyars looked to their lord for a lead. Fedor gave none. He listened to his sister. It appeared that he was satisfied and that the incredible situation was accepted by him. There was nothing for the Boyars to do, and Sophia, none hindering her, continued her education in the Council hall.

In the Terem she now had a spacious room where none, not even Princess Tatiana, might enter without an invitation. Men came to that room not to listen to singers or story-tellers but to discuss the day's state matters – Medvedev, a priest, Polotzky's great friend and pupil, Prince Vassily Golytzin, by far the most enlightened Westerner in Moscow, Yazykov, who had much to do with the army, Likhachev, a noted jurist, and many others.

In 1680 Tsar Fedor married a girl of no great social consequence, one Agafia Grushevska. Within a year the young Tsarina bore a son Ilya, who survived his mother by a bare few days. Agafia's death was followed by a prolonged illness of the Tsar. Sophia, fully conscious of standing near the most important threshold in her life, hardly ever left her brother's bedside. It was more or less natural that during his long convalescence she should slip into the rôle of an intermediary between the sovereign and his government. Sophia had enemies without number, but even those were compelled to admit that the Tsar's sister had 'a man's brain and clarity of judgment'.

Meanwhile the lichen-grown yoke of the Terem grew lighter month by month. Princess Tatiana was no martinet, and it served Sophia's purposes to have her aunts, sisters and cousins share with her at least a few of the liberties she had wrested for herself. Formalities about strangers entering the Terem were being dispensed with one by one. The ladies no longer veiled their faces in the presence of men, cosmetics began to be used almost too lavishly, and intimate suppers were given, with wine and mead appearing on the table. At Kolomenskoye, Tsarina Natalia was heard to accuse her stepdaughter of dallying with the Evil One. For all her many occupations, the stepdaughter found time to gather and digest information about Kolomenskoye, now definitely an enemy camp from her point of view. Her half-brother, little Peter, had a more than indifferent tutor, one Nikita Zotov, known to have a greater passion for the juice of the grape than he had ever had for letters. Peter's real teachers were engineers and artisans from the German Quarter of Moscow. Sophia heard much about the boy's intelligence, energy and temper. She also learned that he was interested in nothing except military games and that he was known to excel in the beating of the drum.

Early in 1682, in the last desperate hope of begetting an heir, Fedor married Marfa Apraxyna. Within a few weeks he took to his bed – never to leave it again. The Terem saw hardly anything of Sophia. With her brother's approval, she now attended the sessions of the Duma, seated in a chair placed at her orders just a little lower than her brother's throne.

All was confusion at the Kremlin. The young Tsar's strength ebbed from day to day. His bride had an uncommon gift of tears and nothing much else. To sharpen everybody's uncertainty, Fedor refused to name his heir. In bald fact, there was nobody for him to name. His younger brother, Ivan, was wholly unfit to govern. Little Peter's accession would mean a prolonged regency, and Fedor could not see his silly stepmother and her unprincipled kin as regents. When Patriarch Joachim, a close ally of Tsarina Natalia, begged the Tsar to name Peter as his successor, Fedor did not reply. Sophia, present in the room, kept silent in her turn.

Those were difficult days for her. She realized that Prince Vassily Golytzin, even then already supposed to be her lover, remained her only partisan of consequence. Prince Ivan Miloslavsky and his kin certainly hoped that their cause would win and just as certainly had no wish to see a woman, however closely related to them, at the helm. Sophia had no known adherents at the Duma. Medvedev, Yazykov and Likhachev were staunchly loyal but of no marked standing in the administrative circles.

Sophia was twenty-five, her very peculiar genius in full accord with her ambition. The Tsar's will being sacrosanct, Fedor's last wishes would have been carried out even if they were at wild variance with tradition, and it would not have been difficult for Sophia to influence her brother, accustomed as he was to turn to her for advice and encouragement. She did not so influence him. She remained in the foreground, and she forbade herself to make the least move and waited for events to decide her future.

They moved rapidly. On 27th April 1682 Fedor died, the abolition of hereditary precedence and the encouragement of letters the main achievements of the six years' reign. The very same day Patriarch Joachim held a secret meeting at his own palace, having had his servants summon a vast crowd to the Red Square. The mob, following instructions which they had neither time nor intelligence to understand, began shouting: 'We want Peter for our Tsar . . . Peter . . . Peter. . . .' The Patriarch and the Duma at once summoned Tsarina Natalia and her son to Moscow. The Naryshkins and all their friends hurried to the Kremlin. From one staircase to another rang excited, angry voices calling Sophia a traitress to tradition, a friend at once of the Jesuits and the Turks, a whore and a heretic. All the doors leading to the Terem were closely guarded by Sophia's adherents.

In her own room, she and Princess Tatiana consulted together in privacy. The elder woman, jealous for her niece's honour, wept and murmured that they should wait for a right moment to come. Her eyes dry, her voice calm and cold, Sophia replied that the right moment was come.

Protocol demanded that Fedor's coffin was to be followed by his widow in a curtained litter and by Peter on foot. Since Fedor's successor was but a child, his mother decided to join the procession – also in a litter. To the amazement of the household, the government and the people in the Red Square, Sophia had every member of the Terem following Tsarina Natalia's litter. The ladies crossed the square on foot, brief veils fluttering over their faces. Natalia's litter reaching the cathedral porch, she got out, turned, saw the ladies immediately behind her, lost her temper, and left without waiting for the service to begin. Sophia and all the others followed the little Tsar and remained in church till the very end of the service. Then Sophia led all her relations back across the square. At the gateway to the palace, she stopped, turned, drew back her veil, stared at the silent, bewildered crowds, and began a loud lamentation:

'Ah, here we are left all alone, with nobody to protect us. . . . My brother Ivan's rights have been passed over most unjustly. If there is any wrong imputed to him and to myself, we had best leave for abroad and live among truly Christian folk who have no hatred towards us. And it should be known to all in Moscow that wicked people hurried on my poor brother Fedor's death.'

On the surface, the incident suggests a desperate move made by someone aware that the last chance had slipped out of her grasp. It was nothing of the kind. Sophia had never faced a crowd before but she knew by instinct how to handle the people. She did not linger for their response. The last word said, she turned and the gates of the palace closed on her and the other ladies. The crowds dispersed in ominous silence. Many among them recalled the dark stories about suspicious medicines prepared for the late Tsar and Matveev's subsequent fall from grace. Once away from the Kremlin, people took to muttering. Fedor's reign, for all its brevity, had endeared him to the Muscovites. He had been generous to many and gentle with all. Now folk said that Matveev was on his way back to Moscow. A mood of unease fell on the city. A mere boy for a Tsar and his mother's feather-brained kin to rule the country. . . . 'Where is Tsarevich Ivan?' asked someone. 'Nobody has seen him anywhere. . . . ' And there was no reply to the question.

That day Sophia made her first public appearance. Certainly, she was ambitious. But she was also a stateswoman of no mean degree. She knew that the Naryshkins and their friends could not govern and that Natalia was no more fit to be a regent than an infant in its cradle. Sophia knew, too, that the boy Peter, however brilliant and unusual his natural gifts, had never been taught to control his temper or bridle his will, or even to occupy himself except in the ways which pleased him – drums, guns, the building of miniature fortresses and various mechanical contrivances absorbed him utterly. His studies were still entrusted to a man least able to prepare him for the throne. Sophia certainly reflected gravely upon her own future, but her intelligence, to call it by no other name, forbade her to withhold the contribution she knew herself capable of making to the national courses.

Yet a single public gesture, however moving, was hardly enough to assure Sophia's foothold. Once back in the Terem she summoned all her adherents to a secret conference.

'*Strielzy*', the musketeers, the most powerful military element in the land, did not like the idea of a woman at the head of the government, but they liked the Naryshkins even less, and the boy Peter's constant preoccupation with the Dutch, the Scots and the Germans was an affront to great numbers among the men. Agents, trusted by Medvedev and Likhachev and paid by Sophia, discovered that murmuring had broken out among the musketeers on the very day of Fedor's death. The way seemed increasingly easy for further and deeper propaganda. Within a week nineteen musketeer regiments declared for the Miloslavsky faction and clamoured for Tsarevich Ivan to be Tsar. Sophia learned that she had evoked a tempest beyond her strength or cunning to control. It was no longer a matter of appealing to the people and dropping hints about possible future calamities. It was not even a matter for the people. The military, always held in high favour at the Kremlin, had control of the capital.

On 15th May 1682, massed regiments, all discipline ground to dust, stormed the palace, shouting that Tsarevich Ivan had been murdered by the Naryshkins and they were there to avenge the innocent blood. Shaking like a reed in the wind, the young prince was led to the upper steps of the porch. His appearance led to a moment of shamed silence and all might have gone well if old Prince Dolgoruki, head of all the musketeer regiments, had not shouted a harsh command at the men, and that was enough to release the wild beast in them all. They rushed up the steps. They no longer thought of either Peter or Ivan as Tsars. They thirsted for blood.

That day's ghastly massacre when Artamon Matveev, some of the Naryshkins and a number of their adherents were literally torn to pieces in the Red Square, is supposed to have left an indelible stamp on Peter's mind. They should have hurried the boy to the back of the palace. Instead they let him witness the horror.

In the end, blood-lust amply satisfied, the musketeers demanded that Ivan and Peter should reign together, with Sophia as regent during Peter's minority. The hierarchy and the Duma had no choice but to accept the will of the military, and none knew better than Sophia that the musketeers' support offered as much security as a leaking boat on a stormy sea.

In the tangled mass of wildly contradictory evidence, it is somewhat difficult to determine the extent of Sophia's direct responsibility for the May massacre. She had not, and even her bitterest enemies allowed it, summoned the musketeers to the Kremlin on that morning which was to leave the stones of the square red-stippled from end to end. On the other hand, Sophia was such a consummate actress that nobody could tell her genuine reaction to the massacre. It is obvious that the musketeers' final demand was in full accord with her own wishes. From the ethical point of view, she cannot be absolved from indirect responsibility for the terror let loose in the Red Square. If she had not planned it, she certainly did not protest against it.

✳

Now she was regent. Quickly but unhurriedly Sophia formed her government, with her uncle, Prince Ivan Miloslavsky, for treasurer and Prince Vassily Golitzyn for foreign affairs. She entrusted education to Medvedev and justice to 'a very honest man', one Sokovnin. She singled out an obscure civil servant by name of Shaklovity and made him State Secretary. In reality, Shaklovity, already Sophia's lover, was given an office equivalent to that of a modern prime minister. His ability certainly deserved the honour. He and Prince Vassily Golitzyn shared Sophia's favours at the time. They should have been rivals. They were friends, and both men served their mistress loyally to the end.

There remained the army. There seemed nobody fit for the office except Prince Khovansky, once governor of Moscow, but Sophia was far from being satisfied with that appointment. Good-looking, wealthy and vain, Khovansky made no secret of his hopes to marry the Regent. None the less, he was a good soldier, and his name spelt magic to the musketeers. Their pleasure at the appointment was but another reminder that Sophia's position rested on no other security than the will of the military. The musketeers were sternly admonished for their violence in May but they were not punished, and Sophia wondered if prudence might not be carried too far. She disliked Khovansky, whose manner occasionally brushed against impertinence. She also disliked the idea that her regency depended on the good will of the musketeers. 'I must change it all.' she said to herself.

Meanwhile a thousand tasks awaited Sophia's attention, and her first concern was to see her brothers crowned Tsars. There being no precedent for a dual coronation, court officials, goldsmiths and others had to work at high pitch to have everything ready by 26th June. Barely were the silent, vacant-looking youth and the bright, vivacious boy anointed than the first breath of danger came near Sophia.

There had been much trouble with the Old Believers during the preceding two reigns. In the summer of 1682, emboldened by Khovansky's appointment and by favours shown to the musketeers, many among whom were of the old persuasion, the leaders of the schism raised their voices again, hurling such a volume of invective against the hierarchy that the Regent decided to have an open debate between the bishops and the schismatics. It was to be held at the Kremlin with her presiding.

The Old Believers took heart and thought they had won the day. In the end, there was no debate but a turmoil. After much shouting and swearing, one of the Old Believers struck a bishop. Sophia at once ordered the offender to leave the assembly. Sullen murmuring broke among the musketeers on guard at the bottom of the hall. It was not fitting, they grumbled, for a woman to preside at an assembly of men. If the Tsarevna had no wish to go back to the Terem, there were enough convents in Moscow to receive her. Little by little, the men's voices reached Sophia. Her face impassive and her voice composed, she said that her brothers and herself could leave the country. 'And what will the people say once they know we have been driven away?' she ended in as casual a tone as though she were asking a clerk to fetch her a fresh quill.

The threat worked immediately, but Sophia at once remembered that Prince Khovansky was an Old Believer and the idol of all the musketeer regiments he now commanded. He was present in the hall, his handsome face inscrutable, but the Regent, having more than once repulsed his ardent wooing, recognized danger when it faced her.

The measures she took were apparently fantastic. She had her two brothers, all the relations and the court assembled in one of the private halls and told them she knew that the Kremlin was no longer safe for them. The very same day all of them together with the government left Moscow and went to one of the country palaces in the neighbourhood of the capital. They did not stay there long. They moved from one palace to another, from an abbey to a convent, and the Regent made it known everywhere that they could neither stay in Moscow nor remain for long at any spot since a terrible conspiracy had been formed against the two Tsars and herself, and she mentioned the existence of that conspiracy some time before she knew anything about it. They travelled, heavily guarded day and night. Sophia did not neglect the government business but for any official to see her meant running the gauntlet of most searching inquiries.

Soon enough she was proved right. A plot had been hatched in Moscow. Prince Khovansky, by virtue of his Rurik descent and relying on the support of the military, meant to seize power and proclaim himself tsar. The lengthy report reached Sophia when she was at Izmailovskoye Palace. At once she summoned the Duma and the list of Khovansky's transgressions was read out to the members. In the end, Khovansky was indicted on several counts. The sentence of death was passed on him *in absentia*. The session having been held behind closed and guarded doors, the Regent made all those present swear by the cross not to divulge their decision to anyone.

That done, Sophia sent a messenger to Moscow with an invitation to Khovansky to come to Izmailovskoye. He accepted light-heartedly, well aware that all the musketeer regiments were solidly behind him. But he was never to meet Sophia again. He had barely dismounted at the gateway of the palace when the guards overpowered him. Within a few minutes Khovansky's handsome head was rolling down the grassy slope and the guards were kicking his body out of sight.

When the news reached Moscow, all the musketeer regiments lost heart. Their leader gone, they dared not start a mutiny, and waited for the Regent's wrath to break upon their own heads, but Sophia, well aware that most of them were involved in the plot, reaped a triumph when she granted a free pardon to all the regiments.

Before winter broke upon the country, she was back at the

Kremlin, often working unto the small hours. Once again she proved that she was not Polotzky's pupil for nothing. The finely trained mind faced each problem in a most methodical way. She had indeed some hours of abandon with her two lovers when her senses responded to the delight each of them could offer her. But at her desk, absorbed in the business of governing, Sophia was not even androgynous. There she stayed icily sexless, all her faculties gathered together for the great and continuously exciting business of governing the country she sincerely loved and served so well. Within a bare two years Sophia had the entire army reorganized, lessened brigandage and other lawlessness in the country, drew up plans for the very first land survey, and busied herself with other home matters in a manner well ahead of her generation. She was the first to introduce measures against the appallingly high incidence of fire and certain of the precautions were embodied in the law. In Moscow and some other towns streets were to be kept clean and penalties were imposed on public brawling. She allocated great sums for the printing of books and attempted, however ineffectually, to fight the general illiteracy.

But illiteracy was not the only dragon for her to fight. There was graft up and down the entire length of the administrative ladder. There was the deadening hand of inertia and the leaden excuse that things used to be done in such and such a way a hundred years ago, which was a valid enough reason for getting them done in precisely the same way at the end of the seventeenth century.

Yet she did not despair. 'Trade must go on expanding,' she said to the Duma. She signed commercial treaties with Sweden and Poland, encouraged home industries by a careful easing of taxation, and saw textiles and iron added to the list of exports. During the regency, trade with England, the Low Countries, Brandenburg and Saxony expanded to a remarkable extent. 'They always need furs in the West,' she said to Prince Golytzin, 'and there is Siberia – but we must not cheapen our prices. They want the furs. They must be made to pay the prices we fix.'

Yet Sophia was only Regent. When foreign ambassadors went to the Kremlin, they were received by two Tsars and their sister who sat a step lower than the two thrones. The ambassadors reported that Tsar Ivan seemed always asleep, that Tsar Peter looked a bright and intelligent boy and that quite obviously their sister governed the hour. Yet Peter was ten when she became Regent and Sophia never forgot that his minority would be over at sixteen.

There does not exist a really authentic portrait of her, and all contemporary descriptions differ wildly one from another. Some called her beautiful and others stressed her ugliness. We know that she was tall and carried herself as befitted her rank. Even her enemies could not deny her brains, and an ambassador from Germany went the length of comparing her with Elizabeth Tudor. Prudent, even-tempered, Sophia was never drunk, or heard using coarse language, or behaved cruelly to her personal attendants. Whatever reforms she envisaged would not have lessened the exigencies of protocol. The Regent moved in traditional splendour, did not favour low company, and never wavered in her piety. The veil off her face and touches of colour on cheeks and mouth were by her judged sufficient to prove her outward adherence to a new way of life. But she was still veiled when present at religious ceremonies and she never appeared at public banquets.

In 1683 Turkey invaded Austria, who turned to Poland for help, and Poland did not refuse it. Yet Sobiesky's triumph was all too speedily forgotten in Vienna. The Crimean Tartars once again began ravaging Polish lands in the south, and Poland turned to Moscow for help. The Regent did not hurry with her reply. The Sultan, the Crimean Khan and the Emperor in turn sent embassies to Moscow to inch their way towards 'a closer understanding', but Sophia was somewhat chary of such advances and her real plans were hooded by pleasant generalities.

In the end, with the full consent of the Duma, she promised to help Poland by opening a campaign against the Crimean Tartars and, whilst memories of a beleaguered Vienna were still fresh in Europe, Sophia sent her own embassies to practically every capital to urge the necessity of meeting the Turkish peril by concerted action. The emissaries from Moscow were rebuffed everywhere, Denmark excepted. The West had different problems to consider. Still, in spite of the chilly reception, those embassies were not quite fruitless. For the first time since the thirteenth century official

Russian voices had been heard in the West – not to discuss this or that export but to give warning of a danger common to all countries. The Regent did not feel deeply disappointed at the apparently barren results of those embassies. It would take time for Muscovy to win confidence in the West. 'It would never do for them to know that we are distressed,' she told her counsellors, and Golytzin, Medvedev and, above all, Shaklovity agreed with her.

Sophia needed a consort to lessen the insecurity of her power. Khovansky's rank would have qualified him for such a marriage, but the man's disloyalty and greed of power determined Sophia's decision to repulse him. Vassily Golytzin might well have been her husband. Unfortunately, he was a married man and – odd as it seems – still devoted to his wife. Shaklovity was a commoner whom she could never marry. Her immediate kin offered little enough help. Her uncle, Prince Ivan Miloslavsky, preferred to sham illness whenever she needed him most. The numerous cousins saw in Sophia a pleasant embodiment of their personal ambition and looked no further. With Tsarina Natalia living in retirement away from the capital, all was peace in Terem. Tsarina Praskovia Saltykove, Ivan's wife, however quarrelsome by nature, stood in great awe of her sister-in-law. Moreover, Tsarina Praskovia was passionately interested in food and preferred to keep away from 'all grave matters', since they were apt to interfere with her digestion. She ended by presenting her imbecile husband with four daughters, and greatly amused the other ladies in the Terem by her incredible capacity for pancakes and rissoles.

But Sophia had not much leisure to spare for Terem matters. The business of governing grew and grew. Soon she was an autocrat, co-equal in authority with her brothers, and St Sophia's day was observed as a national festival together with the Tsars' feast-days. Her name and titles appeared on all the official documents and her power was recognized even in Peking where she sent an embassy to settle the thorny question of the banks of the Amur.

Yet, her few counsellors apart, Sophia stood very much alone. Neither her aunt Tatiana, nor her favourite sister, Martha, could follow her all the way. She might have created a strong party to oppose her undoubted enemies in the Duma, but she never did so since there were not enough men of standing she felt she could trust. She had crowds of low-born and faithful adherents, but to create a new aristocracy lay beyond her power. Even anointed Tsars could not ennoble. The only title in pre-Petrine Russia was that of a prince, and all those who bore it were direct descendants either of Rurik or of Guedemin. Public services would be rewarded by grants of land, serfs, jewellery, costly furs and money, but no Tsar could bestow blue blood. Sophia might well have put a coronet on Shaklovity's head, but she was too much of a realist to launch an innovation which would have confused and irritated the people accustomed to the idea that aristocrats were born and not made. It would be left to her brother to swell the thinning ranks of nobility with princes, counts and barons, but his prince-pieman remained a pieman all his days, and Peter's great-grandson's barber remained a barber for all the dignities a count's rank bestowed on him.

It was in 1687 that the first cloud appeared in Sophia's sky. She had kept a careful watch on all the happenings at Preobrazhenskoye Palace for five years. Peter was now fifteen, and the old capital hummed with endless stories about him. A giant in stature, the young Tsar spent little time with his mother and sister and appeared at the Kremlin very rarely. Diplomatic functions bored him and ecclesiastical ceremonies irritated him by their length. Sophia refused to believe that her half-brother, openly inimical to the national ethos and flagrantly contemptuous of the people's sanctuaries, would ever capture a great following. She heard much of his incredible intelligence and illimitable energy. She knew enough about his terrible temper. The names of the mistresses he enjoyed in the German Quarter of Moscow were familiar to her. She knew of his devotion to the Dutch and the Germans, his ceaseless preoccupation with military matters and his marvellous capacity for drink. She shrugged all of it away. By far the most important weapon she had was Peter's coarse contempt for national sanctities.

And now, all suddenly, her half-brother appeared at a Duma session. He did not stay long. He never spoke. He was not particularly polite to her or to anyone else. But he came – as was his right to do. He sat on the throne so seldom occupied. He listened to what someone was saying about the Astrakhan fisheries. He fidgeted, bit his nails, and went. There was nobody to ask him why had he come at all.

Sophia refused to feel troubled. The Astrakhan fisheries were a small enough matter. The Duma had far weightier business on hand, the opening of the Crimean campaign which started in the spring of 1688 and ended in a disastrous retreat supposedly due to treason among the Cossacks. In reality, the *débâcle* must be laid at Sophia's door: she stumbled into her first major mistake by making Prince Vassily Golytzin her commander-in-chief. A diplomat of no mean stature, he had as much ability to direct a difficult campaign as his own horse. The Regent's reasons for that unfortunate appointment remain an insoluble riddle. The allegation that she meant her lover to gather laurels is rather nonsensical: Golytzin's high reputation rested securely enough on his handling of foreign affairs. That she was blind enough to be assured of his abilities in the field is proved by her letters to him during the campaign.

Yet her popularity stood so firm that people did not murmur at the defeat. The return of the routed army to Moscow was marked by splendid festivities to recompense the men for the undoubted hardihoods they had endured. The weather, the difficult terrain and the Judas-like behaviour of the Cossacks were all blamed for the lack of palpable success. It was, noticed, however, that young Tsar Peter abstained from all the festivities and refused to meet Golytzin on his return.

'I suppose my brother is far too busy with his fortresses and boats,' remarked the Regent.

In January 1689 Tsarina Natalia, in the vain hope of weaning her unruly son from his constant debaucheries, had him married to Eudoxia Lopukhina. The bride was virtually forsaken after the first few weeks. When Sophia heard of her pregnancy, she did not feel particularly disturbed. Peter was seventeen but nobody talked about ending the regency.

In late spring the armies, led again by Golytzin, this once reinforced by Gordon, a very gifted Scottish mercenary in Muscovite service, left for the south again. It was a force of some 200,000 men, and everything went well. They laid siege to Perikop which, if taken, would have enabled the Russians to control the entire Crimean Peninsula. But when the Khan asked for a truce, Golytzin at once raised the siege in spite of Gordon's protests. The terms of the armistice were so favourable, Golytzin explained to Sophia on his return to Moscow, that he thought it unwise to reject them. This time there was no pealing of bells and no fireworks to mark the return of the army, and the sense of an approaching crisis began creeping into the old city. Peter's marriage had if anything sharpened his taste for casual affairs. Tsar Ivan divided his time between sleeping and praying, and occasionally he remembered that he had a wife to sleep with. It was whispered – very cautiously – that Tsar Peter had contracted 'the German disease' at one of the brothels in the German Quarter. The hierarchy, headed by the aged Patriarch, bided their time. Boyars in the Duma remained sombrely non-committal. Yet, in spite of the repeated failure in the deep south, all the military and the common folk of Moscow were staunchly on Sophia's side.

The first clash between a hot-tempered brother and his gravely collected sister broke out on 8th July 1689, the feast of Our Lady of Kazan, a day on which Moscow commemorated the deliverance from the Polish invaders in 1612. The sovereign, ceremonially dressed in long embroidered robes of gold brocade and carrying an ikon in velvet-gloved hands, walked in solemn procession from the Kremlin to the Kazan Cathedral in the city. It was a function which even Peter could not afford to ignore. Sophia had attended it every year since 1682. Now, she appeared as usual, all her ladies, their faces fittingly veiled, standing behind her. Tsar Ivan welcomed her with a solemn bow. Tsar Peter's face darkened with anger and he told her to return to the palace. Sophia took no notice of his words. He lost his temper, handed the ikon to a priest behind him, shouted for a horse, and galloped out of the Kremlin. The Regent took her accustomed place a step behind Tsar Ivan and the great procession started on its way. That day the Muscovites said to one another it was obvious their younger Tsar had sold his soul to the German devil.

But Sophia was not so sure. The incident had shaken her badly for all the calm of her manner. A nucleus of an army, excellently trained by foreign officers, was now known to guard each of Peter's three country palaces. The Regent's intimates kept assuring her that all the military in Moscow were unswerving in their loyalty to her. She replied that she did not wish to see bloodshed. Nor did she think it was the right moment for her to lay down her authority.

'Yet the Tsar is now in his eighteenth year,' her Aunt Tatiana reminded her.

He was. Juridically, the regency should have ended the year before, but nobody had asked for it. And now Sophia asked herself if her brother should reign at all. 'Can he reign?' she wondered, and could not find an answer.

Peter was at Kolomenskoye Palace. One night late in July a wild rumour of a non-existent plot against his life reached the palace. Peter lost all control of himself. Still in his night-shirt, he ran to the stables, leapt on the first horse he saw, and rode furiously to hide himself in a neighbouring wood where presently some members of his household found him and brought him clothes. But he refused to go back to Kolomenskoye and they rode on to Trinity Abbey where Peter, sobbing and shaking in every limb, told the abbot that he had escaped assassination by a hair's breadth.

There certainly was a plan to dethrone Peter, its details worked out by Shaklovity and Medvedev, with Sophia's full knowledge. There was never any plot against Peter's life. To begin with, if Sophia had ever meant to have him killed, she would hardly have waited till after the end of her regency as by law appointed. To have Peter dethroned was a different matter, and on that point, at least, Sophia may stand absolved from all narrowly personal motives. All the evidence proves that her half-brother was wholly unprepared to assume sovereign power.

Now, had Peter taken refuge with his foreign friends in the German Quarter of Moscow, the next few days would have followed a wholly different course. But he had sought refuge at Trinity Abbey, one of the most revered national sanctuaries, and the aged Patriarch joined him there. Step by uncertain step, the mood in Moscow began changing colour. The young Tsar stayed on at the Abbey, and Sophia's enemies whispered that it was a sure sign of Peter's conversion, and they went on whispering until even Sophia's adherents began having doubts about their own allegiance.

At the Kremlin, the accustomed rhythm continued from day to day. The Regent maintained that it was her brother – and not herself – who had started the quarrel. She had nothing but warmly affectionate feelings for him and it was for him to offer reconciliation. She waited for some days. Then she wrote and had no answer to her letters. She sent messengers to Trinity Abbey, and they came back to report that they had not been admitted into the young Tsar's presence. At the end of August Sophia decided to cut the Gordian knot herself and started towards Trinity Abbey, but her carriage was halted midway by soldiers in her brother's service and she was compelled to return to Moscow.

On 1st September, the New Year's Day in the Russian calendar, Sophia made a superb and deeply moving speech to the crowds assembled by custom in the Red Square. She said that her conscience was clear, that, though a sinner like everybody else, she had never contemplated the heinousness of fratricide, and she asked the people to judge her by the fruits of her seven years' regency. But rhetoric, however moving, no longer served Sophia. The crowds heard her. They did not respond, and the palace doors closed on the Regent's last public appearance.

Within the next few days all the regiments Sophia had relied on declared for Peter, nobody concerning themselves about Tsar Ivan relegated to the most shadowy corner of the Kremlin. Shaklovity was arrested at Peter's orders. Himself in imminent danger, Vassily Golytzin begged Sophia to escape either to Sweden or to Poland. Her name was greatly honoured abroad, he reminded her, and her repute stood high in the West. She refused the suggestion promptly and proudly. 'I am a Tsar's daughter. To flee my country now would be to acknowledge myself guilty of whatever they accuse me. I shall stay where I am and where I have belonged all my life.' And even as Sophia spoke, the very hours of her liberty were numbered. Troops sent by Peter arrested her and had her taken to a convent outside the walls of the Kremlin. She neither struggled nor protested. At her request, her sister, Tsarevna Martha, was allowed to accompany her. The convent became a prison, and nobody from the outside world ever saw Sophia again.

The regency was ended. Not so the case of the regent. The new administration was headed by the feather-brained Leo Naryshkin who supplanted Vassily Golytzin. There was not a single man of note at the Kremlin. Prince Romodanovsky's name went down in history as the worst sadist in his generation. The new government, inevitably baffled by the suddenness and the multitude of Peter's commands and wholly in the dark about the future, stumbled from one blunder into another. Within a few months, the programme so laboriously built up by Sophia, by which reforming elements were to be introduced in the spirit of moderation, was destroyed.

Her case dragged on for several months but the most searching and ruthless investigation failed to establish the existence of any conspiracy engineered by her against Peter's life. Yet accusation was piled on accusation where Sophia's adherents were concerned, and Romodanovsky, who presided at the court of inquiry, had a busy time of it. Alone of them all, Vassily Golytzin had his life spared and was exiled to the remote north. Shaklovity, Medvedev and many others, dying after prolonged and unspeakable tortures, denied to the very end the existence of any plot against Peter's life, though some among them admitted that there had been a design to get him dethroned 'for the sake of the country's future'.

Tsarina Natalia and Tsar Ivan were dead by the time the very last curtain fell upon Tsarevna Sophia, closely guarded in her convent outside Moscow. The last revolt of the musketeers started during Peter's absence abroad. Discontent having first broken out in three or four regiments stationed at a great distance from the capital, it was ludicrous to associate the beginnings of the storm with a princess kept in most rigid isolation and guarded day and night. Little by little, however, angry waves of the mutiny began beating against the walls of Moscow. There were many causes for the revolt – anger against the stupidity and harshness of the government, despair at the Tsar's prolonged absence from the country, and a deepened sense of insecurity. To add to it all, there was a rumour that Tsar Peter was no longer alive, that he had been poisoned 'by the Germans, his body pickled and enclosed within a barrel, and that barrel sunk in a foreign sea'. The fantastic story did not fail to grip the people, ever willing to give credence to a fable, and even after the Tsar's return many Old Believers insisted that it was not Peter but 'another' in the Tsar's likeness.

The mutiny had already been dealt with by the time Peter heard of it, and from beginning to end there was not a shred of incriminating evidence against the ex-Regent, but the musketeers, whose lot had certainly worsened since 1689, were in the revolt to a man, and that fact alone convinced Peter of his sister's share in the uprising. He was then on his way to Venice, but he hurried back home to write one of the bloodiest pages into his country's history. Musketeers were butchered in their thousands and all their regiments ceased to exist. The Tsar himself assisted the hangmen, and the intervention of Patriarch Adrian served no purpose at all. Later, some of the hideously mutilated bodies were left hanging outside his sister's windows. Peter did not kill her, but he forced her to take the veil. She died, as Sister Suzanna, in 1704.

❋

That the country prospered during the seven years of Sophia's administration should be obvious to any student of the period, but for nearly two centuries she was adjudged to be some kind of a royal adventuress wholly blinded by a personal ambition which made her destroy every obstacle along her way. If such had indeed been the case, neither Ivan nor Peter would have died in their beds in 1694 and 1725 respectively.

Alone, Catherine the Great came to acknowledge Sophia's quality as regent, but Catherine's appraisal found faint echoes among future historians. To quote from an anonymous textbook published in St Petersburg in 1909, 'Providence was indeed good to Russia in laying bare the fearful plot against the Reformer's life. . . . The wicked and arrogant Tsarevna Sophia meant to murder her brother and to bring about the ruin of the country. . . . Fortunately, her terrible design was discovered in time and the great Tsar was spared to lead Russia to glory and prosperity. Sophia's friends were severely punished, but Peter's great heart would not allow him to shed the blood of his own family. . . . He spared his sister's life and permitted her to end her days in the peace of a convent.'

All in all, Sophia's achievement was less than a flickering candle beside the blinding dazzle of her brother's legend created by his contemporaries and faithfully repeated by posterity.

Certainly, her character had many unpleasing traits. She had cunning, a keen penchant for intrigue and decidedly low ethical standards. The unbroken evenness of her temper suggests something of a hypocritical leaven. The two major mistakes of her regency during the Crimean campaigns cannot be excused even if we allow that peace and not war was Sophia's forte. Yet the most detailed catalogue of her faults cannot wholly condemn her and, her upbringing and environment considered, she might well have stumbled into a multitude of errors. The ambition she nursed so jealously was made of a texture where purely personal threads were interwoven with the national tissue. Finally, pupil of a great Westerner that she was, Sophia had enough vision to see that great reforms had to be introduced gradually and never at the expense of humanizing elements. The West as envisaged by her was infinitely more than dockyards, factories and kettledrums, and she felt on all her pulses that her own country possessed something of its very own to offer to the West.

But her power and her popularity rested on the quicksands of the approbation of an army whose fidelity could never be trusted. Her country's future course came to be set in a different direction and many years were to pass before the Empress Elizabeth and later Catherine the Great with her incomparable brinkmanship succeeded in bringing the Empire more or less within the comity of Western nations.

With all her faults, Sophia at least possessed too sound a knowledge of her country's history in particular and of mankind in general not to realize that more than four centuries of well-nigh cloistral isolation could never be swept aside by a hurricane of materialistic reforms.

IV

The First Emperor

*Peter I, fourth son of Tsar Alexis. Born in
1672, succeeded in 1682, died in 1725*

QUITE APART from the legend created by his contemporaries and
embroidered by many who came after, the life of Peter the Great
presents a number of difficulties to a modern biographer. His
undoubted achievements have now been enlarged almost beyond
credulity and again belittled to the point of absurdity. Latterly,
Peter has been blamed for what he did and what he left undone as
though a single life-span could have been long enough for the
labours of several generations. From an objective point of view, it
might be said that Peter's personality had far too many facets for
him ever to arrive at the mere threshold of integration. From his
childhood until his death, Peter's several selves were never at peace
with one another. They were responsible for the flashes of superhuman genius and for the crude blunders, for the moments of well-
nigh incredible foresight and penetration and for the occasions
when he appeared incapable of seeing the very grass under his feet.
They were alsc responsible for all the contradictions within him.
His was the kind of genius which burned as fiercely and wildly as a
torch, never with the steady and steadying light of a great star. But
there is always some unexpected curve in the flame of a torch, and
its very vehemence comes as a challenge. Peter can disgust, irritate
and often stir us to anger. But he never bores.

That very peculiar genius of his cannot be discerned either in his
childhood or during his early youth, both periods unfortunately
denied the blessing of fruitful and evocative influences. His father
died before Peter's fourth birthday. His brilliant half-brother Alexis

the Younger had gone two years before Peter's arrival. Tsarina Natalia lavished all her love on him, but she lacked the intelligence needed for the right upbringing of such a son. Tsar Fedor's constant ill-health interfered with most of his domestic concerns.

The boy's high spirits could not be kept under control in the Terem, and very early on his temper and impatience revealed a passionate dislike of protocol, cumbersome clothing, long prayers, and the interminable gossip of the ladies. The smell of incense was said to sicken the child. There were, however, a few mild diversions. Tsarina Natalia liked whatever amusements actors, dwarfs and fools could contrive for her, and all manner of motley pleased Peter. Buffoonery, however coarse its kind, began answering a need in him at an early enough date.

He should have had a Polotzky or an Ordyn-Natchokin for his tutor. Had some such advantage been Peter's, his finer qualities – and he had quite a few – would have been given an opportunity of an orderly and gradual development. Unfortunately for himself and his country, a sycophantic civil servant by name of Nikita Zotov became Peter's tutor. Later, the man would play the unenviable part of the buffoon-in-chief at his pupil's court.

Many repellent streaks in Peter's character have been rather exaggeratedly linked with the May massacre of 1682. Undoubtedly all he then saw, one body after another being tossed on to the pikes of the men waiting below the high steps of the palace, must have left an indelible print on his memory. But if the seventeenth-century Moscow was not used to quite such outbreaks of mob violence, it was certainly hardened to cruelties. Most ghastly executions were held in Lobnoye Square in full view of great crowds and even children were accustomed to scenes of a horror all too often beyond all description. Normally, a sovereign's children led a sheltered enough existence, but such was not the case with Peter, and we know that the tempestuous hatred of tradition, alleged to have started in May 1682, had been rooted in him some time before. He was a hard-hearted child. Not even the Petrine legend affords any glimpses of deeply felt affection for any members of his family. Outside that circle, the boy's attachments were many and varied, but he gave his friendship only to such as could be of use to him and later on to his country. His second wife would prove about the only exception.

The musketeers' revolt enabled Peter to snatch at wider liberties than had been his before. Tsarina Natalia left the Kremlin for a palace in the neighbourhood of Moscow, and there were no longer any daily duties linked with the tedious rhythm of Terem life. Zotov ceased to be a tutor and became a servitor in the basest sense of the word. Natalia shed many tears at her son's absorption in guns, boats, little fortresses and drums. She could not prevent his mustering a miniature corps recruited from among the sons of low-born people in the neighbourhood of Preobrazhenskoye, nor could she protest against Peter's friendship with Dutch and Scots carpenters, engineers and others from the German Quarter in Moscow. She wept on and on, but neither then nor later did a woman's tears have the least effect on Peter. Once permanently away from the Kremlin, he leapt out, as it were, from the dusty Byzantine frame into a new and exciting world where liberty opened the road to incessant work and curiosity involved a prodigious expenditure of energy. Preobrazhenskoye and the German Quarter were small enough in physical space, but to Peter their importance was assessed in global terms. His vision, however pale the colour and blurred the shape, enabled him to see possibilities far beyond the old capital and its environs.

Zotov had not taught him much. Now the boy Tsar was learning hungrily and breathlessly: geometry, ballistics, fortification, physics, geography, the carpenter's craft and the shipwright's, a smattering of Dutch and of German – all was grist to Peter's mill. The process certainly lacked method and much of the information acquired so haphazardly could not be digested until later, but the mind refused to stand still even for a moment. All the time away from studies was given to strenuous physical work – the building of miniature fortresses and of boats – and to drill. Peter's manner of life created amazement among the household and the common folk of Moscow. For a Tsar to stain his hands with manual labour was unthinkable.

Of statesmanship Peter as yet knew nothing. That discipline lay wholly outside Zotov's province and the young Tsar's foreign intimates from the German Quarter could not be expected to initiate him in the art of governing. Indirectly, though, those friends were instrumental in leading the genius in Peter to stumble on one point of overwhelming importance to the country.

When he was about twelve, Peter began learning boat-building under the guidance of one German, Brandt. Small craft they all were, and the boy had the freedom of a few rivers and a lake to sail on. But he longed for much wider waters. Such a vast country would be his to rule one day, and she had no other outlet than the White Sea frozen for eight or even nine months in the year. Once having grasped the rudiments of seamanship, Peter knew that he must win a foothold on the Baltic shores and another on the Black Sea.

He was enjoying great and unprecedented freedom. Yet there still remained tedious and tiring encroachments, particularly those occasions when, dressed in the heavily bejewelled robes he detested, Peter must sit on the throne set beside that of Tsar Ivan and endure the interminable formalities of ambassadorial receptions. His brother sat like a badly carved statue, his eyes closed. Peter fidgeted, glanced up and down the hall, and enchanted the foreign diplomats by his vivaciousness and curiosity. Clothes and protocol apart, Peter would have enjoyed those occasions whole-heartedly. The ambassadors certainly enjoyed meeting him. Peter's mere presence made one think of a brightly burning flame, a generously opened window, a zest for life as sparkling as a diamond:

The staid image of tradition he had inherited from his forebears was now wholly rejected. As yet Peter had no other image to put into its place. He knew he was Tsar, but he understood sovereignty in terms quite unintelligible to his people, though he could not explain his ideas to anyone, and the fatal cleavage began early enough.

To Peter, Moscow was by no means the Kremlin and the numerous sanctuaries within and without its walls. Moscow was first and foremost the German Quarter, 'Niemétzkaya Slobodá', where foreigners, not all of them in the Tsar's service, lived, worked, worshipped and spent their leisure in ways condemned by the Muscovite mind. But the German Quarter was not all workshops, factories and trimly curtained houses of respectable citizens. Even before the days of the first Romanov Tsar, many alien adventurers of shady beginnings and rather mottled morals had established their foothold on the banks of the Yaouza. All of them worked hard and drank even harder. Sober conditions of staid family life said nothing to them. There were brothels in the German Quarter and the Kremlin administration preferred to close their eyes so long as no Russian-born female was known to frequent those places.

About 1687 Moscow had its first real shock. The younger of the two Tsars was known to take part in drunken orgies and to enjoy the favours of 'Lutheran whores'. The story flew from corner to corner, from street to street. Tsar Peter had already dishonoured himself by manual labour. Now he was known to have committed a defile-ment unthinkable in the case of an anointed sovereign. The com-mon folk murmured. The hierarchy expressed their anguish in loud enough accents. The Duma passed censure by its silence. But nobody spoke to Peter himself except his most ineffectual mother. Natalia reproached and Peter frowned. Natalia wept and he lost his temper. Copulation was of no great importance, he told her roughly, and the wenches certainly gave him pleasure. To this day it is not known whether it was in the German Quarter or during his first foreign tour that Peter contracted a disease which would in the end triumph over his iron constitution and bring him to an early grave.

Was the young Tsar truly a son of Alexis, Moscow began asking, and no answer could then be given to the question. But it was obvious that neither unbridled promiscuity nor drunken orgies inter-fered with Peter's capacity for work. At last, Tsarina Natalia, driven to despair, decided to have Peter married. It is one of several paradoxes in his story that, flaunting tradition right and left, he allowed himself to be betrothed to a girl he had not even seen. In January 1689 the young Tsar became the husband of Eudoxia Lopukhina, who had the singular misfortune to be born into one of the most conservative Muscovite families. Her father, once approached by Tsarina Natalia, consented to the marriage, and Eudoxia had no voice in the matter. The fourth and the youngest Tsarina of the day was permitted to have a brief spell of married life and to conceive a child. Within a few months Peter thrust her aside and returned to the arms of a girl in the German Quarter. Even the birth of a son early in 1690 did not make him come back to Eudoxia who was nothing to him except a reflection of a Byzantine icon. Natalia's longing to see Peter steadied by marriage was en-tombed soon enough. A few years later she died, asking God's mercy on a son she had never understood. Her stepson, Tsar Ivan, paid her homage by attending the funeral. Peter did not appear.

The storm of 1689 came and went. Now Peter was Tsar *de jure* and *de facto*, but, once his ministers were appointed, he left the administration to them. He had no time for anything except war, with the Black Sea for his final objective, though the breathlessness of earlier years gave place to a carefully measured pace. Determined not to repeat the mistakes of Sophia's commanders, Peter spent six years in meticulous preparation. Not until the spring of 1695 did his armies, trained by foreign experts and equipped far beyond the visible resources of the Treasury, make for the south to fight the Turks. To the despair of his Government, the Tsar decided to stay in the ranks and went as a humble bombardier.

However carefully planned, the campaign ended in a fiasco which greatly pleased the Western Powers. The fortress of Azov did not surrender and the siege had to be abandoned, though the Russians did not retreat in a rout.

That year, 1695, may well be taken as the beginning of an epoch. The Tsar returned from the south, his mood suggesting triumph rather than defeat. The unfortunate end to his very first military venture seemed to have endowed him with superhuman energy. His government learnt that the second campaign was to start the very next year. They pointed out that the state of the exchequer alone forbade any such venture in the immediate future. Peter sent the bearded noblemen to the devil, ordered rises in taxation and a gigantic muster of labour, and left Moscow for Voronezh on the Don, there to install himself in a workman's hut, to supervise and to take his own share in the building of a navy. A depleted Treasury and a bewildered government were of no moment to the Tsar.

By the spring of 1696 the impossible was achieved, and Peter had some reasons for hoping that the plan of attacking Azov from land and sea would not fail. He had two warships, twenty-three galleys and numerous smaller craft ready for launching from the newly-built shipyards on the banks of the Don. In July 1696 Azov surrendered.

The sheer psychological value of the victory stood beyond all reckoning. For the first time the invincible Turk was beaten by the barbarian Russian. The fall of Azov led to a spate of comment and conjecture in the West. From Sweden down to Tuscany they speculated about the next step to be taken by the young Northern giant.

Was the Baltic to be his next objective? Or would he turn away from the sea, crush Poland and threaten the frontiers of the Empire? Nobody could tell and there were no evidences of further warlike preparations. The Tsar was back in Moscow. Festivities in honour of the victory went on from week to week. He did not visit his forsaken Tsarina now living in unbroken retirement at a country palace near Moscow. He all but ignored his six-year-old son, Alexis. The child, left to his mother's care and brought up in an atmosphere of deep piety and cautious criticism of his father, was presumably the heir, but here again nobody could be certain. Tsar Peter's domestic landscape wounded and puzzled his country-people, but it did not concern the West.

Then all suddenly the news reached European capitals. The Tsar of Muscovy was not launching into another war whether on land or at sea. He was sending 'A Grand Embassy' to the Low Countries, England and Venice, his own identity being screened under the name of Peter Mikhailov. Some fifty young men of the best families were going abroad strictly *in statu pupillari* to learn shipbuilding, military sciences and languages, Golovin, one of the Tsar's most fortunate 'finds', and Lefort, the 'Swiss wonder' of the German Quarter, being in charge of the young men. Education was the apparent purpose of the mission. Underneath lay another. Golovin, already no mean diplomat, was to convince the West that the Turkish menace could not be ignored except at their own peril. The Tsar fully trusted Golovin to prove the case. A treaty with Turkey having been signed, Azov and Taganrog now belonged to Russia, but Peter realized that it was but the threshold of an enterprise he would never accomplish without allies.

But he had forgotten the failure of Sophia's embassy ten years earlier and he could not have chosen a less fortunate moment for his mission. Wholly unversed in diplomacy, at sea in the current European drifts, Peter failed to consider the Western interests of the day. There, the imminence of the War for the Spanish Succession had overshadowed all else. If anything, continued hostility between Russia and Turkey would have been welcomed both by Britain and by Holland in that it would prevent the Sultan from offering help to France. In vain did Golovin discuss the Ottoman peril in Holland and England. In vain did he grow eloquent about the possible plight of Austria in the event of some gigantic conflagration in the near future. They listened to him politely enough but made it obvious that the Russo-Turkish matter had not yet attained the importance the Tsar's Prime Minister gave to it. In the end, Peter was forced to admit that the shaping of alliances could be far more exacting than a series of pitched battles. It is doubtful that he would have been successful even if the future of the Spanish throne did not hang in the balance: the West mistrusted the first Muscovite sovereign to appear abroad.

Yet there remained Venice, and the Tsar pinned much hope on finding at least one ally. It so happened that he never reached Venice. In the summer of 1698 he hurried post-haste to Moscow there to deal with the musketeers' revolt already quelled by his government. The official report, received just as he was making for Venice, informed Peter that the danger lay behind. All the ringleaders having been captured and executed, the mood in Moscow was tranquil enough.

None the less, Peter hurried back. In his thought, Sophia, the unfortunate Eudoxia and all the musketeers' regiments down to the last man were implicated in some vast conspiracy his government had by no means squashed. He had no trust in the assurances received from Moscow. His enemies meant him to prolong his absence long enough to wrest the power out of his hand. He had convinced himself of the existence of a conspiracy. In reality, he sped back to deliver the first thundering blow to the ancient 'res publica' of his country. The failure of 'the Grand Embassy', the possible friendship of Venice and the probable peril from Turkey, all were forgotten.

Peter had then been abroad for about seventeen months. He had never made any allowances for the vehement impact made by his departure and his prolonged absence on the same people he was now determined to force into an alien mould. The fact remains that down to the very end of his reign uncounted numbers of men and women would live and die in the conviction that they had no Tsar living. The angry giant who came back to Moscow in the autumn of 1698 was an offspring of Anti-Christ, if not Anti-Christ himself, said the common folk, and it would be wrong to pretend that those people had no case, however clumsy a garb they gave to their belief.

The Tsar came back both as judge and as executioner, and the horrors commanded by him certainly equalled, if they did not outrival, the atrocities during the reign of Ivan the Terrible. The total extermination of musketeer regiments and crowds of other 'suspects' went on for weeks, and the gibbet offered by far the most merciful manner of death. There were not enough hangmen for the business, and the Tsar had Romodanovsky and a handful of others to help him. The city reeked of blood from end to end since Lobnoye Square, where public executions were held, did not afford adequate space. Mutilated bodies lay here, there and everywhere, no orders being given for mass burials. The common citizens of Moscow stayed behind their shuttered windows. Churches were all but empty and market chaffering came to a standstill. In the very thick of the terror, Patriarch Adrian, a man unremarked for his courage, became greater than he was and, an icon in his hands, he made his way to the shambles there to implore the Tsar to desist from further cruelties. A bloody axe in his hands, Peter sent the old man about his business.

During those weeks the Tsar did not live at the Kremlin. The day's 'work' finished, he would make for Lefort's house in the German Quarter there to start the night in a drunken carousal and to end it in the arms of some girl preferred for the moment.

Peter's wrath did not fall on the musketeers alone. Sophia and her sister were forcibly turned into nuns. Tsarina Eudoxia, unacquainted with the very alphabet of a conspiracy, was imprisoned in a convent and her son removed from her. Peter ordered the bishops to begin drawing up the instrument of divorce. The bishops replied that a divorce was out of all question so long as the Tsarina remained a laywoman, and the hapless Eudoxia became Sister Elena.

Only towards the end of September was Moscow given a respite. The exact number of victims never came to light.

Those cruelties and debaucheries certainly stained Peter's humanity and sullied his office. And yet he had a case of his own. The long sojourn abroad had taught him to gauge unerringly the wide gulf between the West and his own country, though even his genius could not see that violently introduced reforms did little except create a confusion, to give it no harsher name, in the national consciousness. Opposition against him was immense and he tried to destroy it with the only weapon to his hand. Cruelty as such was nothing phenomenal to a Muscovite. Tsar Alexis's '*Oulózhenie*' imposed penalties that make one shudder today, and his subjects were not particularly squeamish about them. What Peter failed to understand was the tissue of the enmity he had let loose and its consequences on the future of the country. He was loved – and also feared – by those who surrounded him, who could respond to his peculiar genius, and follow him, however tentatively, from one step to another into a difficult but invariably exciting adventure. But millions of Peter's subjects never came near him and were never given an opportunity to catch even a brief glimpse of that ceaseless titanic activity which, all the mistakes notwithstanding, was redeemed by the absence of narrowly personal objectives.

Peter began destroying archaic surfaces by cutting off beards and enforcing Western clothes on his subjects. But during that apparently trivial process, he destroyed something else.

He would die in 1725. Not until the Napoleonic invasion would the nation be again conscious of the living link between themselves and God's anointed. The Byzantine image of sovereignty standing in his way, Peter swept it aside, and that may well have been necessary, but a different image should have been offered to the people, and it was not. The national consciousness was robbed of the sense of mystery in which the Tsar moved, all his ordinances, however unpalatable to his people, derived from a sacrosanct source. The Tsar stayed remote, the rank and file away from the capital had no personal knowledge of him, and they did not need it. The immeasurable distance between the throne and themselves was something as inevitable as the passing of the four seasons. The Tsar's office, rather than his person, was a star fixed in an otherwise dark sky. The office answered the deep-seated hunger for a symbol in conformity with what they believed to be God's will for their country. They did not need any immediacy which would have interfered with the awe-inspiring sanctity of the symbol.

Such an archaic outlook was certainly bound to change little by little, and a gradual change would have been for the ultimate good of the people. But Peter had no use for any gradual changes, and in the very hurricane of his activity lay the seeds of no less violent reaction and protest against the violent transformation. The Tsar's crown had been put on his head in a sanctuary, and that sanctuary was now profaned. They were subjects of a man no longer graced and housed within the favour of the Almighty. The common folk remained more or less indifferent to the spate of purely administra-

tive reforms pouring forth from the Kremlin. But a deep wound
could not be ignored. The Tsar kept opening new horizons for
them to learn and driving them towards a glory their ancestors had
never dreamt about. All of it meant less than nothing because a star
had fallen from their sky.

Most of the men surrounding Peter were caught up into the contagion of an activity so miraculously unimpaired by frequent
sensual excesses. Many guessed at the causes of the hidden turmoil
within the nation but they kept their peace because those were
topics it was safer not to mention to the Tsar. Moreover, not all his
'eaglets' were of a high mental and ethical stature. There was the
new favourite, Alexander Menshikov, once a pieman, an ignorant,
brutal and corrupt creature, yet Menshikov could go from a harlot's
bed to some workshop, from the workshop to the Tsar's house
either to offer surprisingly prudent counsel or else to prove his
incredible capacity for wine. And Menshikov was a Russian, born
and bred in the Moscow gutters, one out of many millions the Tsar
was determined 'to civilize'. Menshikov, his chin shaved and his
gross body clad in a German coat and breeches, never became
'civilized'. He wenched and drank and enjoyed himself very much
in the manner of his unregarded forebears in the days of Ivan III.
But Menshikov was cunning, and always guessed at the response
expected of him. Peter laughed with him, swore at him, beat him,
and occasionally threatened him with the wheel or the gallows, and
could not do without him.

All because in the rough, adroit, clever Moscow pieman the Tsar
found the embodiment of a justification he needed however un-
consciously. Some people alleged that he had betrayed them with
his constant preference for foreigners. But there was Menshikov, a
bone of the Muscovite bone. Many complained that the Tsar and
his friends scoffed at piety. But there was Menshikov who never
missed a mass or a Te Deum. People murmured that 'to smoke the
devil's herb' was a certain way to eternal perdition, but there was
Menshikov, a pipe always between his teeth, who continued speaking
their own language, and seemed as assured of his salvation as they
were of their own. And in the end Peter raised the uncouth pieman
to the rank of prince. But the pieman never wholly died in
Menshikov.

❋

There were three great enemies for the Tsar to fight – drunkenness, lechery and peculation – and it was the latter that he fought without mercy all through his reign. Graft had become deeply embedded in every cog of the administrative machine since the days when the Tsar's servants received no official emoluments and lived on whatever chance and cunning brought to their door. Conditions were changed under Peter, but graft remained a national habit from the top rung of the administrative ladder down to the bottom. If anything, the increased number of taxes deepened and spread the disease. A tax-collector's job was compared with that of a butter-merchant. No matter how carefully he handled the butter, some of it would adhere to the knife and to the bottom of the tub, and 'would you waste it?' was asked on the right side and on the left. 'Anyone detected in taking bribes shall be sent to the gallows,' ordered the Tsar, and many indeed ended that way, but graft went on spreading. Bribes were taken for information given and information withheld, for the avoidance of compulsory service and for some coveted job on the fringes of the administration, for silence in the matter of a trespass, for faked reports about a friend's imaginary illness. Taxes flowed into the Treasury, but the gap between the estimated amount and the actual receipts continued to widen. Menshikov himself received enormous bribes and got many a beating from the Tsar, who, however, valued him too much to send him to the gallows. But a terrible example was made of Shafirov and Cherkassky, two of Peter's intimates caught red-handed in 'secret machinations'.

In spite of all the penalties peculation was never to vanish from the national scene.

At the end of 1699 Peter realized that further operations against Turkey were more or less out of the question for the moment. But he kept repeating that the country must have an outlet to the sea, and there was the Baltic offering a clear passage to the West, but the Baltic was held by Russia's immemorial enemy, Sweden, and how could Peter fight Sweden without a single ally to help him? The West would have none of him, but he thought of Poland, another ancient foe of Moscow, now ruled by an extravagant and licentious Saxon, Augustus II, who was supposed to have so many mistresses that he could not remember all their names.

Early in 1700 the Tsar went to meet Augustus. The idea of an alliance seemed to tempt the king but Peter found it hard to pin the Saxon down to definite terms. Augustus being a wonderful host, Peter was most royally entertained, the king waxing most eloquent on the subject of women, wine and food. One evening after supper, he gave Peter the receipt of 'a most succulent dish'. 'Take a well-fed duck and plunge it into red wine for twenty-four hours. Then fry its entrails in butter together with cloves, orange peel, red pepper and cinnamon. Boil a little Indian rice and mix it well with the fry. Take four eggs and make a smooth batter. Have the duck part-cooked in a hot oven. Then take it out, stuff it with the fry, place it in a deep dish and smother it in batter. My chef says it must be cooked in a very hot oven. Use the red wine for the sauce, adding a pinch of cinnamon, a little sugar and some lemon peel.' 'What is it all about?' asked the bewildered Tsar.

'Why, the duck named after me, because it is a dish fit for a king. You have just had two helpings of it,' replied Augustus. 'Food? Food?' Peter rapped out. 'I eat whatever you give me when I am hungry. What time is there for you and me to discuss food? I am talking about Sweden.' The King heard and sighed.

This is legend, not history, but in this case the legend is certainly flavoured with authenticity. In the end, a Russo-Polish alliance was concluded, Peter's lack of experience enabling Augustus to glean many advantages. Golovin was commanded to arrange the terms of a peace treaty with Turkey. In August 1700, no formal declaration of war having been served on Charles XII, the Tsar's troops burst into Livonia, and the Great Northern War was started. It was to continue for seventeen hard years.

It would certainly bring glory and important territorial gains to Russia, but in 1700 those benefits were in the future. In 1700, the war meant waves of penury spreading all over Peter's dominions from the exchequer in Moscow down to the humblest landowner with a couple of acres and four lean cows to his name. In 1700 the war meant vast reaches of agricultural land left untilled because peasants were being taught the use of musket and bayonet and one recruitment followed swiftly on the heels of another. In 1700 the war started by the Tsar made the West pour much contempt on an arrogant and untrained barbarian who dared to challenge the greatest military power in the north of Europe, and Charles XII's victory at Narva confirmed the European hopes that the Muscovite bear would be chased back to his lair never to venture out again. The Tsar's flight to Novgorod provided material for many scathing lampoons and King Augustus, whose sense of honour was almost wholly undeveloped, began devising the best means of ridding himself of an alliance which bade fair to end in a disaster for Poland.

The detailed chronicle of the Great Northern War lies outside the scope of this book, but the wonder of the background cannot be left unmentioned. Fighting a hitherto invincible army from the shores of the Baltic down to the heart of the Ukraine, perpetually preoccupied with a million tasks necessary for creating the sinews of war, Peter still found time to carry on a ceaseless flow of interior reforms, planned and founded a city soon to rival the beauty of Venice, dealt with one minor uprising after another, reorganized the ancient administration from top to bottom, flung a new alphabet at the nation, settled the business of the Church in such a way that the hierarchy became the servants of the state, spared no efforts to develop the natural wealth of the country, established schools in St Petersburg and Moscow, and would often say to his 'eaglets': 'as soon as we have learned enough, we shall turn our backs on the foreigner and make him dance to our tune.'

Eight years were to pass before Poltava proved to Europe the barbarian's fighting worth and Sweden's great might began melting away. Those were crucial and cruel years for Russia. The Tsar's physical strength was such that he could twist a horseshoe out of shape and pull a young tree up by the roots. His reforms swept over the country in much the same vehement fashion. The new wine was poured into old bottles, and some of the bottles were too old to contain it.

❋

That Peter's legend had genuine streaks in its foundation cannot in justice be denied. The work he had planned was on a Herculean scale and those who laboured by his side, themselves swept into that tumultuous stream, were certainly convinced that their leader towered over them all not only by his great bodily stature. Peter was loved and even worshipped. He was also feared because his wrath was like the combined breath of a hundred furnaces. But few, if any, among his own generation were able to gauge the work, either inchoate or completed, in cool objective terms.

The Tsar built for the future and fought his wars with a very clear purpose in his mind. He was successful in the north but not in the south, the Black Sea remaining beyond his grasp. Yet Peter's campaigns, for all they occupied most of his reign, do not really exhaust his story. There is always the immense landscape behind the front. There are the people whom he treated much in the same manner as a horseshoe to be twisted this way and that.

To begin with, the Tsar seldom thought of them as people. To him they were so many cogs in the great machine of the state. Being an intelligent mechanic, he took great care of the cogs. Numberless measures were commanded by him in order that the harsh living conditions might be made a little less unendurable, and there was hardly an aspect of social life left untouched by Peter's spate of decrees. Medical care in child-birth, less cumbersome clothes, protection against fire, brigandage and the extortions of usurers, tentative approaches to a standard of cleanliness in the streets, the ban on compulsory marriages and the end to Terem conditions, all those ordinances and many more became law or, at least, its letter. In reality, the new observances came to be limited to urban life only. The yoke of the Terem remained unshaken in many country manors almost to the end of Elizabeth's reign. As to compulsory marriages, they had not ceased – at least among the merchant class – even during the reign of Nicholas I.

There was something else too. Under Peter, 'the element mechanical' was kept well to the forefront of all national necessities, whether it was some cunning German contrivance for a better time-piece or the latest Swedish design for a mortar. 'The element mechanical' could be discerned even at the so-called assemblies, rather clumsy expressions of the Tsar's struggle to end the Muscovite segregation of sexes, those gatherings where men and women must dance a precise number of rounds, drink an appointed amount of liquor and, in general, amuse themselves within the rigid framework of regulations which were not concerned with any individual preference. The Tsar's passion for the mechanical found its way into the educational programme where humanities, linguistics apart, must cede the pride of place to mathematics, astronomy, ballistics and physical sciences.

Yet Peter had many selves and those led to inevitable contradictions. The creation of St Petersburg was certainly a most fortunate contradiction. He had no use for the arts, music bored him and pictures made him yawn, and there is no evidence that he felt attracted by nature. But St Petersburg was the embodiment of an artist's vision. A huddle of some nineteen islands lying between the mouth of a great river and the reaches of the sea, a muted, troubling landscape of soft grey, violet, pale green and grey again, always open to the anger of the sea, its climate governed by the unpredictable whims of wind and of water, a huddle of unregarded islands, their breast so thinly covered by soil that nothing but scrub, stumpy firs and an occasional silver birch grew there – out of it all Peter created a city, its beauty rivalling the compulsion of Venice. Why? How?

The first question poses no difficulties. A stronghold at the mouth of the Neva was a necessity, and to Peter necessities must be acquired whatever the cost. The second question is something of a puzzle because Peter had no perception of beauty. Yet an instinct must have been alive to guide him from island to island until out of mist-swathed formlessness an exquisite form was born, its very stones in miraculous accord with cloud and water, and an identity was given to a wilderness, its signature far more compelling than any *ukazes* signed by Peter.

St Petersburg, its foundations laid in 1703, exacted a high price in labour and in human lives. Wholly alien to Moscow and its Byzantine tradition, the new city proved a link with a far more ancient past than Muscovy could boast of. It harked back to the days of Scandinavian Rus when Rurik the Viking founded the first Russian kingdom in A.D. 862, and planted a Scandinavian garden on the banks of the Dnieper. And later came Alexander, Prince of Novgorod, who defeated the Swedes on the icy reaches of the Neva in the thirteenth century. The Neva and her tributaries, to say nothing of the Gulf of Finland, spoke of the old sagas, and the violence gone to the making of the new Russian capital echoed the same accents. Tsar Peter, caring but little for history, none the less shaped it in a most particular and exciting way when he laid the foundation stone of St Samson's church on one of the nineteen islands. The affection he so seldom showed to his own kind was poured out on his new creation. The first triumph of the Great Northern War, with Narva fallen to Sheremetev, must be celebrated on the banks of the Neva. By that time, Menshikov's enormous stone mansion was nearly completed on Hare Island, and the Tsar's small wooden house on the south bank faced the newly begun fortress and cathedral to the north of the Neva. Peter's tenure of those nineteen islands was anything but certain in 1703, and an ultimate Swedish victory would have razed St Petersburg to the ground, but Peter was certain that no such defeat would ever break over his head. So he ordered his government to leave the Kremlin for a city most of them considered to be 'unfit for human habitation', and nothing was left to old Moscow except the privilege of having the sovereign crowned within her walls.

Boy and young man, Peter had all but idolized the foreigner. Now, his youth gone, the feeling was changed. He still went on 'taking lessons' from abroad and his new administration was built on a pattern borrowed from Sweden. The Tsar was also rather too obviously anxious for matrimonial alliances with the West; he had his two nieces, daughters of Tsar Ivan V, married to the Dukes of Mecklenburg and Courland. He would have no Russian bride for his son, or Russian husbands for his two daughters. But the earlier sense of uncritical admiration for all things foreign was gone never to return. When in 1707 a corps, commanded by Ogylvie, was routed by Loewenhaupt's greatly inferior force and Charles XII rode into Grodno a bare three hours after Peter's flight, the Tsar wrote to Menshikov and ordered him not to entrust the command of the rear to 'foreign fools' ('*inostránnym dourakám*'), words which would never have been used by him in earlier years.

None the less, the Tsar's second wife was an alien. She had not always been a wife but a *maîtresse en titre*, the cast-off 'friend' of at least two other protectors, Sheremetev and Menshikov, known to a great many as Martha Skavronska, and opposition against the Tsar hardened when he decided to make her his lawful wife. She was duly received into the Orthodox Church and given the name of Catherine. Soon enough even the Tsar's enemies had to admit that she was his necessity quite apart from bed and board.

Her earlier story abounds in such a tangle of fabled threads that it is impossible to tell truth from fiction. Her origins are supposed to be either Livonian or Swedish. Naturally, in view of the high fortune ultimately fallen to her, all the mottled details of her past came to receive a more than indulgent treatment. None the less, it is a fact that Skavronska was a camp follower, that her looks pleased quite a few, and that her amiable nature attracted many men. Wholly rootless, early accustomed to hardihoods, and somewhat greedy for pleasure when it came to her, Skavronska was never heard to complain of her lot. Unlike most women of her kind, she took delight in prosaic tasks.

Peter could hardly have made a more fortunate choice. A wife who knitted his socks, washed and mended his shirts, did not grumble at having to sleep in a tent, was satisfied with the rough victuals he preferred, had more than a common share of common sense, was not given either to day-dreaming or sentimentality, was generous with her caresses and did not hesitate to give him the rough edge of her tongue, such a vulgar, large-hearted and perfectly genuine companion answered all Peter's needs. Their ethical concepts being more or less on the same level, they would be unfaithful to each other, but neither ever neglected the other for long.

The Tsar's 'amiable Katinka', as he called her (*lubéznaya Katínka*), was uneducated but her instinct guided her towards a less imperfect understanding of her husband's numberless activities. Her presence, manners and habits brought no wounding reminders of a past he hated to remember. Moscow was little more than a place-name to her. His abhorrence of etiquette accorded well with her own inclination. She learned how to face his anger either with silence or with caresses. The whirlwind climate of his reforms did not disturb her. She seemed to know when to argue and when to agree with her husband. And Peter needed some such harbour, particularly through the years which widened the gulf between him and his son.

Born of Eudoxia in 1690, the child was left in her care. Reared in the strict seclusion of the Terem, delicate from birth, extremely gifted, gentle and shy, little Alexis was forcibly removed from his mother's roof at the end of 1698 and handed over to two strangers appointed to be his tutors. He barely knew his father and was frankly terrified of him. Quite unwittingly, the boy became the centre of the country's opposition to the Tsar. Himself unaware of it, Alexis epitomized all their hopes for an eventual return to the honourable ancient ways. Gradually he came to learn what his mere name stood for among the masses, and it scared him.

The tutors' reports on the boy's progress would have pleased any other father. They did not please the Tsar. Alexis was pronounced to be brilliant at languages; he had learned Latin, Greek, German and Italian with an astonishing ease. His history studies were also remarkable, and he had a strong taste for classic poetry. Mathematics and physical sciences, however, had proved thorny going from the beginning, and the art of war bored him. The tutors' closing remarks dealt with the Prince's constitution. Far too thin for his height, he appeared delicate and tired very easily. His chest often gave cause for anxiety.

All of it was gall to Peter. To have a physical weakling for his only son was quite enough of a humiliation. To hear about that son's progress in Greek drama and Latin poetry was even worse. Ignoring the tutors' comments about Alexis's physical weakness, the Tsar decided to have the boy hardened. An extensive course of military training was followed by a command to join the Tsar at the front, and Alexis's terror at meeting his father was obvious to everybody.

Years before the ultimate catastrophe Peter saw that nothing he could do would ever shape the boy into the desired mould; Alexis belonged to an alien world altogether. 'Away from that climate he could not breathe. There was just nothing in him to make him respond to his father's vehement drive, and Peter mistook the inherent inability for rebellion. He had Alexis married to a shy, pallid princess of the Brunswick-Wolfenbüttel house. Having borne a son and a daughter, the girl died within three years of her wedding-day. Alexis, whose moral fibre had been greatly weakened through the years spent at the dissolute court, took a peasant girl, one Aphrosynia, for his mistress. The Tsar would not have minded if his son got drunk every day and had a dozen mistresses so long as he followed the only course Peter wished him to follow, and Alexis could not. The infrequent interviews with his father chilled the blood in the young man's veins. He stammered and stuttered and shook like a reed. Such was his terror that on return to his own apartments he often fell into a coma.

Meanwhile, opposition against the Tsar was not idle. His marriage to 'a German whore' helped increase the popular conviction that 'the real Tsar' had died abroad in 1698. There were many small-meshed conspiracies, and there is no doubt that eventually Alexis found himself involved in one of them, but the mere idea of an active struggle against his father terrified him. In the end he escaped abroad. His wife's brother-in-law, the Emperor Charles VI, offered him protection, and Alexis imagined himself safe at a castle near Naples. He had no wish to succeed his father. He wanted nothing except Aphrosynia's companionship and peace for his studies.

By that time, Peter, fully conscious of the immense opposition against him, believed that none other than Alexis headed that movement. He sent a deputation to Naples, headed by one Tolstoy, with instructions to lure the Prince back to Russia. Alexis was promised a full pardon for all the offences he had never committed. Tolstoy was a man of deep cunning and it did not take him very long to persuade the Prince that his continued stay abroad would bring lasting disgrace on the Tsar and Russia. 'Anyone would think that his Majesty was a monster,' argued Tolstoy, 'and here I have brought you a full pardon signed by his own hand.'

Alexis let himself be persuaded. In this instance, Peter proved himself a monster indeed. On his return to St Petersburg the young man was imprisoned. His father's senators and generals sat in judgment on a prince whose only fault lay in an innate inability to follow in his father's steps. Peter might just as well have expected the sun to rise in the west. The judges, having amassed a great volume of evidence relating to the opposition against the Tsar, linked every point of it with Alexis's name. Tainted evidence notwithstanding, he was charged with having plotted against his father's life.

In the end, after prolonged torture, Alexis was killed, the actual manner of his death unknown to this day. The Tsar absolved himself from perjury in view of 'the revelations proving the terrible guilt' supposedly come to light during that parody of a trial.

Here we look at a page in Peter's story which even his legend could not whiten. Perjury, cruelty and unbounded cynicism dance their repellent measure from beginning to end, and they even succeed in softening the admittedly unpleasant traits in Alexis's character. Perpetually gyved by his terror of the Tsar, the Prince was cowardly, given to bragging when in his cups and also to lying, and was not above betraying a friend when it suited his purposes, but he possessed neither the ability nor the strength to stand at the head of an organized rebellion. That many such suggestions were made to him is a fact, but all of it went no further than furtive conversations held in shuttered rooms. It almost looks as though in decreeing his son's murder the Tsar was avenging himself upon the opposition he could never crush entirely.

The manifesto announcing Alexis's 'premature demise, willed by the Almighty God,' deceived nobody. The Emperor Charles VI's peremptory order to his representative to leave St Petersburg was symptomatic of the general reaction. For all the victories and the reforms, Russia was adjudged to be still under the yoke of barbarism.

Yet a wholesale condemnation does not really meet the case. Peter's guilt must remain but he did not bear it alone. In the matter of his son and himself, the father vanished in the sovereign and the individual in the state. No eithical standards were recognized by the Tsar where the welfare of the country was concerned. From the point of view of sound statesmanship Alexis was no more and no less than a pale cipher. To the masses of the opposition he was painted in the colours of an able and wholly dedicated pilot one day to steer the nation's ship back to the harbour built by their forefathers. Peter's enemies, and their name was legion, shared in the shaping of Alexis's doom. In the eyes of Peter's adherents, of course, Alexis's death was a proof of his father's victory at home.

It proved something of a Pyrrhic victory. That year of 1718, for all the far-flung victories over Sweden, threw a shadow over the destinies of the reigning house. The heightened sense of national pride and the extravagant celebrations in the palace and on the Neva could not quite disperse the darkness of a dungeon in the newly built Fortress of SS Peter and Paul, with the pitifully mangled body of a Romanov being prepared for burial. At court and else-where they whispered about the increased frequency of the Tsar's nervous spasms, of sombre moods, and of a temper now so fright-ening that not even Menshikov dared intrude upon him. Alone, a common, boisterous, deep-bosomed woman, once a mistress, now a wife, and soon to be crowned Empress, had the gift, not to say genius, of quietening her husband in a manner none would have tried to imitate. Catherine never made a mistake about a moment's most urgent need. She knew when to efface herself and when to take Peter to task for refusing his food because of the black night in his thought. He trusted her. He was big enough never to forget those days by the banks of the Prut when, had it not been for Catherine's sagacity and quickness of judgment, he would have fallen prisoner to the Turks. By 1718, she was more of a necessity than ever. The deeper issues involved in the matter of Alexis may have said little enough to her alien blood. The reaction which gripped her husband spoke a language she could understand.

Meanwhile, the Great Northern War was ended. St Petersburg and its environs were secured by a treaty which rang the knell to Sweden's hegemony in the north. The Baltic lay open to Russian shipping, and Peter had Prussia and Denmark for his allies, with France beginning to show unprecedented cordiality. Britain still refused to be wooed. Not the Tsar's defeat of the Swedes but his continued dalliance with the Jacobites irritated George I, who remained unfriendly to the end of his life, and the Tsar's representatives in London had rather a thin time of it.

But the animosity of the King of England did not trouble Peter. Faulty enough at the beginning, his reading of the European map was far less imperfect now. He had meant to win a foothold on the Baltic and he had won it. For the moment there was nothing more he wanted from the West. He turned his attention eastwards, wresting Baku from Persia and sending expeditions into Central Asia. He even hoped that his armies would reach India one day. Now that his northern dominions were safe from the Swedish threat, the Tsar had more troops to spare for the south, and he was planning another campaign against Turkey since Azov and Taganrog were but a threshold.

But Peter no longer accompanied his armies. He remained in St Petersburg, still living in the tiny wooden house on the south bank of the Neva. The city grew almost from week to week, and it now boasted one of the longest streets in Europe, Nevsky Prospect, a wide and noble thoroughfare stretching for something like five miles. All Peter's 'eaglets' had magnificent stone mansions built for them, and there was also the Summer Palace for his own use, mostly open for the receptions given to foreign ambassadors when the Tsar had to change his shabby clothes for a velvet coat, satin breeches and silk hose, and looked as uncomfortable as though he were sitting on hot bricks.

✳

The battlefield days were over but his work did not slacken. Day by day the Tsar either devised new reforms or grappled with his subjects' mishandling of the innovations already introduced. His senators were clean-shaven, they wore Western clothes, and massacred French and German with equal ease. It was all very much of a veneer. Underneath the hurriedly acquired polish, they remained men of Muscovy, born in the preceding century and not really divorced from its habits. They liked good food and drink, they never missed their after-dinner sleep, and took much time to arrive at a single decision. And through every government department graft still stalked unashamedly. Whenever some particularly glaring example was brought to the Tsar's notice, blood would rush into his face, his voice grow thick with fury and, fists clenched, he would shout that he ruled a nation of thieves, fools and lazybones. If Catherine were present, she would point out that people would not cheat so much if it were not for their poverty.

Here was the wounding heart of the nettle. Peter had hoped to establish prosperity, but the sinews of war were no baubles to be purchased in a cheap market. The development of natural resources was still in its cradle. By the end of Peter's reign, the Empire was bled snow-white by taxation. Yet that penury was no consequence of his personal extravagance. He abhorred all luxuries, his clothes were shabbier than a dockhand's, and he had no use for expensive knick-knacks or fine furniture. Boiled beef, herrings, pickled lemons and cucumbers were his diet. The only jewellery he ever bought was for Catherine. His other mistresses were fortunate if they got a cheap turquoise pin at parting. Peter despised feather-beds, sheets, cushioned armchairs and all manner of bodily ease. Catherine certainly longed for comforts and luxuries, but she controlled herself until he had gone from her.

In 1721, the Nystad Treaty signed, the Tsar proclaimed himself 'Emperor of Russia'. The step infuriated Austria and led to much mordant criticism in the West, the French government together with a few others pointedly ignoring the new title, and millions of Peter's own subjects never really accepted the new dignity. The sonorous word '*imperator*' did not come easily to peasant lips until the very end of the dynasty.

Peter was emperor without an heir. In 1722 he issued his famous Act of Succession* which gave the ruling sovereign full liberty of choice in naming his or her successor. The following year, to the deep indignation of the Muscovites he had Catherine crowned Empress at the Assumption Cathedral.

* Repealed by the Emperor Paul I in 1797.

By then he was wholly spent. At fifty-one he looked an old man. Tic and other nervous ailments tortured him more and more often, and no remedies devised by his doctors brought relief. 'The German disease' he had suffered from for years took a sharp curve for the worse. He was glad to return to St Petersburg, the one creation of his titanic will which never poisoned a single waking moment. It might almost be said that his feeling for the city was that of a bridegroom for his bride.

But Peter was a rapidly ageing bridegroom. Sexual excesses, drinking orgies, herculean physical labours, all those were now asking to be paid in terms of dulling thought, slower gait, increasing weariness, and attacks of melancholia, and the question of succession gave Peter little peace. By 1724 the dynasty consisted of himself, Catherine, their two daughters, Anna and Elizabeth, born out of wedlock but legitimized, the Tsar's grandson, Peter, a boy of nine, and two daughters of Tsar Ivan V, the Duchesses of Mecklenburg and of Courland, the former having one little daughter, the latter being childless. But Peter named none of them as was his right to do, and in the end the matter was left to the Senate or, more accurately, to the court factions.

The question of succession was by no means the only thorn in the Tsar's flesh. Would there be anyone to carry on his work? He had indeed found a number of brilliant men for his service and had trained them himself, but none among them came up to his own stature, nor did it seem that their training would enable them to follow the road once Peter was taken from among them. Peter had a quality to evoke enthusiasm all but merging into worship; he gave his commands in the most lucid form imaginable, he unfolded any new plan of his in all its details and entrusted the work to men he judged most fitted for it. But he was no teacher in the truest sense of the word. His very genius was at once a curse and a blessing in that it guided him towards decisions he knew to be right, but their why and wherefore were never communicated by him to others. No man living could possibly have enlarged on any of his ventures, or quickened the vehemence of his own pace, and no man, however talented and well trained, could continue that rhythm after Peter's death. And that was a tragedy since in 1725 so many of Peter's undertakings were inchoate.

✳

It used to be fashionable, and the fashion held firm for nearly two hundred years, to consider Peter as the first reformer of Russia. Far too little attention used to be paid either to the medieval Rus which maintained a flourishing trade both with the West and with Byzantium and married its princesses to foreign rulers from Norway down to France, or to Westernizing influences begun many years before Peter was born. The West imagined Muscovy as a somnolent bear in his well-nigh inaccessible lair until a young genius forced his way in, and started the process of a remarkable metamorphosis whereby the bear was turned into a human being, taught to shave his chin, to wear German clothes, and to acquire Western polish. But, of course, the bear's nature could never be exorcized.

As has been mentioned earlier, technology was Peter's temple, and technology said nothing at all to the masses. All his magnificent undertakings did little more than sweep along the fringes of his immense dominions which, in a way, explains his failure to destroy the past – soon enough proved to be as indestructible as the air, beliefs, customs and superstitions holding their own right into the present century. And even where the fringes were concerned, Peter's efforts to transmit civilization could not succeed because he himself was an alien in that country.

Being wholly dedicated to technology, Peter saw his subjects in terms of human material to be well shaken, moulded and used for the good of the state. Certainly, his reign made history, but he lacked any sense of history. Otherwise he would hardly have robbed the masses of the mystique surrounding their concept of sovereignty. It would be irrelevant to argue whether such an idea worked for the people's advantage or not. It formed the focal point of the covenant they lived by, something shrouded in mystery and hallowed by distance, but always as certain as the four seasons of the year, an awe-inspiring essential for a hard-driven, inarticulate people, whose lot was no easier under Peter than it had been during the years of the Tartar yoke. The Tsar shattered that mystique by callouses on his anointed hands, by turning upstarts into princes and counts, by his obvious impatience with the church ritual, by his constant public appearances where neither clothes nor demeanour set him apart from the humblest of his subjects, by a host of other details which ground the mystique to dust. In its place he offered the people an image they considered grotesque, an idea, which, if accepted, would, so they thought, have to be paid for in the coin of ultimate spiritual jeopardy. All of it may well seem archaic today when the general concept of monarchy has become an anachronism over the greater part of the world. But it was most woundingly real to the Russian masses of Peter's generation.

None the less, the epithet bestowed on him cannot be shrugged away. There was more than an occasional streak of greatness in Peter. All he tried to carry out was not for himself but for the people. If he drove them hard, he drove himself immeasurably harder. His vision may indeed have been set into a technological framework, but it was a vision, not a glimpse of a dust-bin in some forgotten back yard.

The root of the trouble is that Peter was born in the wrong country and in the wrong century. A flame burned in him which his own generation found well-nigh impossible to understand. In the ninth century those inexhaustible energies might have united the three Scandinavian kingdoms for a better purpose than that of pillage, or else safeguarded Charlemagne's great heritage from the ravages of internecine war. It is rather tempting to offer a final imaginative twist: Peter would certainly have been at home in his country today.

V

The Ladies' Hour

Six reigns, four of them very brief and all of them together covering about thirty-eight years, separate Peter I from Catherine the Great. In 1796, her son Paul succeeded her, and by that time the Romanov bloodstream was so thin a trickle as to have its very existence doubted by some historians. None the less, the dynasty did not lose its original signature. The consciousness that the first Romanov had been elected by the will of the people was never allowed to die out in spite of all the foreign infusions.

Catherine I, Martha Skavronska before her marriage to Peter I, date and place of birth unknown. Succeeded in January 1725, died in May 1727

THE PREMATURE death of Peter led the Western powers to assume that the work by him begun and still unfinished, would perish with his successor, whose very identity was then unknown. The withdrawal of Russia from the European scene would certainly have pleased the West, already embarrassed and annoyed by Russian encroachments. Foreign residents in St Petersburg, Moscow and Archangel reported on the swelling volume of opposition to 'the new way of life'. Yet the assumption of Russia's return to the Byzantine observance argued nothing except an abysmal ignorance of conditions in the country.

Meanwhile, the government faced the urgent task of finding a successor. The Senate, the hierarchy and most of the old nobility upheld the candidature of Peter, the ten-year-old son of the murdered Tsarevich Alexis, and he might have been elected if the government, the Church and the nobility had possessed one grain of cohesion among them. Having come to an agreement about young Peter, they could not agree about the form of the regency or the number of regents. One faction after another tried to push various names into the foreground and unanimity moved further and further away. Aloof from all factions, Menshikov, Peter Tolstoy and Yaguzhinsky were busily grinding their own axe. The three men had hated one another for years but for once they buried their venom and stood together. To have Tsarevich Alexis's little son for their sovereign, argued those men, would open the door to untold catastrophes since all the enemies of the late Emperor would see in such an election the eventual fulfilment of their hopes. In the end, Menshikov and the other two won over the army and navy commanders, frightened the senators, and over-rode all the objections raised by church dignitaries. Less than a month after Peter's death, Catherine, once a camp follower, became Empress and Autocrat of All the Russias.

Historiographers have been rather unkind to her. Her obscure beginnings and an admittedly spotted past were made to overshadow all else. Yet it would hardly be too much to say that the country lost heavily because of the brevity of her reign, and it remains a matter for wonder that a woman like her should have proved herself in so remarkable a fashion.

Naturally, Catherine accepted the crown not only because she felt it to be her duty but also because the prospect of power pleased her in no mean degree. She pledged herself to walk in her husband's steps but she took that road with a difference. Herself once only too intimately acquainted with penury, misery and humiliation, Catherine gave free rein to a quality her husband had never possessed, namely, compassion.

Within the very first months of her reign taxation was reduced, commerce freed from a host of irksome restrictions, and tentative measures introduced to ease the hardships of the common folk. 'We must have a long respite from war,' she told her ministers on more than one occasion. 'There will be time to think about the Black Sea and Turkey when the country has had a spell of peace.'

She had Menshikov for her prime minister, the man who had most strongly urged her candidature, once her protector, and now her servant. The situation might well have developed into a grotesque melodrama. That it did not do so was not due to Menshikov, whose tact was never on a par with his gift for intrigue, but to

Catherine's dignity. In St Petersburg she was sovereign first and foremost. In the privacy of her palace at Peterhof she indulged in certain minor liberties. The household and sentries on guard might see their Empress enjoy a tankard of iced beer, her plump body wrapped in a dressing-gown, slippers on her feet, her tumbled hair innocent of powder and her beringed hands anything but clean. She did not permit such relaxations in the capital. Ministers, senior servants of the crown, and, very particularly, foreign ambassadors, were received in a formal splendour which would have made the late Tsar lose his temper. On some occasions, however, Catherine was apt to exaggerate her part when, for instance, a senator, received in private audience, would find his sovereign lady in the full panoply of a diamond tiara, decorations and the purple velvet mantle on her shoulders.

Menshikov trod prudently. His enemies were never tired of alleging that he nursed hopes of ascending the throne, the erstwhile mistress his wife, but the accusation does not accord with facts. Vicious, corrupt and ambitious as he was, the Muscovite pieman was no fool, and he must have realized that the identity of Martha Skavronska was buried for ever. The Empress would never have thought of marrying a commoner any more than she would have expected her Peterhof roses to turn into lilacs.

Moreover, Menshikov's was by no means the only voice in her government. She chose another man for her Vice-Chancellor, Osterman, a genius of a statesman, who had come into his own during her husband's reign. Catherine listened to Osterman's advice, sometimes followed it and sometimes trusted her own judgment. Twenty-four years of life with a man who did not govern except when he was asleep and who shared everything with her had been a good education for Catherine. When Great Britain, mistrusting her peaceable intentions, urged Sweden to send ships to patrol the Gulf of Finland, Osterman feared that the situation would develop into a *casus belli*. 'Not unless we choose it to do so,' replied Peter's widow. Eventually, the matter was settled by her own note of tranquil and dignified protest. Wearied of the Senate's procrastinations, Catherine formed her Supreme Privy Council, completed one of her husband's unfinished projects in founding the Academy of Sciences and, though herself wholly uninterested in literature, established the first bookshop in St Petersburg.

The 1722 Act of Succession giving her the authority to choose her successor, Catherine made no secret of her decision. Her little step-grandson, hated by Peter since infancy, now lived in Catherine's palace together with his sister, Natalia. The Empress, busy with matrimonial plans for her own two daughters, proved herself kindly and generous towards the children who had spent so much time in misery because of their unfortunate father. Catherine chose able tutors for the little Grand-Duke to prepare him for the throne and warmly approved of his deep affection for Natalia. 'The children must not be kept apart,' she said. 'The girl has such a good influence over him.'

Yet the first Empress of Russia had one failing. Surprisingly it did not cloud her mind but it ended by shattering her health. Her capacity for drink was phenomenal even in those days of excess. Content with plain food, thrifty with her wardrobe to the length of wearing patched kirtles and darned hose when she was at Peterhof, Catherine was supposed to consume about six bottles of wine daily. The particular number may well have been born of some backstairs gossip and does not matter so greatly. The fact remains that when the first serious illness struck her in January 1727, she had no strength left to struggle against its ravages. Menshikov and Osterman between them took over the reins. All in secret Menshikov devised a plan of betrothing his daughter, Maria, to Grand-Duke Peter. It is not known whether the Empress was told about it, but by that time she was no longer able either to protest or to approve. She died in May 1727, her exact age remaining a mystery.

The two years' reign left a fair imprint. On one of her visits to the newly founded Academy of Sciences, Catherine saw a map of the Empire, all the territories won by her husband marked in bold crimson. She is supposed to have said: 'The country is vast enough, God knows. It is a long peace we need to put our house in order and to get the Treasury on its feet. Wars are so damned expensive.'

But she was not given enough time for the task envisaged by her.

Peter II, son of Tsarevich Alexis, grandson of Peter the Great. Born in 1715, succeeded in 1727, died in 1730

The Emperor Peter II was twelve on his accession. The Regency Council was headed by Menshikov, the other four members of the

Supreme Privy Council, and by the daughters of Peter the Great, Anna, Duchess of Holstein and Princess Elizabeth, whose fiancé, Prince Charles of Holstein, had died of smallpox a few days before their wedding.

The boy emperor had had one of the most unhappy childhoods ever fallen to the lot of a prince. He could not remember his parents: the mother died very soon after his arrival and the father was murdered when the boy was barely three years old. To Tsar Peter, the boy and his sister Natalia, a year older than her brother, were twin reminders of a hated son. The children were sent to live in one of the suburbs of St Petersburg. The Treasury allowance was just about adequate enough for them to escape utter penury and shabbiness, and the grandfather saw to it that the boy's education was entrusted to fairly capable tutors. Otherwise the brother and sister were wholly neglected. Nobody cared for them and nobody wanted them. They grew up rigidly excluded from all family occasions, and at an early date they were told about their father's terrible fate. 'The pup may well turn out like the hound that sired him' – such was Tsar Peter's comment on a grandson he hardly ever met. The children, deeply attached to each other, grew up in the cold atmosphere of insecurity, with indefinable danger spinning its web in some shadowy corner. When new ships of the line were launched in St Petersburg, little Peter would be told: 'well, you should be there – but you can't. The Tsar's Majesty would have a fit if he saw you,' and the child would be laughed at when he burst into tears. Had it not been for his sister's affection, the boy would hardly have endured those years.

But on Tsar Peter's death the children were at once summoned to the palace by their step-grandmother and made aware of their rightful place in the world. That abrupt change did not bewilder either Peter or Natalia. Their hunger for affection satisfied most miraculously, they responded eagerly. Catherine and her two daughters showered care and presents on them. When Peter was asked what he wanted most in the world, he instantly replied: 'never to be parted from Natalia'.

Now he was Emperor, with Osterman for his tutor-in-chief and Menshikov for his guardian. To the sensitive, intelligent boy, the Regent-in-chief was one of the symbols of a dark and unhappy past. Menshikov had been most callously instrumental in bringing about

Tsarevich Alexis's death, and Alexis's son did not hide his feelings. The first clash between them did not take long to come.

Tsarina Eudoxia, Peter's grandmother, still languished in the same prison where her husband had sent her in 1691. The young Emperor's first concern was to have an order drafted for her immediate release, but Menshikov protested. Such an action might well lead to an insurrection in the country, he pointed out. 'You mean that my father's friends will then rally round me,' said the boy. 'Well, I would be most happy if they did.' Menshikov nearly lost his temper. 'I refuse to sanction such an order. I am Regent.' 'But I am Emperor,' Peter replied.

Tsarina Eudoxia was released. She chose to live in Moscow, and the grandchildren went there to meet her for the first time. Within a few days Peter declared that the old city pleased him much more than St Petersburg. However, after a brief stay with the aged Tsarina, the children returned to the north. Little by little, members of the ancient nobility, so openly despised by Menshikov, began drawing nearer the throne. Presently there was no more talk of any betrothal between the Emperor and Maria Menshikova. Men of the Dolgoruki and Golytzin families said quite openly that it was not fitting for a Romanov to mate with an upstart's daughter. Scared by the rumours of a conspiracy against him, the Regent-in-chief formed a clumsy plan of kidnapping Peter and holding him prisoner at his own mansion on Vassily Island. The plan miscarried, and the arrogant dictator found himself on the way to Siberia in September 1727. By Christmas the young Emperor and his sister were most comfortably installed at the Kremlin palace in Moscow. Peter's coronation followed in March 1728.

Now the ancient city became a capital once again. The Supreme Privy Council, the Senate, the Synod and the entire administration left St Petersburg for Moscow at the Emperor's orders. Princes Dolgoruki and Golytzin were regents *de jure*, with Osterman in charge of foreign affairs. The country continued to be at peace with the whole world and, following the death of King George I, Russian relations with Britain grew slightly warmer.

Peter II was kept busy indeed. There were the hours of study, and Osterman himself gave him lessons in statecraft. There were also 'great occasions' when he must receive foreign diplomats. There was the whole of Moscow for him to learn. Finally, there were hawking and hunting expeditions. He was constantly companioned by Natalia and by his step-aunt, Princess Elizabeth, about six years older than himself. At thirteen Peter promised fair to be nearly as tall as his grandfather. In features he resembled his mother. He had a pronounced firm will, something of a temper, a deep hunger for affection, and a discernment surprising for his age.

The young Emperor's engagement to Princess Catherine Dolgoruka was announced in December 1729 and the wedding was fixed for 30th January 1730. The girl's family had doubtless contrived the match to a certain extent. None the less, it was no dryly contractual business, and the flush of his first love certainly comforted the boy after the loss of Natalia in December 1728. The few letters he wrote to his fiancée were artless, ardent and patently sincere. That union promised to be something of a new foundation stone for the dynasty. There was no question of a return to the ways of the past. On the other hand, all the inclinations of the young Emperor pointed to his desire to see much of the old blended with the new. When he was asked if the palaces in St Petersburg and Peterhof should be re-furbished for his wedding, Peter replied that it was his wish never again to hear those names mentioned in his presence. He was the sovereign of Russia and her capital was Moscow.

In January 1730 Peter caught smallpox, and he died in the morning of what should have been his wedding-day, the sixth and the last true-bred Romanov of the male line.

He was barely fifteen, but all the good qualities observed in his forebears could already be detected in him – firmness tempered by gentleness, love of peace, a sense of justice, a deep, however inarticulate, concern for the country. He had much more: gaiety, love of clean fun and true family feeling. All opportunity to prove himself a good son having been denied him, Peter's treatment of his grandmother Eudoxia, his devotion to his sister and to Princess Elizabeth and, finally, his feeling for the girl he was to marry, all of it together presents most unusually rewarding material for the tapestry of those days. Catherine Dolgoruka's memoirs, left unpublished until 1913, speak of Peter as 'her summer sky, my dove of peace, my lovely eagle,' and she wrote those lines in her advanced age.

That day in January 1730 certainly darkened the Russian skies.

The male Romanov line was now wholly extinct. All that day and far into the night the Supreme Privy Council sat in session behind closely guarded doors. The Council consisted of five members, but Osterman, pleading an attack of gout, absented himself. Of the other four, one was a senile and amiable nonentity, rather afflicted by deafness, who kept nodding his head at every name being put forward. A successor to Peter II must be found, but where could they look for him? Princess Elizabeth was mentioned by one and the infant son of the late Anna, Duchess of Holstein, by another. The discussion ended in a fiery monologue delivered by Prince Dimitry Golytzin. They had forgotten the most likely candidate, he told them, Anna, younger daughter of Tsar Ivan V, the widowed Duchess of Courland. 'She has no children,' someone interjected. 'She is barely thirty-seven and she may well marry again,' retorted Golytzin. 'Anyway, she is a Romanov born and is reputed to be in good health.'

Golytzin had much more to say once his candidate was accepted. There must be no more autocracy, he urged. The Duchess must sign a declaration to govern jointly with the Supreme Privy Council and the Senate. The three councillors did not recoil from the daring idea but pointed out that the Senate must be consulted. The session, its numbers considerably swelled by the arrival of as many old gentlemen as were not prevented by gout and other ailments, began hammering out the clauses of the document to be submitted to Anna. There were nine articles in all, limiting the sovereign's authority in every possible direction until it seemed that her autocracy would not extend far beyond the frontiers of her own household.

The very next day a deputation left for Mittau. In about three weeks a courier from Courland reached Moscow. Anna had accepted the crown and signed the articles. The nobility were overjoyed. Alone, Osterman looked pensive, aware that a limited monarchy would run a disastrous course in Russia. But Osterman had no close acquaintance with the widowed Duchess of Courland.

Shortly after her arrival in Moscow, the fat blonde daughter of Ivan V took her bearings, declared the nine articles to be out of accord with the will of the people and the needs of the Empire, ordered the paper she had signed to be brought to her, and tore it up with her own hands. The army upheld her. The common folk knew nothing of the matter. There was not a particle of opposition, the architects of the Mittau plan being stunned into frightened silence, and Anna was duly crowned as the Empress and Autocrat of all the Russias.

Anna, second daughter of Tsar Ivan V ; born in 1693, succeeded in February 1730, died in October 1740

'SHE IS a most venomous cicatrice and vulgar to boot. She has been known to count the apples on a tree for fear that her gardeners would cheat her. I wish that barbarian Russia joy of her.' So wrote a young baron from the Baltic Provinces to a friend in Sweden.

The description answers up to a point. Anna was something of a cicatrice and, all her intelligence notwithstanding, she was a fool in her blind passion for a man whose proper associate should have been a harlot and not the Empress of Russia.

In 1730 Anna was 37. The hard half-hooded eyes, the buttoned-up mouth, a certain meanness in gait and gesture and the ungraceful bulk added several years to her age. An unhappy childhood spent with a most unmotherly mother, an early and compulsory marriage to a man acquainted with vices she had not known to exist, a penurious widowhood full of petty humiliations out of all accord with her rank, such had been her past. She was not big enough to steer past bitterness. Her experiences left her a sour-minded prisoner of retrospection.

The deputation from Moscow took Anna unawares. She signed the so-called Mittau articles without argument. She would have signed her soul away to be free of Courland where she was despised and hated, of poverty which compelled her to live on lean beef and pickled cabbage and to wear shifts cobbled up by the none too willing hands of her women.

Moscow saw in Anna a daughter of Tsar Ivan V and welcomed her tumultuously. It was good to have a true-bred Russian on the throne with a Romanov for a father and a Saltykova for a mother. Anna seemed the best successor to the boy-Emperor who had preferred Moscow to the alien drifts of St Petersburg. The crowds, milling up and down the streets, had no idea that they were shouting themselves hoarse in honour of the first wholly Germanized Russian. For all their miseries, the years in Courland had wrought havoc with

Anna's Muscovite heritage, and general disillusionment started almost at once. The daughter of Ivan V seemed to have small use for her father's race. She arrived surrounded by a crowd of German hangers-on, chief among them being one Biren, a groom's grandson and her lover.

She left Moscow almost immediately for St Petersburg. The old nobility having planned to diminish her authority, Anna, incapable of forgiving and forgetting, began to persecute them with a coldly calculated ferocity. The Dolgoruki and the Golytzin were the first victims and others followed. Count Tolstoy and some of his friends who had ventured to name Elizabeth as Peter II's successor, did not escape Anna's vengeance. The poor little bride of the boy-Emperor was banished to Siberia for life. Princess Elizabeth was exiled to a lonely country manor and her Civil List cut down to a niggardly minimum.

It might have been supposed that a woman long accustomed to eat the crust of penury would have learned thrift, but the dizzily rapid ascent to the throne plunged Anna into a whirlpool of extravagances. The Treasury dared not protest. Taxation fell heavily on the rich and on the poor. Import dues rose most alarmingly, and various monopolies decreed by the imperial will began determining the price of herrings and candles. The erstwhile hausfrau from Mittau, who had once counted cucumbers and sausages in her larder, now revelled in luxuries never before known at the Russian court. Anna's dressing-table and a great mirror above it were of solid gold. There were stories about baths of white wine, an easing-stool of silver studded with sapphires, toothbrushes with rubies on their handles, and 'robrones' embroidered all over with pearls and amethysts. Some of it was idle tittle-tattle from the market-place and the street-corner. Much of it was unhappily true, and the Empress's lover enjoyed a large share of all those extravagances. Biren's apartments, sumptuously furnished, adjoined Anna's own at the Summer Palace. None the less, she had a magnificent mansion built for him on one of the islands. A special state department was created to look after the favourite's brood mares and stallions. Biren's plate amazed foreign ambassadors, and so did the diamonds showered by the Empress on his complaisant wife. In less than a year the groom's grandson became the largest landowner in the Empire, his estates reaching as far as Siberia. To crown all her benefactions the

Empress exalted her lover to the ducal rank when the Duchy of Courland fell vacant.

No parvenu, having reached the top of the ladder by more than devious means, can feel safe. Biren was capable of imagining a deadly conspiracy in a street-urchin's laughter at the clumsiness shown by his wife on entering her coach, and he never missed a chance of communicating his suspicions to Anna, who, well remembering the design against her power, became more and more convinced that her own life was in perpetual danger. Her lover urged that the support of the army alone was hardly enough to assure her safety, and she agreed. So an unholy inquisition, known as the Secret Chancery, came into being, Biren's green-coated hirelings carrying their slogan, '*Slóvo i délo*', 'Word and Deed', up and down the country. The new institution was named most aptly: its trials were held *in camera*, its sentences were never made public, and its records were kept in cypher. At the palace, frightened pages now had to taste every dish before it was served to the Empress.

Yet hers might have been a glorious reign. Necessity had sharpened her political acumen. She could see the advantages or otherwise of a suggested treaty far more quickly than her ministers, and she was no figurehead in the Council hall. She had men like Osterman, Münnich and Lacy to serve her, and she knew how to use their genius. The Turkish wars during Anna's reign were certainly costly in lives and money and by the Treaty of Constantinople in 1739, the conquests of Münnich, who had held the Crimea in the hollow of his hand, were cancelled out – mainly by French intrigues. None the less, those campaigns were not fruitless. Generals in the Russian service proved again and again that they could master the Turk, and the southward progress of Anna's armies was watched most anxiously from Sweden down to the Italian states. The Empress's own notes to her ambassadors abroad were proofs that Russian diplomacy was no longer ignored, and she was fully resolved not to let the Constantinople Treaty be the last page of her chronicle.

She had reached her forty-seventh year. The succession seemed assured through the marriage of her niece, Princess Anne of Mecklenburg-Schwerin, with a pallid nonentity labelled Anthony-Ulrich of Brunswick-Wolfenbüttel. The Empress had them come to St Petersburg where a son was born to them in July 1740. There was much rejoicing at court and very little satisfaction elsewhere. In the following October, Anna had a stroke while seated at dinner. She rallied enough formally to name the infant great-nephew her heir and to appoint Biren regent during the long minority.

The belfries throughout the Empire pealed to announce her death. But, Biren and his family excepted, there were few to mourn her.

Ivan VI, eldest son of Prince and Princess Anthony-Ulrich of Brunswick-Wolfenbüttel and great-nephew of the Empress Anna. Born in July 1740, succeeded in October 1740, dethroned in December 1741, murdered in May 1764

A four-month-old infant, his maternal grandmother being his only link with the dynasty, became Autocrat of the All the Russias. At the Summer Palace, the so-called Brunswick quartet, which consisted of his parents, a lady-in-waiting, Julia Mengden, mistress of Prince Anthony, and a chamberlain, Count Linar, lover of the Princess, resembled marionettes obedient to the most trivial order of Biren until Osterman and Münnich released them from the bondage by discovering a rather clumsy conspiracy. At the end of November, the ex-Regent, his family and the majority of his hangers-on were *en route* for Siberia, and the little Emperor's mother became Regent. The business of governing being wholly beyond her comprehension, the Empire was virtually ruled by Osterman. The Brunswick quartet had their time fully occupied by French plays, *fêtes champêtres*, dancing, cards, gossip and the building of pleasure pavilions.

1741 might have been a disastrous year for Russia if Osterman had not steered the ship of state clear of the rocks. The War of the Austrian Succession having broken out, there followed the customary re-shuffling of alliances. Turkey seemed restive once again, the mood of the Crimean Khan tautened in consequence, and forces had to be sent to the south to prevent any likely hostilities. In early summer Sweden turned a misunderstanding into a cause for formal rupture, declared war on Russia, and invaded Finland. Though the Swedes were repulsed by General Lacy in command of the Russian armies in the north, other perils remained, not the least among them being the thickening discontent in the country. Itinerant preachers never absent from the Russian scene, wandered from one province to another, reminding their listeners that nothing except sorrows awaited a land whose ruler was a child and whose government lay in the hands of men out of communion with the only true Orthodox Church. Poor harvests in some parts of the country were inevitably interpreted as signs of God's anger against Russia. The Secret Chancery kept a ceaseless vigil lest the smallest sign of a budding conspiracy were to come to light. But there were no conspiracies. Eleven years of sharply-fanged hardship and weariness were taking their toll. A breath of something like apathy began moving over the country.

One starlit frosty night in December 1741 the Emperor Ivan VI was lifted out of his cot by the hands of strangers. Having never been aware of his sovereignty, he could not know that the fourteenth month of his reign marked its close. It is said that he cried lustily on being woken. Strangers tried to soothe him. Wrapped in shawls and furs, the tiny Majesty of Russia was carried down the wide stairs and put into a hooded sledge waiting near the porch of the Summer Palace. That brief journey from the nurseries to the porch was Ivan VI's last public appearance. That very night, his parents and their motley retinue were made prisoners by order of Princess Elizabeth, elected Empress by the will of the guards regiments.

The child never saw his parents again. His appointed place of exile shifted from a fortress on the Baltic border to Kholmogory in the north and, finally, to Schlüsselburg at the mouth of the Neva. All the official records referred to the dethroned sovereign as 'the nameless prisoner'. He grew up in an intolerably close confinement which allowed him neither exercise nor privacy. His speech was slow and incoherent and his mind was housed in a twilight none among his jailers tried to disperse. Both Kholmogory and Schlüsselburg were places of stone and iron. Ivan VI was never permitted to learn a world where grass pushed green in spring and leaves burned crimson in autumn, and where men and women moved about, apparently unshackled and free to choose their habitation, clothes and food. Nor did Ivan know that in the same world, its very existence unsuspected by him, he was still remembered, pitied and prayed for. His very name might not be mentioned in public.

Ivan VI never knew that in spite of his captivity, its very site unknown to the masses, his name remained a challenge to the occupant of the throne. All in secret there were men to plot for his restoration, and one such attempt, carried into the walls of his dungeon, caused the young man to be killed by his jailers in 1764. They did not bury him at the Cathedral of St Peter and St Paul, the mausoleum of the dynasty. His body was laid in the grounds of Schlüsselburg Fortress. The report spoke of 'the fatal accident befallen to the nameless prisoner', a great-grandson of Tsar Ivan V, born into the purple, guilty of no other trespass than that of providing his great-aunt, the Empress Anna, with a legitimate successor.

*Elizabeth, second daughter of Peter I and Martha
Skavronska (Catherine I); born in 1709, ascended
the throne December 1741; died on Christmas
Day 1761*

The new reign did not start at a sovereign's deathbed, in a palace, or in a hall of the Senate, or at the altar steps of a cathedral. It began in the noisome, smoky atmosphere of the grenadier barracks with half-dressed, tousled men leaping from their wooden bunks and wondering if they were still asleep because of a tall beautiful woman, a soldier's cloak over her shoulders, a brief pike in her right hand, a woman accompanied by none, standing in the opened doorway, with torchlight falling upon her face and the fluent folds of her cloak. The men stared in silence. Then she spoke, and to them her words brought music of the morning into the midnight hour:

'You all know whose daughter I am. And I have come to you in my father's name. Will you promise to serve me?'

The grenadiers, now wholly awakened, shouted their consent.

The scene certainly invites the efforts of a composer, a painter, or a novelist. It was undoubtedly stirring, slightly melodramatic and – as will shortly be proved – entirely against the existing Russian law. Later the government, the rest of the army and the people accepted the *fait accompli* since there was nothing else for them to do.

But the grenadiers alone formed the vanguard and they were the first to swear allegiance to Tsar Peter's daughter, who, by her very appeal for their help and service, was breaking a law made by her father. The grenadiers were most likely ignorant of any such law. Members of the administration and many others knew perfectly well that in the juridical sense Elizabeth was an usurper. She wrested the crown out of the Brunswick hands for the undoubted good of the Empire. None the less, the law remained broken.

Peter the Great's Succession Act of 1722, whatever its merits or otherwise, empowered the sovereign to name his or her successor, and the Empress Anna was absolutely within her rights in naming the infant great-nephew as her heir. Ivan VI was Emperor *de jure*. By dethroning him, Elizabeth violated her own father's will. Not a drop of blood was shed either during that night or later during her reign, but the Brunswick ghost would haunt her threshold all down the years to come.

That December night in 1741 those who were aware of the usurpation kept a prudent silence. It seemed enough that the swift and bloodless revolution should be in full accord with the nation's wishes and hopes. The oath of allegiance to Elizabeth came from the people's heart.

What manner of woman was she?

The magnificent hurricane of her father's reign, the gyved years that followed, and the splendour come to flower under Catherine the Great, all those rather dwarfed Elizabeth's own achievement, and few were the historians who admitted that much accomplished by Catherine the Great had been initiated by her husband's aunt.

Elizabeth was thirty-two at her accession, and reputed to be the most beautiful woman of her day and the finest dancer in the whole of Europe. Her father had hoped to see her become queen of France but the Bourbon sensitivity and pride of race recoiled from the idea of a matrimonial alliance with the daughter of a camp-follower. After a few equally barren attempts made elsewhere, a far less important bridegroom was found in Prince Charles of Holstein, but he died a few days before the wedding. It pleased Elizabeth to continue – and that for a long time – to show evidences of a grief she may or may not have felt.

Badly brought up and most casually educated – to the end of her life Elizabeth could not remember that Great Britain was an island – she was not yet sixteen at her father's death. Having danced, sung, ridden hard and laughed since her childhood, she went on doing so until 1730. Her gaiety, simplicity and courage endeared her to all who knew her. Peter II was deeply attached to that vivacious step-aunt, who seemed to have no other purpose in life than to be in love with it. Already in 1726 there floated rumours about Elizabeth's lovers. Some of the stories were good-natured tittle-tattle – 'if she wants to enjoy herself, why should she not?' Other rumours proved true.

She did not really resemble either of her parents. Indolent, indifferent to food, passionately devoted to open-air sports, wholly at sea in the least important technological details, devoid of ambition and seemingly unconcerned about her own future, Elizabeth went on her way much in the manner of a gaily painted butterfly. Her beauty troubled. Her gaiety was contagious. Her candour was apt to serve her badly at times. She disliked foreigners and made no secret of it. Osterman, when he came to power, made her pay for many an unguarded remark.

The crisis of 1730 brought danger close to Elizabeth's door, but she did not appear to realize it. Having seen her nephew buried at the Assumption Cathedral, she stayed where she was. The common folk would have gone to the gallows for her and voices of some important people were raised on her behalf, but Elizabeth chose to stay in the background. Very likely, it was the safest thing for her to do. To Dimitry Golytzin, the architect of the Mittau plan, and quite a number of others, Elizabeth was first and foremost Peter the Great's daughter, reputed to be something of a wanton.

Things certainly changed for the worse with the arrival of the widow from Courland. Anna feared and mistrusted her cousin, and there followed ten years of exile in the country, a shamefully meagre allowance being appointed to Elizabeth. There were no large-scale conspiracies, but quite a few men were sent to the gallows for drinking the health of 'the North Star'. Remote from all current social drifts, neglected by the court, caring nothing for politics, Elizabeth stayed unforgotten by the people. Abroad, her name would be mentioned often enough. France watched narrowly and waited for developments. None came. Elizabeth's palace in St Petersburg stayed shuttered. She lived on at that country manor, employing her time in riding, hunting and shooting. She could not afford to have a great household, nor to entertain much. There were stirring little tales about her shabbiness and the poor fare she had. But her spirits remained the same. People in the countryside round about nearly worshipped her. Biren's sycophants in St Petersburg called her a whore.

In November 1740, her exile ended, Elizabeth appeared in St

Petersburg. The Princess-Regent and her court seemed friendly enough. Osterman watched her jealously, but Elizabeth did not provide him with the least reason for arraigning her. Her fortune restored to her, the Tsarevna gave parties, bought jewels and horses, supped and danced at the Summer Palace, brought expensive toys into the imperial nurseries, and was known to yawn whenever any political discussion was started in her presence. The years of humiliatingly penurious exile had not embittered her in the least. Gaiety and ebullience unimpaired, Elizabeth seemed to say, 'Please, I am still young, and let me enjoy life. I ask for no more.'

Such an ingenuous attitude lulled Osterman's anxieties to a certain extent, but he did not altogether relish Elizabeth's return to St Petersburg. With Münnich retired in high dudgeon and Biren exiled to Siberia, Osterman was Russia's virtual ruler, but there remained certain family matters about which the Princess-Regent did not consult him. Osterman knew well that in Elizabeth's eyes he remained a German nobody who owed an incalculable debt to her father. Unable to prevent her from regaining possession of her palace in St Petersburg, Osterman still had some opportunities to remind Elizabeth of the power under his hand. The Treasury was compelled to take orders from him. Within a few months Elizabeth's extravagances outran her means. She asked for an increase of her revenue, and it was refused. The French ambassador came to her rescue. The gold from France came to Elizabeth in such a way that Osterman never heard of it.

Nor did he find out that the gay supper parties at the palace overlooking Mars Square now ended in serious discussions held behind well guarded doors. Evening by evening, Elizabeth's intimates, her lover – soon to be her husband – Alexis Razumovsky, her chamberlain, Michael Voronzov, the two brothers Shuvalov, and her French physician, Armand Lestocq, talked about the conditions in the country, the ineptitude of the government and – most particularly – the mood of the army. Evening by evening, trusted go-betweens brought reports about the prevailing climate in St Petersburg barracks and elsewhere. On one such evening a momentous decision was shaped and taken. But nobody accompanied Elizabeth to the grenadier barracks that December night of 1741.

The indolent self within her did not die that night but it went to sleep for several years. Another, wholly surprising self came to life.

Activity replaced laziness and gaiety was tempered with gravity. Unprepared for her high office, untrained in the very rudiments of statecraft, Elizabeth seems to have looked reality in the face, assessed its burdens as well as its privileges, and proved herself capable of matching her response to the challenge she should have met in 1730.

All the aliens in the government were dismissed and many were exiled. Everybody wondered about Alexis Bestouzhev, Osterman's brilliant pupil and second-in-command who, when still a young man, had acquitted himself most remarkably during the Russo-Swedish negotiations of 1718–21. His was a difficult and unlovable character, and Elizabeth felt irked and repelled by it. If anything, she disliked Bestouzhev more than Queen Victoria disliked Gladstone. Bestouzhev had enemies without number and the barbed wire quality of his manner and conversation had won him no friends at all. People were certain that he would follow Osterman to Siberia and so he did – to be recalled almost immediately.

'I loathe the man but I am in need of his genius,' said Elizabeth to Alexis Razumovsky. 'There is plenty of trouble for him to settle,' and she amazed everybody by making Bestouzhev her Vice-Chancellor. The glories of her reign would certainly owe much to the man with whose opinion and policy the West had to reckon.

Elizabeth could hardly have taken the throne at a more difficult moment in Russian history. The Swedish question remained unsettled, and Sweden's rout in Finland had disturbed France, whose ambassador, La Chetardie, received instructions to offer French mediation, his government leaning rather heavily towards the possibility of Russian concessions since an enfeebled Sweden did not answer French purposes at all. In this instance, La Chetardie's clumsiness fully equalled his brazenness. Having first assured his government of certain success because of the Empress's ignorance of statemanship, La Chetardie decided to appeal to her as a woman to show herself generous towards Sweden, the friendship of France being the reward of her complaisance. But it was the sovereign – and not the woman – who answered him in her faultless French:

'What will my people think of me if I allowed myself to cast a slur on my father's memory by ceding to Sweden the very same lands he had conquered at such a high cost?' Unprompted by Bestouzhev, though aware that he shared her views, Elizabeth refused to negotiate except on her own terms, and the war continued until the Treaty of Abo in 1743 left the southern part of Finland in Russian possession.

'But there must not be any quarrel with France,' the Empress warned her Vice-Chancellor. 'European affairs are your business, but I have an Empire to govern, and God knows we need a breathing space.'

Whatever the mistakes of the home administration, Elizabeth hoped to govern on the simple principle of being the mother of an enormous family. The inevitable delegation of supreme authority was made even more unsatisfactory by the difficulties which stood in the way of all provincial communication with the centre. The rigours and whims of climate and the scarcity of good roads helped to swell the authority of local administration sometimes to the point of tyranny. A governor's unjust practices could be appealed against – in theory. In hard practice, appeals to the Senate and even more so petitions to the sovereign seldom achieved their purpose, chiefly owing to the leprosy of peculation. Nevertheless, a direct approach to the throne ceased to be as dangerous as it had been during the reign of Anna when a private petition against some injustice in provincial courts was all too often misinterpreted and treated as a gesture of rebellion against supreme authority. Elizabeth abolished the Secret Chancery and capital punishment. With no aliens to harass and order them about, the masses were relieved of at least one burden. The Tsarina, however remote in distance, remained the North Star.

In St Petersburg, his dingy office scarcely in keeping with a Vice-Chancellor's dignity, Bestouzhev, his ultimate purposes hooded even from his colleagues, was working hard. He well knew that the Treaty of Abo had earned him the undying enmity of France, but for the moment that troubled neither his mistress nor himself. Bestouzhev leant a little too heavily on the friendship of Austria and Saxony, mistrusted Prussia, and was doing his best to establish less icy relations between his country and Great Britain, but London would have none of him. Public opinion in England remained staunchly pro-Brunswick. Where were the Princess-Regent and her family? Why could they not be sent back to Brunswick? Were they alive or not? St Petersburg vouchsafed no information whatever.

'They were all Russian subjects,' the Empress said to Bestouzhev, 'and I will not have the British meddle in our home affairs. Was their late King pleased with the help and sympathy my father showed to the Jacobites?'

The ex-Regent, her husband and children, with the exception of Ivan VI, were kept at Kholmogory near Archangel. Soon enough Bestouzhev's enemies, urged on by French gold, realized that the deposed Emperor might become a useful tool in their hands. It was argued that the Vice-Chancellor must inevitably thirst after greater power than Elizabeth allowed him, that the respect he had felt for Osterman could not have died out and that, finally, the restoration of the imperial infant would involve a prolonged regency, with Bestouzhev inevitably at the helm. Those arguments proved that his enemies did not know him at all. Much poisonous gossip was brought to the Empress. She brushed all the stories away as though they were so many cobwebs on the ceiling. She disliked Bestouzhev as much as ever, but her trust in him continued deepening.

Nor had she much leisure for any gossip. She was preoccupied with a dynastic matter. Her late sister's only child, the fifteen-year-old Duke of Holstein, was summoned to St Petersburg. The Empress made him waive his rights to the crown of Sweden and had him made a member of the Orthodox Church. Grand-Duke Peter was declared her heir, and she must get him married to assure the continuity of the dynasty. Elizabeth chose the least important German princess for her nephew's bride. Early in 1744 the girl and her mother arrived in Russia. The Princess's father, Augustus of Anhalt-Zerbst, was in King Frederick's service. There was undisguised pleasure over the betrothal in Berlin, but the King wrote to his minister in St Petersburg: 'I cannot reckon on the Empress's friendship unless Bestouzhev is swept out of the way.' Mardefeldt and La Chetardie joined forces to bring about the Vice-Chancellor's downfall. He discovered the plot at the eleventh hour and the secret dispatches of the French ambassador, having been perlustrated and copied, were brought to the Empress. The innuendos against her minister's integrity made no impression on her, but when she came to read La Chetardie's remarks about herself, Elizabeth lost her temper very much in her father's fashion.

The Frenchman's imagination had really run too far. He wrote pages about Elizabeth's profligacy, vanity and absorption in pleasure.

He mocked at her lack of education. He made scathing references to her mother's early years. Some of it was true. Most of it had been harvested among gossip-mongers. As a result, La Chetardie was sent out of the country within forty-eight hours and Elizabeth wrote a spirited protest to the King of France.

But that storm came to be forgotten when in September of the same momentous year King Frederick invaded Bohemia. Elizabeth was badly shaken. Not so Bestouzhev who had never expected Frederick to keep faith with Austria. Yet he had a difficult time with his mistress. He urged her to send help to Vienna. Her reply was ambiguous. She wished for no quarrel with Prussia. 'I can't afford a war, man,' she kept telling Bestouzhev, 'and so far I have nothing against King Frederick.' 'He is asking for our help, Madam,' the Vice-Chancellor said, and the Empress retorted that she could not afford to help anyone. 'Austria must manage on her own.'

Frederick, having despaired of bringing about Bestouzhev's downfall, began using different tactics. Bribes far above his official emoluments were offered to the Vice-Chancellor. He refused them all. The Prussian minister complained that Bestouzhev's personality was out of accord with the national character. 'You might as well try to bribe the Archangel Gabriel,' he wrote to Berlin.

Unknown to Bestouzhev, the Empress heard about the rejected offers, one of which amounted to one hundred thousand crowns, a fortune to a man who, possessing neither estates nor any other inherited wealth, subsisted on his salary. Elizabeth's respect deepened, but she neither praised nor rewarded the man who knew that she knew because of her refusal to give any help to Prussia.

Relations between the two countries worsened from month to month. Now St Petersburg and Berlin took to watching each other in the manner of two wild animals crouching for a deadly leap. Apart from the stilted and elegant verbiage of official documents, neither the Empress nor the King troubled about any restraint of language. To Elizabeth, Frederick became 'the penny Shah of Berlin', 'the Prussian fox', 'the garbage gatherer'. To Frederick the Empress appeared as 'a she-bear', 'a savage cat', and on one public occasion he compared her with the Turk. Where Prussia was concerned, Elizabeth and her Chancellor marched hand in hand. But there was one thorny thicket of a divergence between them.

Bestouzhev saw clearly that Austria, once exhausted by the war, would prove a broken reed as an ally at some critical future moment. He therefore began toiling harder than ever to bring about an Anglo-Russian understanding, and the Empress made dust of all his efforts. In the first place the British attitude to the Brunswick matter had incensed her from the beginning. Next, she was convinced that any such alliance would result in small profit to her own Empire, there being far too many divergencies of interest. But Bestouzhev persevered until she gave her consent late in 1755. He thought he was reaping a triumph when he got a treaty signed early in 1756. It proved Dead Sea fruit and even worse; it was one of the causes of his ultimate downfall.

Those early months of 1756 were a diplomatic whirlpool. Frederick, stealing a march on Russia, had signed the Treaty of Westminster. France, contrary to all the assertions of Bestouzhev, joined Austria against Prussia. His life-work lay in ruins and the Prussian invasion of Saxony started the Seven Years' War. Secure of British friendship and monetary help, assured by his agents that the Russian finances could not meet the costs of even a brief campaign, Frederick saw his dominions stretching to the banks of the Danube and even beyond.

And it certainly seemed at the beginning that the Prussian hopes would be justified. Elizabeth's resources were stretched to the very utmost. Her commanders wasted what few victories fell to their share. Her hurriedly recruited armies were no match for the Prussian forces. The help given by Maria Theresa was of a kind which prompted Elizabeth's firm and dignified protests against the unfairness of expecting Russia to pull all the Austrian chestnuts out of the fire. To thicken the shadows, some letters of Bestouzhev to General Apraxyn were intercepted at Elizabeth's orders, high treason was read into them, and the Vice-Chancellor had to stand his trial. In the end the ominous charge was withdrawn, but the Empress would not re-install him, and she called on Michael Voronzov to serve her – a loyal enough man, but no genius in statecraft. All of it, together with the disappointment in her nephew and heir, who shared none of her views and continued professing his friendship for 'the Prussian fox', told heavily on the Empress. Her sudden illness in the autumn of 1757 raised Frederick's hopes that she would not recover. But Elizabeth cheated him by rallying. Her greatly depleted strength notwithstanding, she prosecuted the war with a heightened vigour.

General Saltykov's victory at Künersdorff amazed Europe. King Frederick seemed crushed, and Great Britain chose the moment to suggest that peace negotiations should begin without delay, and Austria and France were of the same opinion. Alone, Elizabeth refused. Her health already undermined, her thoughts distracted by the unhappy family climate, she held on. From 1759 onwards her firm stand alone barred the way to the allies' disintegration. 'The Shah of Berlin must be rendered harmless once and for all,' she declared to her ministers, and she made it clear to all the ambassadors at her court that she was resolved to fight to the end even if it meant selling all her jewellery and her immense wardrobe. In October 1760 Chernishev's corps occupied Berlin. France at once instructed de Breteuil to put concrete peace proposals before the Empress.

At a historic audience given to the French and Austrian ambassadors, Elizabeth spoke words which were to prove prophetic:

'I am certain that Europe will come to rue the day unless Prussia's power is broken utterly. Should King Frederick be successful, his heirs will never be content with Prussia alone. They would venture much farther than Saxony and Bohemia.'

She stood firm, and she spoke in the manner of one aware of her leading position. She told Prince Esterhazy that she would withdraw her help from Austria unless the latter fulfilled her own obligations in a proper manner. Apologetic letters from Maria Theresa were sent to St Petersburg. Elizabeth wrote to France that the European matters of the hour were of paramount importance and that France should stop her preoccupation with America and the Indies. In the autumn of 1761, when England declared war on Spain, Elizabeth ordered a Te Deum to be sung and said to her ministers: 'Now London will have no money to waste on the Prussian fox'.

'You expect me to call a truce?' she said to de Breteuil. 'The business is not yet finished. You never expected to see my soldiers in Berlin, did you? Your country and mine are allies today, but I know that quite a few governments in Europe would be happy to see Russia breaking up, once peace is concluded. I am not greedy. I shall ask for nothing except Ducal Prussia. My people have earned it by their blood. No, it is far too early to think of truce.'

Admittedly, it is difficult to gauge the extent of Elizabeth's sin-

cerity in denying her territorial ambitions, and the West was hardly
prepared to believe her, the Treaty of Abo still fresh in diplomatic
memory. Yet with Elizabeth the matter of Prussia went much further
and deeper than any desire for territorial aggrandizement. She
sensed on all her pulses that King Frederick was nursing a hope for
a German hegemony and that it was her business to prevent him
from attaining a goal that would spell disaster, so she felt, to the
whole of Europe. To that end Elizabeth struggled on and was prepared to make any sacrifices the task demanded of her. It was precisely her unswerving policy which would pave the way to the
splendours of the reign to come. Not under Peter I, still less under
Amma, did Russia enter the European comity – but under Elizabeth.
The West and indeed many among her own subjects were apt to
regard her views on Prussia as exaggerated chiefly because of her
personal dislike of King Frederick. The future which Elizabeth was
not to see would prove her right.

With Berlin occupied by her soldiers and with Western statesmen
pondering over the Empress's utterances, it might be supposed that
the Russian home landscape presented a correspondingly rewarding
tapestry.

Alas, the ever-growing necessities of a difficult and costly war
proved exactly the opposite. Taxes kept rising. Many projected
plans for cultural enlightenment had to be shelved because of lack
of funds. Bestouzhev's successor, prevented by the Empress from
committing any major blunders, was not exactly a star in the diplomatic firmament. Away from the capital, the administration
resembled a cart trundling along at a snail's pace and occasionally
losing one of its wheels in a rut. Enormous reaches of arable lay
neglected because each new recruitment kept encroaching on land
labour. Nothing was done to improve the means of communication;
only the roads leading westwards were kept in passably good repair.
The Empress's personal extravagances were not of much help to the
harassed Treasury. She had a passion for building new palaces, and
the great Rastrelli served her in St Petersburg and at Tsarskoe Selo.
One of her palaces having been burned down, she had another built
within less than two months. Her jewellery, clothes and furniture
were discussed in Paris, Vienna and Dresden. Her charities knew no
boundaries. Her love of dancing did not weaken with the advancing
years, and she may well be called the foundress of the Russian ballet.

Many educational plans were more or less at a standstill. But Elizabeth greatly cherished the Academy of Sciences, and she never lost her ability to recognize genius so that a fisherman's son from Archangel was enabled to fulfil his rich promise in more fields than one. The name of Lomonossov was to remain one of the richest jewels in Elizabeth's crown.

And to the very end Elizabeth kept her hold on the people. She went on pilgrimages, walking along dusty and stony roads in company of monks, bakers' wives and peasant women. She shared their rough food and joined in their devotions. She stood godmother to many babies born to serjeants and privates of Guards regiments. She swore lustily, using full-blooded idioms the common folk could echo. She rode in the manner of a cavalryman and, all her simplicity notwithstanding, she knew how to keep her dignity whether she wore a purple velvet mantle or a shabby riding-habit.

But all was far from well at the palace. There was not even a semblance of any family life. Elizabeth's nephew and heir, Grand-Duke Peter, ended by poisoning her solitude. The boy never grew up into a man. He amused himself with toys and childish diversions. What was far worse, he worshipped at the Berlin shrine. Elizabeth, having married him to the Anhalt Zerbst princess and having waited for nine years for a son to be born to them, despised Peter and distrusted and persecuted Catherine, who deserved none of the harshness meted out to her at the Empress's orders.

Having recovered from her illness in 1757, Elizabeth took to leading a most peculiar life. She slept all through the day, dined at midnight, and gave audiences in the small hours. The fall of Bestouzhev and the all but treacherous blunders committed by her generals made her give way to most unreasoned suspicions until she feared the least shadow in a corner. Barely fifty, she looked an old woman and her pitiful failing could no longer be hidden even from a casual visitor at the palace. Elizabeth drank at meals and drank between meals, and her enemies, including 'the Prussian fox', alleged that she stopped drinking only when she slept. The toll exacted by such a life grew harder and harder to pay. The spirited words to the French ambassador at the beginning of 1761 prove Elizabeth's very last utterance of note. Moods of inertia rather than indolence increased in duration and in frequency.

Her government and the court were gripped by anxiety. There was some talk about the Empress disinheriting her 'damned fool of a nephew' as she came to call Peter, in favour of his seven-year-old son, Paul. But the hour of important decisions had gone from her for ever. When her intimates, only too well aware that Grand-Duke Peter was unfit to reign, mustered enough courage and begged the Empress to consider the consequences likely to fall upon the country, she merely shrugged and said: 'Ah that fool will lose the crown soon enough. My people will never stand his licking the Prussian boots.'

The closing months of 1761 went on leaden feet. Within perpetually curtained rooms, ablaze with the shine of numberless candles, in unimaginable loneliness, the last true-bred Romanov sovereign lived from day to day, sometimes seeking spiritual counsel but refusing all medical aid. Reconciled to Grand Duchess Catherine, Elizabeth would not have her nephew admitted into her rooms.

On Christmas Day 1761 Elizabeth died. 'The Shah of Berlin' was overjoyed. The Empire almost tottered under the blow. For the masses, the drunken, moody, suspicious, unhappy and prematurely aged woman had never existed at all. They still thought of her as 'the North Star' who had delivered them from the hateful alien yoke.

Peter III, only child of Duke Carl-Frederick of Holstein-Gottorp and Anna, elder daughter of Peter the Great.
Born in 1728, succeeded on Christmas Day 1761;
abdicated in June 1762, murdered in July 1762

Unlike most princes of the blood in his generation, Carl-Peter-Ulrich of Holstein-Gottorp was born of a love match. His parents had to struggle hard before consent was given to their marriage, but their happiness was very brief. Anna died in giving birth to her son.

There were no softening influences in his infancy. His father, crushed by the loss of his wife, did not neglect the child, but the Duke's ideas about his son's upbringing were odd even for that age. The prince had orderlies for nurses and officers for tutors. His childhood spent in the icy climate of a barracky castle, Carl-Peter-Ulrich was early taught to look upon military minutiae as the sole justification of existence. They drilled him without any regard for his strength and health. They trained him for the guardroom, the parade ground and eventually for the battlefield. For quite a few years nobody troubled to develop him in any other direction but the boy had to have some personal outlet. The buffoon within him, undoubtedly inherited from his imperial grandfather, was by no means subdued by his tutors' harsh treatment.

At the age of eleven, the boy became Duke of Holstein-Gottorp and heir to the crown of Sweden. He seemed to care little enough for either dignity. He did not know his mother's tongue at all; he spoke roughly accented German, was able to stumble through a few phrases in Swedish, and could massacre French when the occasion asked for it. Some Latin having been whipped into him, the little Duke ploughed his reluctant way through Caesar and Tacitus. But he never grew up and his real self was very much in evidence when he happened to be engaged in some foolish prank always at the expense of his intimates' comfort.

Swarthy of skin, morose of temper, untidy in his personal habits, a clumsy liar and a most unconvincing braggart (he was heard boasting that he had routed a Danish army at the age of eight), Carl-Peter-Ulrich was none the less greatly to be pitied, and there was nobody to pity him. His numerous German relations disliked having their clothes slashed to ribbons, finding bloody remains of rats and mice under their pillows, or else discovering that a salt-cellar had been emptied into the coffee-pot. They nicknamed him 'the imp of Kiel', made wry faces at his arrival, and were thankful to see him leave. Unluckily for them and also for himself, Carl-Peter-Ulrich was too important a boy to be ignored altogether.

Elizabeth, become Empress, brushed all those unpleasant chronicles aside. To her, the boy was the only child of a greatly beloved sister, half a Romanov by blood, and the only possible inheritor of the Russian crown. She insisted that all the stories spread about him were born of jealousy on the part of his German kin, and she summoned the boy to St Petersburg, ordered him to waive his rights to the Swedish throne, had him enter the Orthodox Church, and created him a Grand-Duke. Finally, in 1745, the Empress had him married to the 16-year-old Sophia-Augusta-Frederika of Anhalt-Zerbst.

But it never seemed to occur to the Empress that her nephew should have been prepared for the future. Peter had a large household, enjoyed a generous allowance, and found himself at liberty to continue with his childish pastimes.

Marriage did not turn him into an adult. Peter took a violent dislike to his bride, neglected her from the very beginning, and made no secret of his sordid and inevitably casual affairs. Nor did he conceal his true sympathies. We cannot tell if Peter believed in God. He certainly believed in Prussia, and King Frederick became his friend, counsellor and idol. At the outbreak of the Seven Years' War, the heir to the Russian crown was known to pray for the ultimate Prussian victory. The Empress, long since disillusioned in him, realized that it was out of all question to have the Grand-Duke join her armies, even at the rear. Past his thirtieth birthday, Peter led the life of an ill-mannered and uncontrollable twelve-year-old – with the exception of his excessive drinking and wenching.

State business bored him to tears. He felt ill at ease in St Petersburg and greatly preferred his palaces at Oranienbaum and Peterhof where nobody interfered with the beating of a large drum from one room to another, building fortresses out of cardboard, and finding pleasure in fashioning diminutive soldiers from cornflour and glue. Peter court-martialled a rat he had caught eating one of his puppets, had a tiny gibbet erected in the room, and hanged the rat with his own hands. For a slightly more serious occupation, the Grand-Duke had his Holstein battalion for the daily drill in strict accordance with the Prussian army regulations. In maudlin moods, which generally followed a drinking bout, Peter was known to bewail his fate and to long for his native Holstein. His mother's country, its faith, language and customs were of no use to him except in so far as they provided material for most grotesque ridicule. Peter would swear in German at the difficulties of a language 'fit for savages and pigs', grimaced and guffawed during church services, parodied his aunt, her ministers and bishops at parties in his rooms, and toasted the King of Prussia at a time when unnumbered thousands of his aunt's subjects were shedding their blood at the front.

In 1754 a son was born of that most unfortunate marriage. If the Grand-Duke had a single true friend to give him counsel, he might have learned that the most salutary course for him was to ask the Empress to let him cede his rights to his son and to return to Holstein. Elizabeth, who allowed neither Peter nor Catherine any voice about the child's upbringing, might well have consented to her nephew's departure. But an independent decision of such magnitude lay beyond the Grand-Duke's enfeebled intelligence, and he had no true friends. He spent his days surrounded by a sycophantic crowd.

A few years before the Empress's death, Peter found a mistress to please him permanently. She was Elizabeth Voronzova, sister of the famous Kitty Dashkova, with whom she had about as much affinity as there exists between a loaf of bread and a poodle. 'Lízanka' amply answered every need of Peter's. She capped his coarse language with her own, all but rivalled him in the telling of salacious stories, had a marvellous capacity for drink, and enjoyed her lover's buffoonery even when he ruined her elaborate coiffure by pouring a jug of milk over it. When, wrapped in a velvet curtain for a chasuble and wearing a saucepan for a mitre, the Grand-Duke mimicked the old Metropolitan of St Petersburg, Lizanka's deafening laughter did not come from any dutiful response of a sycophant. She truly enjoyed the performance, begged him to repeat it, and called her lover a genius so often that Peter ended by believing it himself.

Yet 'Lizanka' had a trait which she was cunning enough not to hang on the window-sill for all the world to see. She had unbounded ambition, and loved the prospect of a crown even more than she liked her beer.

For all their shared interests and preferences, Peter's attachment to Lizanka remains something of a question-mark to a psychologist. Peter's hatred of all things Russian had long since ceased to be normal. Not only was Lizanka a true-bred Russian but she was apparently untouched by the veneer of Western usages. She certainly wore clothes of the French cut, had her hair powdered, and enjoyed the social freedom introduced by Peter the Great, but inwardly she belonged to the East, Byzantine rather than Muscovite. The foreign covenant, its demands and challenges, spelt pure gibberish to Lizanka, and yet she proved the only woman Peter loved. Coarse, unshapely and incredibly ugly as she was, to her lover she stood for an embodiment of Aphrodite, grace flowering on her lips and music breaking in her walk. He learnt of bliss when he lay in her arms, and she knew that she sustained him when she kept repeating that the sun would shine on him once he was Emperor.

Little by little Peter grew convinced that on his accession he must divorce Catherine and make Lizanka his Empress. 'Will you send her abroad?' Lizanka asked. 'That might be dangerous. Better have her shut up in some convent in Siberia.' Peter loathed religious houses and never went near any of them. Now he agreed that they had their use in an emergency, and between them Catherine's future was settled comfortably enough for their own comfort.

On Christmas Day 1761 Peter became Emperor. He did not exile his wife to Siberia that same evening. He had far more pressing matters to deal with. His first sovereign act was to send couriers to King Frederick and all the generals at the front. The war was ended. The five years' expenditure of blood, energy and money was thrown overboard within a few hours. When the French ambassador dared to protest against such an abrupt ending to the alliance, Peter rudely said that the alliance had not been arranged by him and that the King of Prussia was his sole ally in the world. That sudden withdrawal of Russia naturally enabled Frederick to dictate his own terms, and Peter would welcome them.

His next command was for a banquet to be served in a hall adjoining Elizabeth's private apartments where her body was already being prepared for burial. Presently her chaplains crossed the hall on their way to begin the appointed offices for the dead. None of the Emperor's guests dared take notice of the black-robed clergy. Their new sovereign having ordained a banquet, it was their duty to eat, drink and remain unaware that death had visited the palace but a few hours before.

'Lizanka' was formally installed at the palace. Crown heirlooms, Elizabeth's personal jewellery and many trinkets filched from Catherine were in possession of the mistress. Peter still talked about divorcing his wife but he took no steps in that direction. 'She cannot escape me,' he kept saying to his mistress, 'and there is no hurry now that I am Emperor'.

For the first time in his life Peter was busy. There followed an avalanche of *ukazes*, and some of them are sad proofs of what Peter III might have been if his childhood and youth had been entrusted to people capable of developing his qualities. During his brief sovereignty he proved that he was neither wholly buffoon nor libertine. Compassion zigzagged its way through many documents he signed, and compassion was a rare quality to find in Russia at the time. His aunt had abolished capital punishment. He put an end to torture. He fought against graft. He issued orders to ease the lot of merchants overburdened with taxation. He exempted nobility and gentry from compulsory state service. On the other hand, Peter III secularized all ecclesiastical property and refused to be crowned in Moscow. 'What does it matter if I get crowned in St Petersburg?' he asked, and even King Frederick's appeals for him not to hurt national feelings did not make Peter III change his mind. 'My coronation?' he wrote to the King. 'There is plenty of time. I must first settle with those impertinent Danes.'

Indeed, there seemed plenty of time to divorce his wife and have her shut up in some remote Siberian convent, to be crowned at St Alexander's Abbey in St Petersburg, and to settle his differences with the outraged governments of France and Austria. There was plenty of time to marry his 'adorable Lizanka' and to place the imperial crown on her head. Why, he had only been Emperor for a few months, but he must first of all punish Denmark for her stubbornness in holding on to the Gottorp lands which belonged to him as Duke of Holstein. Peter threw himself wholeheartedly into the preparations for the absurd campaign. When an admiral reported that some of the ships of the line could not be adequately manned because a fever epidemic had broken out among the men, the Emperor thundered that illness formed no part of a sailor's duty and commanded all the sick men 'to get well without delay'.

Peter kept so far from reality that he never thought of reckoning with the mood of the army. They were at the end of June 1762. Peter, having insulted his wife at a public dinner in St Petersburg, had ordered her to have a banquet at Peterhof on his feast-day, the 29th June. Meanwhile he and Lizanka were at Oranienbaum. The Danish campaign was to start in a few days and she was to accompany him. 'When we are back,' said Peter III, 'and that will be soon because the Danes are rotten fighters, I will have Catherine imprisoned for life and you shall be my Empress.'

He had no idea that at dead of night his wife left Peterhof and drove at breakneck speed to St Petersburg there to be proclaimed Empress. Not a drop of blood was shed. Peter offered no fight. He abdicated almost eagerly. They parted him from his mistress, his pet monkey and his violin, and sent him to Ropsha, an isolated manor to the west of the capital. In grovelling terms Peter wrote to his wife – now become his sovereign – and begged for his mistress, the monkey and the violin to be restored to him. The monkey and the fiddle were duly sent to Ropsha, but not the mistress, who was already on her way to a prison in Siberia. Within a week Peter III was dead – either strangled or poisoned. Nobody knew for certain and none among his jailers at Ropsha were punished.

Responsibility for the murder cannot be shifted from Catherine's door. Nor can Elizabeth be wholly absolved because 'the imp of Kiel' should have been left to pursue his bizarre buffooneries in Holstein.

VI

'We, Catherine the Second'

*Sophia-Augusta Frederica, eldest daughter of Prince
Christian Augustus of Anhalt-Zerbst and his wife,
Johanna Elizabeth, née Princess of Holstein-Gottorp.
Born at Stettin in May 1729, married Grand-
Duke Peter of Russia in September 1745, became
Empress Consort in December 1761, deposed her
husband, the Emperor Peter III, in June 1762,
died in November 1796*

BOTH TO contemporaries and to posterity the infancy of any great
personage suggests a most temptingly blank piece of canvas. There
is a suggestion of hagiography in a point of view undisciplined
enough to discern signs of greatness in the way a baby clutches at its
rattle. In her case, however, even Catherine's rather elaborate efforts
to weave glamour into her earliest memories failed to convince.
Hers was a most ordinary childhood, she being an unimportant
princess born of an obscure family. The great chance of her life
came to Catherine not because of her origins or merits, but first
because the then Empress of Russia, Elizabeth, once affianced to
Catherine's uncle, was a sentimental woman who clung to the young
man's memory with a tenacity scarcely justified by an engagement
illustrating the old saying that a bird in hand is preferable to two
in the bush. Secondly, and even more importantly, the German
matrimonial market of the day had few potential brides quite as
insignificant as Sophia, daughter of a prince who ruled over the
eighth part of the none too big principality of Anhalt. The girl would
have been fortunate to find some equally obscure princeling for a
husband. Otherwise, she would have drifted into the stagnant water
of grey spinsterhood, like so many of her aunts and cousins, who
were perpetually short of money, devoted themselves to the care of

crippled animals and birds in their draughty, bleakly furnished castles, wore gowns which would have shamed a merchant's wife, scrounged wine, game and travelling expenses from their wealthier relations, and divided their leisure between the Bible and patience cards. That such a life did not fall to Catherine's lot was a stroke of good fortune.

She owed her good education to her father who, though the dullest officer in the Prussian King's army, was no fool. Figgy, as she was known in the family, was brought up by a clever, honest and exciting French governess, whose conversation even more than the lessons enlarged the child's horizons. Of good colouring, with most attractive brown eyes, she was certainly pretty, and the rough manners of her earliest years were somewhat mended by the time she reached her teens. Figgy had a well-developed wit and an un-slumbering regard for her own self. Such a dowry, linked with a possibly meagre marriage settlement, would have been unlikely to tempt many bachelor princes. Moreover, she was the daughter of a vain, feather-brained and most indiscreet woman, whose behaviour and conversation promised fair to cripple the daughter's chances. In brief, had smallpox or any other mischance carried the girl off before 1744, her name might never have appeared in the German annals of the time.

But, though much was against her, Figgy nursed ambitions and made no secret of them. She meant to be a queen one day. Her governess reproved her. The others, on hearing about the absurd day-dream, laughed at the eleven-year-old girl unlikely to win even the least important duchy in Germany.

As has been told before, Elizabeth of Russia had been concerned about the succession ever since she deposed Ivan VI in November 1741. Unmarried, she decided that her sister's son, then aged fourteen, was the only possible successor for her. Therefore Elizabeth began looking for a suitable bride, her nephew's own preferences being ignored all through.

Figgy was not yet fifteen when the invitation to come to St Petersburg reached Zerbst. Nobody saw fit to tell her anything about the reasons, but she was shrewd enough to realize that she was being summoned to Russia very much in the manner of a bundle of brocade a customer wished to see on approval. She knew that if she failed to please the Empress (nobody seemed to think of the Grand-Duke's reactions), her future would be sunk in utter obscurity.

Yet to her fool of a mother, the marriage was 'a foregone conclusion' long before the Russian frontier was reached, and she gloated over the idea that she had been briefed by the King of Prussia to win Elizabeth's friendship in the teeth of Chancellor Bestouzhev's opposition. In the case of success Johanna-Elizabeth's reward would be a considerable estate in Pomerania, relieving her of many a burdensome debt she should never have contracted. The princess, who was not particularly good at managing her own tiny household and who was utterly at sea in diplomacy, plunged into the perilous waters of a deep political intrigue on her arrival in Russia. Naturally, she failed from the beginning, and all but wrecked her daughter's chances of winning the most important bridegroom in Europe.

That did not happen because Elizabeth, having once met 'the child from Zerbst', liked her. The foolish mother was not forgiven her foolishness but the daughter did not suffer for it. The betrothal took place at the appointed time and Figgy became Grand-Duchess Catherine. In September 1745 she was married to Peter at Kazan Cathedral in St Petersburg in great and wearying splendour, and the Empress began looking forward to the autumn of 1746 when, as a great-aunt, she would see the succession firmly assured. Princess Johanna-Elizabeth, now scorned by the Russian Court and out of favour with King Frederick, went home immediately after the wedding, having been told in no kindly terms that there would be no further invitations to St Petersburg.

Now Catherine found herself the second lady in the land, bride of a young man, her own first cousin, who puzzled, exasperated and disgusted her by turns. They were not strangers to each other. She had met Peter some years before at Eutin where his bragging had revolted her. Now he was eighteen and he bragged just as much. He also complained. He hated Russia and longed to be back at Kiel.

Having drunk very heavily at the wedding banquet, the Grand-Duke tottered into the nuptial chamber, got into bed with his boots on, and at once fell asleep, not to wake till late in the morning. Such was the beginning of Catherine's married life, and so it continued for some time, the Grand-Duke preferring to find his pleasure elsewhere.

Her mother's all but fatal blunder had taught young Catherine a
lesson she would not forget for many years. Barely seventeen, her
early ambition was sharpened and clarified. To marry a prince she
detested and could not respect was but the first step along the path
to the throne. In St Petersburg Catherine had no friends either able
or willing to guide her along that difficult road and she preferred
to tread it alone. She realized that she must walk so prudently that
nobody at the Empress's court would suspect the least serious
purpose being contemplated by a very young, merry, light-hearted
Grand-Duchess, who made no secret of her hunger for endless
pleasure. Gay supper parties and dances were held in grand-ducal
apartments almost every evening. Such pastimes humoured Peter's
temper, and in those early days the Empress remained indulgent
and kindly except for an occasional rebuke tossed at Catherine
because of her undeniable extravagances.

All the members of the household had been chosen by Elizabeth,
but Bestouzhev took no risks. An inveterate enemy of Prussia, he had
opposed the match from the very beginning, trying to convince the
Empress that such a marriage might involve the Empire in the
Prussian matter. But, Elizabeth having brushed all such arguments
aside, the Chancellor had to accept her ruling. Now two of his best
and most adroit agents were sent as footmen to the grand-ducal
household. Not a single conversation took place but all its details,
however trivial, were reported to the Chancellor. These regular
reports made him wonder if there could be anything to fear from a
child-bride, whose chatter was certainly witty, but whose mind
seemed engrossed in clothes, jewellery, the lastest fashion in scent,
and whatever dishes were sent up from the palace kitchens.

Bestouzhev knew nothing of those long and lonely hours when the
Grand-Duchess, grossly neglected by her husband, thought neither
of clothes nor dancing. She had mastered the difficult alien language
with an incredible rapidity, and now all in secret was preparing herself for the future by reading anything on Russia that the library of
the Academy of Sciences could send her. The sight of books
scattered about in her rooms did not seem to disturb the Chancellor's
agents. As months went on, however, they stumbled on an important
discovery. On hearing of it, Bestouzhev lost no time in asking for a
private audience with the Empress. The fact laid before her bewildered and angered her, but she would not be convinced. She

refused to believe that Catherine was wife in name only and dismissed it for gossip.

At that time, only very few intimates of the Grand-Duke knew about his physical defect. The court, aware of his endless dalliances with female members of the household, suspected nothing at all. Nor did Catherine. 'My dear husband,' so she would write in later years, 'did not occupy himself with me . . . he spent his whole time drilling his footmen . . . he changed his uniform about twenty times a day . . . I was determined to please him but the dullest book was highly entertaining once he left me alone.'

All of it was worlds away from the purpose for which she had been summoned to Russia.

They were now in the spring of 1746. The Empress was getting anxious and ordered her ladies to keep in constant touch with their opposite numbers at the Grand-Ducal court. Catherine's ladies in their turn continued making unequivocal enquiries among the laundresses, but nothing of comfort could be reported to the Empress. The all-important matter of succession remained in as grave a jeopardy as it had been in 1741.

It is indeed odd that the Empress approached neither her nephew nor his wife. A single intimate discussion would have dragged the trouble into daylight. Yet it should be remembered that by 1746 Elizabeth's disappointment in her heir precluded any such conversation, and within a few months after the wedding Catherine had ceased to be the Empress's 'most amiable and beloved Katinka'. Elizabeth blamed her roundly for her inability to influence her husband, for her extravagances, for wearing unsuitable clothes, and for all the unseemly pranks of the Grand-Duke. Meanwhile Bestouzhev went on collecting more and more material for an indictment which was not to be delivered verbally this time. The books and papers in Catherine's rooms, mentioned but casually by his spies, now gave the Chancellor some food for thought. The Grand-Duchess had a number of foreign correspondents. Naturally, her private letters could not be censored. Was the intrigue started by the mother continued by the daughter? And did her letters to Zerbst contain messages meant for Berlin? The Chancellor never forgot the Grand-Duke's pronounced Prussian sympathies.

All of it was embodied into a most scathing report which ended on a note of brutal terseness: 'It is common knowledge among the

ladies and gentlemen of the Grand-Ducal household that their
Imperial Highnesses do not cohabit. Her Imperial Highness is still
a virgin. His Imperial Highness seems to bestow his favours on
maids-of-honour and waiting-women, though not one of them has
so far been put into the family way by him. There is an urgent
matter to be discussed with her Majesty's physicians about his
Imperial Highness's capacities as a husband. It is obvious that her
Imperial Highness has never been instructed in conjugal duties.'

Soon after Easter 1746 the storm broke at the palace, and Peter
and Catherine found themselves sent to school with a tutor and a
governess 'to supervise every matter of importance'. The Choglokovs
were appointed to rule the grand-ducal household, Maria Choglokova being the Empress's first cousin on her mother's side.
Elizabeth said to the Chancellor that she knew of no other exemplary
married couple to fill such a post. 'They have been married for less
than four years and my cousin has already been brought to bed
three times.'

Unfortunately, the exemplary couple did not justify the Empress's
confidence. The tutor ended by falling in love with Catherine, who
loathed the man from the beginning, and Maria deserted her husband
for a married man.

Yet those bombshells were still far off that April day in 1746 when
the governess stormed her way into Catherine's rooms, ordered the
servants to remove all books and writing materials and, alone with
the Grand-Duchess, began delivering the imperial commands. No
letters were to be written abroad except to Catherine's parents and
those would be drafted by a clerk in the Imperial Chancery. Having
come to the end of a maddening catalogue, Choglokova proceeded
to instruct the Grand-Duchess in her 'duties'. The governess's
candour made Catherine burst into angry tears. She felt herself
degraded to the level of a brood mare sent to stud.

In the end the Grand-Duke had his disability removed by surgical means, and he and Catherine became man and wife, neither
having any joy of the other.

But the purely physical degradation was far from being the only
burden cast upon Catherine. From now on she would walk in
danger for sixteen years. The unexpected ban on the wholly
innocuous correspondence with her relations sharpened her wits
and deepened her natural cynicism. The seventeen-year-old girl

stood alone. She read her husband unerringly. He loathed Russia, despised his aunt, mocked at the faith, language and customs of the country, and when in a maudlin mood languished for his native Holstein and for a visit to Potsdam. Catherine, not a drop of native blood in her veins, resolved to become more Russian than the Russians. Her books had been taken away. She dared not engage in serious conversation with the Empress's ministers, and she trusted none among her ladies. Yet there were servants for her to talk to, and she never missed a chance of learning an idiom. And more. The frequent religious services which it was her duty to attend were never wasted occasions. The humility and fervour shown by the Grand-Duchess made no impression on the court, but they were certainly observed and admired by common folk. Within a few years Catherine's name came to mean something to the unregarded rank and file.

She had two miscarriages between 1746 and 1754. Early in 1754 she was pregnant again, and the Empress decided to avoid all possible risks of another mischance. Catherine found herself surrounded by incredible care until she bore a son in September 1754. The infant was immediately claimed by the Empress, the mother being refused a voice in the very choice of his name. To little Paul she remained a stranger all through his childhood.

Catherine was now twenty-five. She had spent ten years at Elizabeth's court. Now that she had given an heir to the crown she was left entirely alone. The Empress, bitterly disappointed in her nephew, lavished all her care on little Paul. His mother could do whatever she pleased, the Choglokov régime having been an unpleasant memory for some time.

By 1754 Catherine had had at least two lovers, Zachary Chernyshev and Serge Saltykov, but Paul was indubitably her husband's son. In a general sense, affinities between two characters should not be taken as proof of paternity. In Paul's case, however, there were far too many traits of a singular enough nature: Grand-Duke Peter and his son both had a passion for very peculiar buffoonery, both had cunning and simplicity, both indulged in generous impulses and in spurts of cruelty. The homage paid to the Potsdam shrine by the father was faithfully echoed by the son. No Russian, such as Saltykov, could have shared that particular passion.

In diplomatic circles the Grand-Duchess was already spoken of

as 'the beautiful wanton', but her lovers were not as important to
her as her many enemies alleged and as her friends deplored. The
years of humiliating bondage proved that a genius had been born in
Stettin in May 1729. Under such conditions a fool would have dissi-
pated her energies in matters of no moment. A woman of an average
intelligence would have been dwarfed under a treatment as cruel as
it was absurd. Yet Catherine grew and expanded much in the manner
of a plant set in some particularly rewarding spot. Each new humiliation devised by the Empress, each fresh insult flung by the Grand-
Duke seemed so much more material to fashion the weapons in
Catherine's secret armoury.

From the rigidly ethical point of view, those years showed much
on the debit side. What sincerity the Grand-Duchess may have had
vanished for good. Contempt, cynicism, a peculiar kind of vanity
which would one day brush against the grotesque, and a deeply
developed cunning, such were the companions on the road Catherine
walked, her gaze steadfast on the ultimate goal – the crown. Still,
there were some more pleasing streaks in the pattern: courage,
patience, endurance, and an unbounded love for the country she had
learned to call her own.

Catherine walked in peril often enough. Sometimes she felt uncertain if the day's ending would find her at the palace or in a
dungeon. From the latter fate, however, her own consummate
prudence always saved her. For an adventuress to possess such
caution suggests a paradox. And, indeed, there were many paradoxes
in that personality which still defy easy analysis. Danger her daily
bread, she never wavered in her resolve, nor did she form a single
plan to achieve it. The glittering goal remained. Unto that end
Catherine schooled herself to wear a morning face with midnight
in her heart and mind. Unto that end she endured the Empress's
tyranny, her husband's cruelty and neglect, Bestouzhev's rock-hewn
enmity, and the inanities of the Choglokov régime, as numerous as
they were incredible. Once when the Grand-Duchess mentioned
Plutarch, the governess said that she was certain the gentleman had
never been presented to the Empress. 'It is my sacred duty,' went
on the duenna, 'to prevent your Imperial Highness from making the
acquaintance of a possible adventurer. With such an outlandish
name one can expect anything at all, even the theft of your Imperial
Highness's diamonds.'

But the Choglokov tyranny reached its ebb, and Catherine's bondage grew lighter. 'Concessions' were made in the name of the Empress – though everybody knew that the Chancellor was changing his opinion about the Grand-Duchess. The ban was lifted from her correspondence, and books reappeared in her rooms. The discovery of Madame de Sévigné's letters and of Bayle's Dictionary marked the beginning of a new mental stage. In particular, Bayle, pioneer and rebel, turned Catherine into a passionate liberal. His fearless insistence on 'the sovereignty of the people' and his scathing condemnation of slavery moulded her principles for many years to come. Catherine dared confide her ideas to none but, stationery being again permitted, she solaced herself by making notes in three languages, and had enough wit to make use of a very secret drawer in her bureau, since most of those notes, if discovered, would have rung an instant knell to her hopes, such as for instance: '. . . Serfdom is dreadful indeed . . . Authority means nothing without trust. . . . The good of a nation and justice for all must walk together. . . . There should be two main rules for a prince's education – make him virtuous and make him love truth. . . . '

She would dismiss her ladies immediately after a party or supper, lock her door, and plunge into a world all greening with the promise of robust and delightful mental travail. She read avidly and made notes, many of them lacking cohesion and logic but all charged with a neophyte's passion to learn. She thought of Luther and his challenge. She read all she could find about Peter the Great and his reforms, so many of them inchoate at his death and still unfinished by mid-century. To govern creatively, as Catherine thought, meant to improvise and to reform. In the end, she escaped mental cabbage-dom by way of Bayle, Montaigne, Descartes and Montesquieu, whose 'Esprit des Lois' became her Bible.

Such studies would hardly have won the approval of an academic purist. Catherine read voraciously, no counsellor at hand to teach her how to tell one authority from another. She formed numberless misjudgments, and accepted one set of criteria only to replace it by another, and much of her reading proved far beyond her mental grasp. But Catherine's studies were never an intellectual pursuit. She read to fill in the lacunae left in her early education, to add colour to a bleak horizon, to deepen her acquaintance with a world immeasurably larger than any of the palaces where she lived. The scrambled-egg process certainly did not turn Catherine into a scholar, but it immersed her into a world of reality, made her more keenly aware of the inexorable law of cause and effect. Finally, and most importantly, it prepared her energies for the future.

1754–61 proved Catherine's most formative years. The Empress's health worsened month by month. Grand-Duke Peter neglected his wife wholly. Little Prince Paul was under his great-aunt's care and saw his mother about once a month, and that did not greatly disturb her. From an enemy Bestouzhev became a friend, sharing his fears and anxieties with her. Catherine listened, but for some time she did not permit herself either to approve or to criticize the Chancellor's plans for the change in succession in favour of her own little son, with herself as Regent. It was now clear to Bestouzhev, as it was to the majority of other statesmen, that Grand-Duke Peter was no more fit to reign than his own valet. The Chancellor well knew the Empress's own mind on the matter, 'but, Madam,' he said to the Grand-Duchess, 'she is dilatory. She detests his Imperial Highness and will not commit herself to disinherit him. However, I have a paper for her to sign when the opportune moment arrives.'

Wider and still wider liberties being now hers, Catherine met ambassadors, talked to them, and enchanted them both by her beauty and her wit. Little by little she learned to read the day's map of Europe. They began mentioning her name abroad. All her gifts so long undeveloped were now reaching their flowering, and her conversation would have revived a shrivelled dandelion. She was admired. She was also censured for her 'affairs'. She took Poniatowsky for her lover and had a daughter by him. The infant, officially recognized as a Romanov princess, died within a few months, and the Grand-Duchess did not mourn her. The travail of the body excepted, she had done with motherhood after the birth of Paul.

Meanwhile, her husband, in between drilling a miniature army, building toy fortresses, and cursing his aunt's commanders for their victories over the Prussians during the Seven Years' War, reached a questionable lasting harbour of his own with his beloved Lizanka.

Poniatowsky left Russia, and Catherine did not weep at his going. She now had Gregory Orlov who certainly excited and pleased her. In emotional terms, however, he proved but one incident out of many.

Inch by carefully measured inch the Grand-Duchess found her way into the complexities of statesmanship. She survived Bestouzhev's downfall, braved the Empress's wrath at the discovery of her correspondence with General Apraxyn, and rode safely through a tumult which would have crushed any other woman.

Elizabeth died, not even Ivan Shuvalov, then *'monsieur en titre'*, having been able to persuade her to name little Prince Paul her successor. Catherine knew that her buffoon of a husband could never rule the country. None the less, he was Emperor. Gregory Orlov and his four brothers in turn assured the young Empress of 'a happy outcome'. She, once again pregnant, slighted in public and in private, would certainly have liked to feel so assured. But she had no money and most of her important jewels were in the hands of Elizabeth Voronzova.

In the end it was neither the Orlov brothers nor the grenadiers who thrust the sceptre into Catherine's hands but her own husband whose six months' misrule had turned everybody's hand against him. Peter III's formal abdication was the most grotesque anticlimax in the whole history of Russia.

Today, those days in June 1762 suggest a German operetta or a chapter from 'The Prisoner of Zenda', and such indeed was their surface, but it screened an epochal event.

Peter III, having completed his arrangements for an absurd campaign against Denmark, was keeping high festival at Oranienbaum with Elizabeth Voronzova, whom he had promised to marry on the conclusion of the war. The mistress already imagined herself as wife and Empress, and she wore the imperial diamonds and rubies even on the days when she was too lazy to change her dressing-gown for more suitable clothes. Catherine was alone with her ladies at Peterhof. There is nothing to tell us what she did through those last few days. There does not seem to have been any communication between Peterhof and St Petersburg. In the middle of a night she was rather rudely woken by Alexis Orlov who had galloped from the capital. He told her that she must hurry to St Petersburg where the Guards regiments were waiting to have her proclaimed as their sovereign lady, and not a moment must be lost.

Day had long since broken over the city of nineteen islands when the carriage halted at the gateway into the grenadier barracks. Later the same day Catherine crossed the threshold of the palace, no longer a humiliated consort but a sovereign mistress.

Events moved breathlessly but, all appearances of suddenness notwithstanding, many years of hard schooling lay behind the triumph. Few among Russian sovereigns reached the throne as well prepared as that girl from Zerbst. The great day in June 1762 was at once an end and a beginning, in that order.

Not a shot was fired in the Emperor's defence. Taken prisoner and driven to the manor of Ropsha to the north-west of the capital, Peter wrote rather pitifully servile letters to his wife. But Ropsha could not be other than a temporary arrangement. The fate of a deposed monarch presented a problem to trouble even experienced statesmen, and where were they in the Russia of 1762 ? Peter still remained the Duke of Holstein, but to have him sent to the Duchy was no solution. There might have been complications with Prussia, and Catherine was in no position to face them. Kholmogory in the neighbourhood of Archangel was already occupied by the younger Brunswick children. Still another deposed Emperor, the luckless Ivan VI, then aged twenty-two, languished at Schlüsselburg at the mouth of the Neva. There was a prison on one of the northern islands – but it was out of all question to have the ex-Emperor in the capital.

We cannot tell what decision was reached at the gathering since it was held *in camera* and its findings never recorded. Peter III stayed on at Ropsha for precisely a week, and then came the end, its details mantled in mystery to this day. The manifesto announcing his death convinced nobody in spite of all the clinical details it gave. There does not exist a single particle of evidence pointing at any direct orders given by Catherine to have her husband murdered, but that affords no proof that no such orders were given since all incriminating evidence would have been immediately destroyed. The men responsible for the ex-Emperor's welfare were never accused of regicide. Indirectly, the whole responsibility cannot be shifted from Catherine's threshold, and nobody in Europe minced their words about it. A German periodical went to the length of comparing Peter III with Edward II and Ropsha with Berkeley Castle. In St Petersburg, the Senate 'ventured' to suggest that the Empress should not appear in the funeral procession, and Catherine played into her accusers' hands by accepting the suggestion.

Weighty reasons were certainly on her side. Her own position anything but secure, the Empress could not have afforded to have two ex-Emperors on her hands. Equally, the country's health might well have been totally ruined if Peter's reign had continued. The misgoverned Empire stood in sharp need of a helmsman. Yet, no matter what fine casuistry be employed to explain the necessity, murder remains murder, and Catherine would not escape retribution – not at her enemies' hands but at those of her own son.

That, however, was still to come. In 1762 Catherine had no leisure to occupy herself with her conscience. Aware of her tenuous grasp on the sceptre, she flung herself into the business of governing, serenely certain of her ability to strengthen her tenure by working harder than any among her subjects.

'The Empire needs peace above all things,' she declared to the diplomats accredited to her court whom she had summoned to explain the reasons for her refusal to reopen hostilities against Prussia. The immediate indignation of France and Austria had no effect on her. Many years of peace were essential, as she saw, to bring the Russian house into order. Her future foreign policy was very clear in her own mind but she shared those ideas with none. She had dreamt and schemed of expansion eastwards, southwards and westwards all through the years of her hard apprenticeship. Now she knew that all such schemes must be shelved for a time.

She considered the great landscape of the Empire she had won. What it had to offer would have dismayed the most experienced statesman of the day. It fired all the energies in Catherine.

The main heartbeat of the government was the Senate, composed of amiable, elderly, mostly gouty gentlemen. They left all the work to their clerks who, receiving a pittance of a wage, considered bribes as an essential part of their hard-earned increment. The Treasury was well-nigh depleted. There was no budget, and nobody seemed to know anything about the national income. All naval matters had been neglected since the death of Peter the Great, though the Admiralty staff still collected their salaries and used an incredible amount of ink and paper on trivial reports meant to be shelved as soon as they were written. The army pay stood in lamentable arrears. The Empire was monopoly-ridden – salt, wine, undressed hides, tobacco, fish, even rhubarb and hemp being included in the list. Legal reforms projected by Elizabeth were at a standstill. Some government departments complained that they had had no funds allocated to them for some years.

And in the palace an unceasing chorus would have driven any other woman to the threshold of insanity. The French and Austrian ambassadors protested against the wantonly broken alliance; General Goudovich grew boring with his pleas that the truce with Prussia should be moulded into a treaty; Nikita Panin, tutor of Catherine's son, and others urged that a speedy rapprochement with Great Britain was essential for Russia's future. Church dignitaries clamoured for the return of all ecclesiastical estates sequestrated by Peter III. Governors from all parts of the Empire flocked to the capital with their reports of increased incidence of arson, murder and brigandage. The stream of petitions addressed to the Empress grew more and more swollen every day. It looked as though the whole nation were shouting at her: 'You wanted the crown. We have given it to you. Now get on with the job if you can.'

In those days Catherine spent seventeen and more hours at work every day. She dismissed Elizabeth's inept chancellor, Michael Voronzov, and she did not replace him. Bestouzhev was duly re-called from exile, but Catherine did not re-install him in the office. She preferred to be her own Chancellor, and she did not know that she was making the first major mistake of her reign. She would train many men in the art of statesmanship – Wiazemsky, Shakovskoy, Bezborodko, Repnin, Alsoufiev, but not one of them would be allowed to lay his hand on the helm.

The Empress improvised from day to day. 'I must rule after my own fashion,' she said to her senators the very first time she attended a session at the Senate. Years before, as a Grand-Duchess, she had written: 'One must govern in such a way that one's people think they themselves want to do what one commands them to do.' 'Trade must have breathing-space,' she declared to her administration, and swept away all the monopolies with one stroke of the pen. Appalled at her senators' ignorance of Russian geography, she sent them to school by buying a map of the Empire 'for your diligent study'. She issued an avalanche of tersely-worded orders dealing with the state of the roads, the tangled-up Admiralty finances, the sale of drugs, the training of midwives, the scrutiny of shamelessly swollen 'expense' accounts among the administration. Tasks kept crowding into her days, but nobody saw her tired. Many, however, saw her angry. Her temper would spiral up – a dark-red column of it – at any example of dishonesty or official ineptitude brought to her knowledge. 'Do these clerks imagine that my subjects can eat omelets made of addled eggs?' was her mordant comment on one such case.

Most meticulously did Catherine make plans for her coronation. The mystical purpose of the anointing said nothing at all to her but she never permitted herself to forget with what deep eloquence it spoke to the millions of her subjects. The coronation meant an encroachment she would have done without. It would thieve hours and days. None the less, it remained a necessity of the first rank, and she decided to hurry it on. When a September date was announced, the authorities in Moscow nearly swooned in despair. How could they have the city prepared within two months, they asked? But Catherine would have no delays. She replied that it was a sovereign's first duty to dedicate herself to her people's service by the most binding and solemn of all oaths in existence, and she could not do it too soon. Triumphal arches, red carpets, re-painted houses and yards of bunting, what did those matter? Nothing was of importance except the great rite in the Assumption Cathedral, and two months allowed enough time to get it ready.

Catherine's insistence on that early date was a gesture made by a genius. The link to be forged between the nation and herself and to strengthen her grasp on the sceptre could not be hammered out by lightened taxes and other concessions. The nation's truest heartbeat lay in its acceptance of symbolism, and she was ready to accord it immediate recognition.

So everybody had to hurry. Less than a week before the great day, it was discovered that the globe used for Elizabeth's coronation was missing from the regalia chest. Someone suggested that its fabulous diamonds and emeralds, prised out of their setting, had been given by Peter III to Elizabeth Voronzova. There followed other variants. The Empress, brushing all the stories aside, ordered a new globe to be made, and court goldsmiths had to work day and night to have it ready in time. A few months after the coronation, the missing globe was found in some forgotten corner of Petrovsky Palace in Moscow, in a coffer full of toys once belonging to Peter II.

'Anything can get mislaid at times,' remarked Catherine, and she had the globe put together with her private jewellery.

One single word can serve as a headline for the whole drift of Catherine's foreign policy: audacity. The first country to be made aware of it was little Courland on the Baltic coast. There, the Empress chose to make her apprenticeship in practical diplomacy, though the latter was hardly a fitting word to harness to an act of pure piracy, prefaced by overt threats.

It will be remembered that the Duchy had been ruled by the Empress Anna's lover, Johan Biren. On his downfall and exile, Courland was governed by a prince of Saxony. The Empress Elizabeth, having recalled Biren from exile, did not reinstate him as Duke of Courland since she had no stomach for an imbroglio with the King of Saxony. Now, Catherine argued, Russia had an indisputable lien on Courland since a Romanov princess had been its sovereign duchess all through her widowhood. The argument was specious and Saxony rejected it as such. The Empress had not expected any different reaction, and her soldiers were already marching westwards. The matter came to no bloodshed, however. The Saxon fled from Mittau, and Catherine succeeded in settling old Biren in a castle which had never belonged to him except by the favour of his imperial mistress. There were uneasy ripples all through the states of Germany and even beyond. The Empress ignored them all. 'Now the Baltic coast, yes, three hundred miles of it, is in the Russian pocket,' she said to Gregory Orlov.

Her next venture was even more impudent. In 1763, on the death of King Augustus III of Poland, Catherine put forward the candidature of her ex-lover, Stanislaus Poniatovsky, and that in the teeth of the man's vehement protests that he had neither the wish nor the capacity to reign. 'How could I be king?' he wrote plaintively to St Petersburg, and the Empress replied laconically: 'by learning to be one.' Poniatovsky's nomination, to say nothing of his election, involved fantastic expenditure, but the Empress considered the money to be well spent, once the crown of Poland was put on Poniatovsky's head. 'Now Poland is settled for many years ahead,' she remarked to her ministers, and once again plunged into home matters. But the first breath of danger came early enough and close enough for her to make the second major blunder of her reign. In the summer of 1764 Catherine paid a visit to 'her' Duke at Mittau. That same summer Europe was horrified to hear that the unfortunate Ivan VI, imprisoned in a dungeon at Schlüsselburg, had been killed 'at the orders of the female Caligula of the North'. The young man was certainly dead. Little else was known. Much came to be imagined. Inevitably, the ghost of Ropsha stirred out of its grave. From north to south in Europe they called Catherine a murderess, and public opinion was specially incensed in England because Ivan VI belonged to the House of Brunswick.

Catherine's personal reactions to the volume of execration remain unrecorded. But she certainly brought it on her own head. The young man's jailers had been given orders to have him killed in case of a mutiny at the Schlüsselburg fortress. An obscure army officer, Mirovich, together with a few accomplices, staged such a mutiny, its aim being to release 'the nameless prisoner', who was stabbed by his guards before the mutineers broke into the dungeon. The trial of Mirovich was conducted with such clumsiness and surrounded by such frenzied and futile efforts to preserve utter secrecy that the case of 'the nameless prisoner', whose shattered intelligence would not have enabled him to reign for one hour, who had no party in the country, and whose very whereabouts were unknown to the majority, reached the proportions of a national crisis and became the most burning matter of the day. Ivan VI's mental condition being known to very few, it was whispered on all sides that Catherine would have lost her throne on a Friday if he had not been murdered the Thursday before. An obscure fanatic's hopeless attempt to rescue Ivan from Schlüsselburg was swollen into a national uprising against 'the usurper'. Pamphlets in three languages appeared in Europe, all depicting the sufferings of Ivan's brothers and sisters at their prison in the far north. Their mother's death in child-birth in 1746, by then virtually forgotten, was now remembered and believed to have been a murder carried out at Elizabeth's orders.

Much of it was due to a mood already tautened and irritated by Catherine's interference in Polish and Baltic matters, and the coolness she exhibited at her court functions was at once attributed to her having no conscience. Yet, with no Brunswick ghost whispering into her ear, the Empress continued with the business of governing.

Splendour was being added to splendour at court, but her private life ran to a will-nigh middle-class pattern. She rose at six and retired at ten. Except for formal occasions, her clothes were of the plainest. A frugal breakfast of coffee and rusks and a no less modest dinner were her only meals. She never drank wine and considered supper an unnecessary indulgence. Her extravagances were many indeed but they spread in different directions and laid the foundations of priceless art collections for the whole nation to enjoy. Idleness sickened her. Once all state matters were done with for the day, the Empress turned to her books, and she read creatively, pen poised in her hand. 'Ideas are like hares,' she said, 'they run away so quickly that you must catch them at once.' All the volumes belonging to her were rich in most telling marginal notes.

But even such reading came as a relaxation. State business was always in the foreground, sometimes occupying the hours of solitude. 'Education is the most important problem of all,' she never tired of saying. 'An unenlightened nation is like a flock of ewes without a ram.'

Education had not been altogether neglected by the first Romanovs, though only a fringe of the vast population had reaped the benefit, and at Catherine's own death the masses were still illiterate. Elizabeth had founded the University of Moscow but there were hardly any schools to prepare the boys for the entry. Naval matters having been neglected by Peter the Great's successors, the Naval College founded by him was staffed by gentlemen whose competence went no further than the rudiments of geometry and the use of the globes. Catherine's own foundations came in spate – military academies, schools of commerce and of artillery, the Mines Institute, 'to encourage the speedy development of studies into the natural resources of the Empire', and, finally, the Smolny Nobility College, the very first establishment for girls, opened in dazzling splendour in 1764.

Certainly the masses did not benefit *en masse*. But, once an obscure have-not herself, Catherine did not fill her establishments from the ranks of the nobility alone. Numbers of 'have-nots', most of them brought to her notice by a fortunate chance, were set by her on the road to great achievement, and not all of them were her lovers. Bezborodko, Roumiantzev, Kutuzov, Trotchinsky, Dimitriev, to name but a few, were given opportunities to prove their genius without being invited to share the imperial bed.

❀

As a Grand-Duchess, Catherine had written: 'A sovereign is at fault if his people are displeased with him. . . . Everything is dead without freedom, and the latter is the right to do everything permitted by law. . . . I shall expect my laws to be obeyed, but I shall not tolerate slavery. . . .'

Those words came from a conviction formed after a deep study of Bayle, Diderot and Montesquieu. Now that she was sovereign, Catherine saw even more clearly that the Empire's laws were crying out for reform. For three years, sharing her ideas with none, she laboured at the composition of a monumental 'Nakaz', i.e. 'Instruction', borrowing much of her material from Montesquieu and Beccaria. 'My book is not very original,' she confessed in a letter to Voltaire in 1767, 'but I trust that Monsieur Montesquieu, now in heaven, will forgive the plagiarism for the good it may do to twenty million people.' And she wrote to d'Alembert that she felt 'like a crow strutting about in peacock feathers. Were I Pope, I would certainly canonize Montesquieu, and that without listening to the Devil's Advocate. . . .'

The Nakaz, so Catherine hoped, would become a guidebook for future legislators, and the fine liberalism of her youth found its way into its pages. The paragraphs dealing with serfdom were particularly revealing. The basic argument that slavery warred against Christian principles was borrowed from Montesquieu, but Catherine amplified it by examining it in the light of prevalent Russian conditions: '. . . with us,' she wrote, 'abolition could hardly be carried out except by a series of long-term arrangements . . . all peasants belonging to a particular estate might be given their freedom on the transfer of the estate to another owner. . . . In some such way, the last traces of serfdom would be gone within two or three generations, or even sooner. . . . Agricultural produce is the greatest asset in central Russia, and agriculture could never really flourish if the land continued to be worked by those who had neither property nor any rights of their own. . . .' There was also an inspiring paragraph on legal procedure: '. . . everybody irrespective of rank or substance, should get a fair hearing in our courts . . . capital punishment should be resorted to only in most grave cases . . . all forms of torture should be abolished since they debase and cripple civilized standards. . . .'

The publication of the Nakaz in 1766 and its translation into two or three foreign languages somewhat softened the Western attitude towards 'the female Caligula of the North'. France alone remained adamant, and the French translation of the *Nakaz* came under the government's ban.

In July 1767 the Grand Commission, summoned to study the forthcoming reforms, opened in Moscow. To have a peasant delegate speak at the Kremlin certainly made history, but the fact that all 'the offending' paragraphs about emancipation were deleted at the insistence of nobility and gentry emphasized the insecurity of Catherine's position even five years after her accession. The 564 delegates, fifty among whom were peasants, came together and hoped for a sequence of fruitful sessions, but by the autumn of that year Russia found herself at war with Turkey. The Grand Commission was inevitably prorogued, and many circumstances combined to prevent it from ever being assembled again. Its findings, however, did not perish.

✳

To fight Turkey in order to gain a foothold on the Black Sea shore was the pivotal point of Catherine's foreign policy, but she meant to choose her own moment to begin the struggle. That was denied her. Russian interference in Polish matters roused the Sultan's apprehensions. A feather-light incident near the Crimean border was skilfully turned into a *casus belli*. Catherine could not afford to refuse the challenge.

Still less could she afford to engage herself in war. Her Treasury was empty in 1767. She had an exhausted, ill-shod and virtually unarmed army. Up and down the countryside mutinies broke out among the peasants who, having heard about the *Nakaz* and the Grand Commission in Moscow, had interpreted it all in terms of immediate and generously endowed franchise. And the Empire possessed no navy.

Catherine's administration were in despair. The Senate began searching for a possible compromise to avoid the conflict. The Empress told them she had small use for compromises, and added that the entire political canon consisted of three words: 'circumstance, conjecture, and conjunction'. It is doubtful if her Senators understood her.

It almost looks as though she flung herself gaily into the first major campaign of her reign. She lost no time in obtaining a substantial loan from the Netherlands and at once created an embryo War

Ministry. She guessed at Roumiantzev's genius and appointed him her commander-in-chief. The shipyards in St Petersburg, Olonetz, Voronezh and Petrozavodsk became as busy as they had been under Peter the Great. Within little more than a year three squadrons were ready for action and sailed down the Baltic under the command of Alexis Orlov. The army, well shod, properly armed, and adequately victualled, began the march to the south. All such vast expenses did not plunge Russia into bankruptcy. Catherine seized Possoshkov's argument that '[with us] a piece of paper would answer the purpose of gold or silver once it be issued at the sovereign's command and bear his likeness stamped upon it. . . .' From 1768, assignats, engraved with the Empress's portrait, became legal tender in Russia.

After eighteen uneventful months, Orlov's squadrons annihilated the entire Turkish fleet off the Bay of Chesmé and Generals Roumiantzev and Golytzin took fortresses considered impregnable.

'We have not finished the war yet,' said Catherine. Russian successes bewildered and disturbed Europe. There were great festivities in St Petersburg, and it pleased the Empress to give frequent diplomatic receptions where victories would be discussed at length and reverses never get a mention.

There were reverses, and the bitterest of them all was thousands of miles away from the front. The Pougachev revolt flamed up in 1770, an uprising of a savage force the Cossack deserter had not evoked and could not control. The mutiny started on the banks of the Yaik and swept westwards and northwards until Pougachev's hordes were threatening Moscow. In her correspondence Catherine permitted herself to make mocking allusions to 'ce marquis de Pougacheff'. In grim reality, the mutiny was far more dangerous than any Brunswick conspiracy could have been. Pougachev proclaimed himself Peter III, 'miraculously saved from his assassins in 1762', but the filched title was little more than a small banner to a revolt which recked little of monarchy. Discontent had long since been simmering in the immense wild spaces south and east of Kazan. All the nomadic have-nots, their lives made intolerable by bureaucratic intrusion and graft, joined the revolt. The Cossacks, hating all officialdom on principle, threw in their lot with the tribes. The bloody struggle lasted for four years. It was savage Asia in little, its loins girded against the barely Europeanized Russia. The rebellion was quelled, but its ravages took many years to heal.

The victory over Pougachev's hordes was in a sense a Pyrrhic triumph: it dealt the first shock to Catherine's liberal principles. The first Turkish war brought great glory and many gains to the Empire, but the Grand Commission was never again summoned to Moscow, and all tentative plans for emancipation began gathering dust on the bureaucratic shelf. The Empress had persuaded herself that the nation she ruled was yet unable to distinguish between freedom and licence.

It was a fateful decision, and the Empress's identification with her husband's dynasty was completed about that time. For something like one hundred and fifty years, the Romanovs, whatever their individual merits or otherwise, remained committed to the inexorable commands of Fate. To call it the will of God did not really change the issue. Pougachev's execution in a Moscow square synchronized with Catherine's recoil from liberal ideas. The evidences of that recoil were not easily discernible at first, and the flames of a reformer's zeal would not be embered until 1789, but the blood-stippled phantom, appearing in 1770, was not to vanish from the Russian skies.

A stranger lived in the Empress's palace, a youth of small stature and unprepossessing appearance, whose complex personality never ceased to baffle his intimates. Courteous and rude, intelligent and foolish, kindly and cruel, generous and mean by turn, the young man lived at the palace by virtue of his being the first gentleman in the land, a dignity which, in his case, was shorn of all meaning. Heir to the throne, ably tutored by Nikita Panin, Paul should have been allowed a voice at his mother's Council table. It never happened. From his childhood, he and Catherine had been strangers to each other.

As was said elsewhere, she could not be blamed for the beginnings of the estrangement. Yet Paul was nearly eight when she wrested the crown out of his father's hands and a happier relationship might well have been begun at the time. It was not. A pupil of Nikita Panin's, Paul might have been drawn by kindness. As things were, he felt afraid of his mother and never learned her at all. In her presence all his good qualities – and he had many of them – vanished. All Catherine saw was a nervous, boorish boy, unsure of his speech and lamentably uncouth in his manner. Her first approach meeting with no response, she left him to Panin's care.

However unloved, Paul was Catherine's only legitimate child and he alone could prevent the total extinction of the dynasty. Therefore, in 1773, when the Grand-Duke was nineteen, the Empress married him to a Hessian princess, who became Grand-Duchess Nathalie. The honeymoon over, Paul expected a summons to a Council meeting. No such call reached him. Catherine wrote instead: 'Come to me for advice when you need it . . . I have decided to set aside a few hours every week to see you in private so that you can learn something about statesmanship, our laws, and my manner of governing. . . . Does that please you?'

It did not please Paul. He had longed for a loaf and been offered a crumb. His inexperienced and indiscreet Grand-Duchess urged him to disregard the invitation, and argued that it was the Empress's duty to let him have a voice in the Council Hall. Paul agreed but he lacked the courage to say so to his mother. Nathalie thought her 'despicable'.

'Look at all her lovers,' she cried, 'She is a harlot. . . . The Empress Maria Theresa said so several times – '

'Her lovers,' replied Paul heavily and not quite sincerely, 'don't matter so much. It is her entire policy that will ruin the Empire one day.'

Here again the Grand-Duke's words took a sharp curve away from the truth. The dislike and mistrust between mother and son had a different root than the Empress's policy, and both were aware of it, and neither ever mentioned it to the other. Nikita Panin, now dismissed from Paul's household, had taught his pupil to respect his father's memory. In the Orlov brothers the Grand-Duke saw his father's murderers and his name for Alexis Orlov was 'that butcher'. The father's ghost stood between the mother and the son. The mere name of Ropsha, never spoken in her presence, was enough to bring horror into Paul's mind.

As to the Empress's lovers, the processional, with the exception of Potemkin and Lanskoy, makes the most boring chapter of her story. Few, if any, of those gentlemen *en titre* were gentlemen by descent. Good fortune swept them up the steps of the palace porch and piloted them into the dazzling imperial orbit. Those men were no more than 'particular' servants of the crown. Potemkin's dark genius lifted him high above the sordid rut, and Lanskoy's quality of heart and mind somewhat redeemed an otherwise humiliating situation, and he alone seems to have unlocked Catherine's heart towards the end of her life. All the others were *messieurs de convenance*, engaged and dismissed at the imperial pleasure.

The triumphs of the Kutchuk-Kainardji Treaty cost much in blood, money and exertion, but the Empress's audacious programme was rapidly gaining shape. The Crimean Tartars freed from the Turk's tutelage, Russian ships enjoying the freedom of the Black Sea, Kuban and the Valley of the Terek being ceded to the Empire, and a most rewardingly vast indemnity – such were the fruits of Catherine's first campaign. The undisguised irritation of the West proved but fuel to her vanity. She had not expected any different reaction from either Britain or France, but she was determined to win Austria's friendship. Amidst all the peace festivities and in spite of the ever-swelling volume of state work, Catherine found time to enlarge her correspondence. Her letters may well serve as models to enterprising publicity agents today. She advertised everything from a rich harvest in a province to a new glass factory in the suburbs of her capital. She felt intensely proud of her Foundlings' Home in Moscow, but she never permitted herself to mention it to any of her friends abroad lest they should think that the incidence of bastardy was on the increase in her Empire. Otherwise, anything served as grist to her brinkmanship mill. Even the fact that she repaid the Dutch loan in gold found its way into many letters, and was she not pleased at Voltaire calling her *'Catherine le Grand'*?

With Grimm alone, her faithful *souffre-douleur*, did the Empress share some of her anxieties, particularly those concerning her son and her daughter-in-law, who, having first been *'une femme d'or'*, soon slipped down to the sorry level of an extravagant, peevish and indolent woman. '. . . [she] is always ill, and who would wonder at it? She always rushes into extremes. . . . If she goes for a walk, she must trudge for twenty versts. . . . If she dances, it must be quite twenty minuets. . . . To avoid excessive heat in their apartments, she orders that they are not to be heated at all, and at once catches a bad cold. . . . In eighteen months she has not learned a word of Russian. She says she means to learn it, and she goes on saying so. . . . Her debts have swollen to twice the amount of her yearly allowance, and yet there is hardly a princess in Europe who receives as much as she does. . . .'

In the spring of 1776 the unsatisfactory Grand-Duchess died in labour, her child being stillborn. In less than a year the Empress had her son married again, to a Württemberg princess who became Grand-Duchess Marie. In December 1777 Catherine, rarely indulging in tears, wept at the christening of her first grandson. Less than two years later that grandson had a brother, and the Empress's private correspondence became one paean of thanksgiving: no longer did extinction threaten the dynasty. 'I feel so happy and I am busier than ever before,' she wrote to Grimm. Indeed she was busy, with the upbringing of her grandsons wholly on her hands.

Catherine was no Empress Elizabeth. The boys were not taken away from their mother within a few minutes of their arrival, and Paul and Marie had freedom of access to the nurseries, but it was the grandmother who appointed the rhythm to be followed in those meagrely furnished rooms. Paul concealed his anger as best he could, Marie did not venture to complain, and the Empress was deeply satisfied with an activity to her novel and exciting. In the end, the little boys had the happiest childhood of any princes in Europe. Their upbringing proved what Catherine might have done for her own son had she not been excluded by the brutality of Elizabeth. The fruit of the Empress's experience came to be embodied in 'An Elementary Instruction' printed by the Academy of Sciences in 1782. It was no more than a collection of random notes but, strangely enough, an element of unity crept into the little book. 'You should never mock at a child; that is dangerous. . . . You can learn much about his imagination if you watch him at play and leave him alone at it. . . . No child should be afraid of his elders: that engenders cowardice and lack of truthfulness. . . . Children should always be kept busy in mind and in body. . . . If you do not know the answer to a question put by a child, do not lose your patience and do not deceive him. . . . Reflect carefully upon any punishment before you inflict it. . . . Self-respect and compassion for others should be developed as early as possible. . . . A child should be told that he comes into the world naked in precisely the same manner as everybody else's child – no difference being between a prince and a peasant. . . .'

Here we face something of a paradox: a wise, kindly and devoted grandmother and an almost revolting failure as a mother. Catherine failed most signally with Paul. It cannot be said that she failed with the others: they meant nothing at all to her. The other four children, a daughter by Poniatovsky, a son and two daughters by Gregory Orlov, were no more than tiresome accidents. Poniatovsky's daughter, acknowledged as a Romanov princess, died in infancy, her mother wholly unmoved by the loss. Orlov's son, created Count Bobrinsky, was smuggled out of the palace within an hour of his arrival and given into the care of hurriedly chosen foster-parents. Later, he had some money settled on him, and that determined his mother's responsibility. Already grown-up, young Bobrinsky ran into difficulties. Catherine heard of them and refused to help. His two sisters were brought up by a society widow as her nieces. They never appeared at court. The Empress, having settled a fairly generous dowry on each, thought no more of them, and their names never appeared in any of her letters.

And yet she was not devoid of family sense. She was devoted to her incredibly boring father, loved her impossible mother, and cared deeply for a most unsatisfactory brother.

The apparent paradox may be explained by nothing except – and that only in conjectural terms – the consequences of the shock Catherine had suffered after Paul's birth. It may well be that Elizabeth's cruelty had then implanted a revulsion to motherhood. The four children born after Paul were accidents Catherine would have been pleased to avoid.

But a new sensibility welled up in her with the coming of her grandchildren. Above all else, they enabled her to look towards a proud and triumphant future of the dynasty and the country. The decade following the boys' arrival certainly accorded marvellously well with Catherine's hopes and ambitions. The first Russian settlement was founded on the Alaskan peninsula, and the Empire became the foremost fur exporter in the world. She had consolidated her footing on the Black Sea shore. Harvests continued miraculously plentiful. What possible discontent smouldered up and down in the country did not break out into revolts. All her educational establishments flourished, and her merchants reached prosperity during a gratefully prolonged spell of peace. Experts from England and Germany were working at the amethyst and malachite mines in

Siberia. The financial *tour-de-force* of 1768 lightened the tax burdens and increased the gold reserves needed for foreign commitments.

Of course, there were many dark streaks up and down the national landscape. Graft still flourished. Legislation limped badly. Cases were still heard *in camera*, and the abstract idea of justice seldom occupied the judges' minds. The incidence of brigandage, arson, murder and lesser crimes stood as high as it had done at Catherine's accession, though her local government reform was about to start its struggle with the lawlessness up and down the countryside.

In her late fifties, she looked a woman of forty. 'I enjoy being busy,' she once said to a friend, and her delight in life was as robust as it had been in the days of her youth. Abstemiousness in food and drink was paying pleasant dividends.

Catherine's counsellor-in-chief was now Bezborodko, once an unregarded chancery clerk, but she remained her own Chancellor. The annexation of the Crimea certainly exasperated the Great Powers, to say nothing of Turkey, and led to the first major clash between the Empress and her son, but she could afford to shrug all criticism away. In moments of leisure, when embroidering or carving in ivory, she dreamt of her ships passing the Bosphorus and the Dardanelles, of her second grandson, Constantine, putting on the crown of a resurrected Byzantium under the roof of St Sophia. With the Turk chased out of Europe, the way would lie open into the Mediterranean, to the very shores of North Africa. . . .

Her enemies hoped for a war to break out after the Crimean affair, but Turkey did not dare to move, the Russo-Austrian alliance standing firm, and Prussia, satisfied with her share of the first Polish Partition, stayed rigidly neutral. The French Government demanded that no Russian men-of-war were to be kept on the Black Sea. Catherine read the note and scribbled to Bezborodko:

'I believe such a note could not be quite ignored. Make it clear to them that we are not accustomed to "demands". Ours is no small Italian state, with a couple of barges and a dozen fishing-smacks to keep in our waters.'

The French protest against the dismemberment of Poland was received by Catherine in the same spirit.

There were two distinct Frances in her mind. The first was the country of Pascal, the great dramatists, Montesquieu, Voltaire and many others who had nourished her mind and enlarged her horizons.

The second, the body politic of France, never ceased to stir Catherine into anger and contempt. *'Ces coquins des Francais,'* she called them. She had not forgiven their condemnation of her *Nakaz*, or forgotten Choiseul's mockery at 'the miserable bottoms' sailing past Gibraltar in 1769. The first attacks on her private life were made at Versailles, and in her eyes the Queen of France was an echo of 'that tiresome and lachrymose St Teresa' in Vienna, who had once compared the Empress of Russia with a Biblical harlot.

The Crimea having been annexed most peacefully, Catherine hoped for a lengthy spell of undisturbed homework. In less than four years she found herself at the threshold of a war neither she nor her country were prepared for.

The celebrated journey to the Crimea in 1787 once again revealed her genius for publicity. None the less, it proved a mistake. The great feast on the shores of the Black Sea, the naval review at Sebastopol, to say nothing of many lesser provocations, upset Turkey, and France at once promised her support. Tension was not particularly eased by a Russian cartoon where fat, loosely pantalooned Turkish soldiers, swords all but falling out of their hands, were drilled by thin, wildly moustachio-ed French officers. Guns, roaring in salute in Sebastopol, presaged a second Chesmé, so it was said at St Germains, and the Sultan knew he could rely on French aid. The Turks wasted no time on preliminaries. They threw Catherine's ambassador into the Seven Towers and sent an ultimatum to the north demanding an immediate cession of the Crimea and the right to inspect all Russian shipping in the Black Sea.

In September 1787 Khrapovitzky, Catherine's private secretary, recorded in his diary that '. . . her Majesty deigned to weep when signing the war manifesto.'

She had good cause for tears. Austrian friendship had grown slightly thinner with the years; Prussia was no more than lukewarm, Britain and France were solidly against Russia. At home, even Bezborodko looked gloomy and the other ministers all but lost their heads 'at the calamity which should never have happened.' Grand-Duke Paul was darkly triumphant, and Catherine's commanders began quarrelling one with another. Potemkin left for the south, telling his sovereign lady that she was not to expect news of any victories. 'We are no more prepared for a war than a hen in some backyard.'

Disasters came swiftly enough. A storm on the Black Sea smote so savagely at the assembled fleet that all hope for an immediate naval offensive had to be given up. On land, the Russian armies were routed again and again. Potemkin wrote that the Crimea must be evacuated. The Empress replied: '. . . Never . . . [you are] my best pupil. . . . Have you forgotten that high spirits can cover up any failure? . . . So long as one can keep in the saddle, why dismount for the purpose of clutching at the horse's tail? Defeats should be used to temper the will and sharpen the energy. . . . Forward and I say again forward. . . .'

So Catherine wrote to Potemkin. She used the same persuasion with her other commanders but those closest to her knew something of her anxiety, though the latter was never made evident anywhere except in the private apartments. Insomnia now attacked her.

She knew she stood alone. She knew that the Great Powers were waiting for her downfall.

It did not come, though the four years of the war took a heavy toll. The triumphs of Rymnik, Ismail and Ochakov were not bought in a cheap market. But at last the Black Sea fleet emerged out of dock, and Admiral Oushakov chased the Turk to the very edge of the Bosphorus. Successive Turkish defeats cooled French enthusiasm, and, spent to the uttermost, Turkey asked for a truce. For Catherine the glory of the Treaty of Yassy was darkened by Potemkin's sudden death.

The four difficult years certainly carried her Empire to heights of splendour. But they also marked the beginning of the saddest chapter in her life. The thunders of 1789 dealt a final blow to what remnants of liberalism still lingered in her mind. Catherine began persecuting those who ventured to be articulate against serfdom. Her treatment of Raditschev and Novikov was a curtain falling on all the splendid visions of the early years. Catherine did not resurrect the Empress Anna's Secret Chancery, but she had her Sheshkovsky and his department, their instructions being 'to detect and to punish anyone poisoned, or suspected of being poisoned, with the pernicious venom of liberal thought.' Thus did Catherine bequeath a grim legacy to her successors. Alexander III's Okhrana stemmed out of it, and so did the Soviet Tcheka and its re-christened inheritors down to our own day.

The Empress, long since convinced that her son was unfit to

reign, decided to make her eldest grandson, Alexander, her heir. But dilatoriness, once utterly alien to her nature, now possessed her, and she put off signing the manifesto. In November 1796 the Empress had a stroke one morning. Consciousness never returned, and she died in the evening of the same day.

Mistakes of judgment and of policy certainly chequer her reign. She would not have had so many reverses during the second Turkish campaign if she had trusted the genius of Paul Jones, whose treatment at her hands was both shabby and foolish. By her active share in the Polish partitions Catherine laid up a most unenviable legacy for her successors. Nor did she implement many of the reforms left unfinished at the death of Peter the Great.

None the less, hers was a great reign. No tie of blood linking her with the dynasty, Catherine succeeded in identifying herself with the Romanovs. Alexis would have approved of her many educational establishments, Sophia would have praised her foreign policy, and the great Peter might well have marvelled that so much energy could come from a mere woman. Even her inchoate reforms carried enough weight to speak to statesmen of a day she was not to see.

Let Catherine's own words be used for the last sentences: '. . . I am certain that I have never undertaken anything without first being convinced that it was for the good of the Empire. Russia has done much for me, and I think that all my gifts used in her service were hardly enough to pay my enormous debt to the country since all I could do for Russia was but a drop in the ocean. . . .'

VII

'A Reign Fantastical'

*Paul I, only child of the Emperor Peter III and his
wife, Catherine II. Born in September 1754,
succeeded in November 1796, murdered in
March 1801*

IN SEPTEMBER 1754 St Petersburg, Moscow and other big cities
in Russia broke into a whirl of festivities that was to last well into
1755 till the coming of Lent ended them. Thus did the Empire welcome the birth of a prince whose arrival assured the continuity of an
all but extinct dynasty. But, as the years went on, men and women
who had danced in Paul's honour did not know that the most important child in the country was growing up in most fantastic and unfortunate surroundings. His parents, living under the same roof, had
no liberty of access to him. His great-aunt, the Empress Elizabeth,
had him surrounded by middle-aged nurses chosen more for their
piety than any other reason. The women, themselves terrified of
Elizabeth, made the boy share their terror whenever she appeared in
the nurseries. They certainly taught him his prayers but, their idea
of the unseen being rooted in a frightening dichotomy, they early
implanted a fear of the dark in the child. Ignorant of any dietetics,
they let him eat what he pleased. Paul's digestion being almost
permanently upset, his nights were fretted by nightmares which the
nurses attributed to the Evil One, to be banished by a few drops of
holy water. That, however, did not ease Paul's stomach.

The nurses were also garrulous. They gossiped about the Empress
and Paul's parents, and about an unknown cousin, once an emperor
and now a nameless prisoner in a fortress dungeon, and they succeeded in peopling Paul's world with phantoms. The tutors, who
marvelled at Paul's intelligence, were unable to quieten him when,

frightened for no reason that they could see, the little Grand-Duke would break into passionate sobbing.

At last it occurred to the Empress that she must make changes in her great-nephew's household. His manners were perfect and his progress at studies big with promise, but his nervousness bewildered and angered her. 'The child must be cured,' she said, and appointed General Nikita Panin to be Paul's tutor-in-chief.

The nurses were certainly inept and foolish, but they filled an emptiness in the child's life. They gave him affection he could not find elsewhere. Terrified of the Empress, a stranger to his parents, Paul was a Grand-Duke to courtiers and tutors, their behaviour in his presence determined by the soulless demands of an etiquette which allowed no room for feelings. But to his nurses Paul was a little boy with a heart in need of affection, and they lavished it on him. The Empress dismissed them rather abruptly and, in going, they took Paul's childhood with them. He was then in his seventh year.

The task fallen to Nikita Panin was no easy one. Elizabeth did not conceal from him that she considered Grand-Duke Peter unfit to reign and that she wished Paul to be prepared for the throne – 'but in such a way that he guesses nothing of my intentions,' she warned Panin. Her health worsening from month to month, the court became a bee-hive of intrigues. Factions were being formed almost daily. Some were – quite unaccountably – for Peter. Others, particularly the Shuvalov clan, hoped to see Paul succeed, with themselves as regents. A few remembered that the hapless Ivan VI was still alive. There was also the Grand-Duchess. Panin kept studiedly aloof from all factions, and nobody could read his mind.

On Christmas Day 1761 Elizabeth died, no manifesto having been signed by her. Panin, well aware of Peter III's distrust of him, daily expected his dismissal but, beyond appropriating Paul's civil list for the benefit of his mistress, Peter III did not meddle in his son's affairs. Once only did the Emperor appear in Paul's rooms when the boy was having his geography lesson. Before going, Peter III kissed his son and praised him for his intelligence. Nothing else happened except that a light lit up Paul's usually sad eyes. That moment sank into his memory for ever. Panin was present; he too would re-member.

❀

On a June morning in 1762 the little Grand-Duke was fast asleep when a valet ran into his room, shook him by the shoulder and shouted that he 'must fly at once. They say his Majesty means to have you killed this very day.' In such a madly distorted way did the news of the day's upheaval reach the backstairs of the Summer Palace, and Paul screamed at the word 'kill' – '*ubit*'.

Panin came in and the valet was sent away, but the child would not stop screaming until the tutor ordered him to get up and dress. Panin's sternness put an end to the sobbing but not to the panic. The day began and ended in a storm. Paul was driven to the Winter Palace there to see his mother, a grenadier's cloak on her shoulders, her face dusty and her hair dishevelled. She stooped to kiss him, and training alone prevented him from shrinking away. Later, she vanished. Then someone told Paul that his father had abdicated and his mother had been proclaimed Empress 'by the will of the people'.

Somehow that frightening, tumultuous day came to an end, and the boy found himself alone with Panin and heard him say to himself, 'it should never have happened in such a way. . . .' Nothing more, and the words Paul could not understand served to deepen his fears. A few days later it fell to Panin to tell his pupil that his father was dead – 'of a severe internal disorder', Panin quoted from the manifesto. Somehow or other, the truth became known to Peter III's son. With a diplomat's adroitness, Panin kept the Emperor's memory alive in the boy's mind. In the end, Paul saw an exquisitely painted portrait of a man wholly dedicated to the service of his country but continually hampered in all his efforts to do good, a man understood by very few, whose terrible death lay at his wife's door. Touch by touch, stroke by stroke did Panin work at that wondrously imaginary portrait. It pleased him to think that in some such way he repaid himself for the disappointment of June 1762 when, as he believed, Paul should have been declared Emperor.

Catherine did not neglect her son altogether. At her wish statesmen, soldiers and diplomats were often invited to dine at the Grand-Duke's table. She interested himself in his studies and amusements, and tried to make up for the years of estrangement. But she failed from the start, and did not try again.

Paul's evident discomfort in her presence and his habitual reserve baffled and annoyed her. She heard from the tutors that 'it was a pure delight to teach his Imperial Highness – so quick and intelligent he is. Had he been born a commoner, able to devote himself wholly to mathematical studies, he might have become a Russian Pascal. . . .' Yet whenever Catherine had Paul with her, not a flicker of that intelligence could be observed by her. His nerves much steadier, he sobbed no longer; his manners were impeccable, but he moved about like a marionette, his blue-grey eyes empty of all expression, his speech studiedly reserved. Catherine did not then suspect that the husband she had neither loved nor respected was, as it were, avenging himself vicariously by means of that fantastic portrait clearly graven in her son's mind.

In hours of leisure, Paul's greatest pleasure lay in 'make-believe' games. They were always of a military kind. He spared no trouble in sketching maps of various 'invasions'. Once when his tin army occupied France, he said to Panin: 'I am now Duke of St Cloud. I am also the Emperor Frederick II; I am determined to amaze the whole world one day. Oh I am also a great many other people. I think it is such a good game so long as you believe it to be real.'

Such words should have disturbed Panin far more than the Grand-Duke's occasional lapses from truthfulness and spells of laziness. But Panin does not seem to have taken any notice, and 'the game' swept through many centuries, and encircled the globe from Stockholm to Constantinople, from America to China.

When Paul reached his teens, signs of dichotomy became more and more evident, and still they attracted no notice. To millions of his mother's subjects he remained 'our sweet hope' and 'our golden heart' because of his kindliness, courtesy and winning smile.

The impress of 'the game' on Paul's mind was disastrous. Already there appeared odd cleavages in his thoughts. He was passionately devoted to military minutiae yet he feared and condemned war. He spent endless hours in tracing his 'conquests' all over the map, and he vehemently disapproved of his mother's policy. Roumiantzev's triumphs provoked Paul to mockery, the victory at Chesmé infuriated him, and Panin encouraged all his criticisms.

Presently, voices were heard in the Senate suggesting that the Grand-Duke should be allowed to have a share in governmental matters, but the Empress, aware that her son disagreed with the whole trend of her policy, would not hear of it. She preferred to occupy herself with the easier problem of Paul's marriage. In September 1773 he became husband of a Hesse-Darmstadt princess, now

Grand-Duchess Nathalie, whose ambition, far more sharply edged than his own, spurred him to present a most curious memorandum to his mother. Nathalie imagined that its contents would compel the Empress to recognize Paul's merits and to give him a seat at her Council table. To the bitter disappointment of both husband and wife, the Empress left the paper without an answer.

'Russia needs rest from war,' so began Paul's memorandum. 'The whole country is in a state of chaos. . . . Everything should be centralized. . . . Field-marshals and privates alike should be subjected to rigorous discipline. . . . All the cities, towns, villages and hamlets should be put on a military footing. . . . All private enterprise should be done away with since it hurts the interests of the state. . . .' From end to end, the paper was a scathing indictment of the Empress's liberal policy. The idea that 'all educational establishments, all markets and fairs, and all manner of private entertainment' should fall 'under the most rigorous military supervision' made Catherine ask herself if her sense of humour were failing her because the document read like a joke and yet she could not laugh at it.

In April 1776 Nathalie died in labour. Paul was stricken by the loss. He had enjoyed her caresses and companionship, and her ready response to his deep passion for Prussia had been a great comfort to him.

By the end of the same year, however, he was endowed with a second bride, a Württemberg princess, soon to become Grand-Duchess Marie. The betrothal inspired Paul to write yet another document of fourteen leadenly worded clauses which would have pleased any serjeant-major in the Prussian army. 'I do not intend to speak about love. . . . The Princess will have to exercise her patience to endure my temper and my moods. . . . [She] must not interfere in State matters. . . . She must never accept any advice from the members of the household. . . . It will be necessary for her so to frame her behaviour as to exclude the least possibility of being involved in intrigues. . . .'

The bride-to-be is supposed to have learned the fourteen clauses by heart. The future Empress of Russia was in love, and her letters during the engagement have something of a Latin abandon. The Grand-Duke would not discuss love but within a few months after their marriage Marie became his necessity. She engentled him.

Intelligent enough to see the disastrous inner halvedness in Paul, she did not recoil from it.

As the years went on, Marie became his good angel. Herself deeply hurt at the Empress's decision to bring up their sons, the Grand-Duchess knew how to control her husband's anger, but even her devotion was powerless to prevent Paul from moving ever nearer and nearer the point where the real lay wholly overlaid by the fantastic. Marie had her first brush with panic on the eve of their leaving for a European tour in the autumn of 1781. All the arrangements had been planned by the Empress, and Paul came to the conclusion that she wished him and his wife out of Russia for a secret and nefarious purpose of her own. Panic-driven, he told the Grand-Duchess:

'My mother is determined to make Alexander her heir during our absence. As the law stands, she will be within her rights, and it would be far less unpleasant to carry it out with us away. Anything might happen during our absence. Why, we have not even been allowed to choose our own cooks!' Marie begged Paul to be careful but he replied sombrely that unwanted people had been poisoned before.

Husband and wife were fêted wherever they went, but the Grand-Duke did not always bridle his tongue. He complained to the Emperor Joseph II of never being permitted to attend his mother's Council meetings. At Versailles, where they called Paul 'ce prince adorable', the king asked him if he had many trustworthy intimates, and Paul replied that if he had a faithful dog, his mother would order it to be drowned. All such 'gaffes', to call them by no harsher name, reached the Empress in time. They did not exactly improve the relations between mother and son.

She did not particularly want him in St Petersburg, but in sending him away from the capital Catherine succeeded in giving him pleasure. She presented him with a big estate about fifty miles west of St Petersburg, a place called Gatchina with a big manor house, a model home farm, a great park with lakes, some few hamlets, and several parcels of arable and pasture. There, the Grand-Ducal pair settled down, Paul plunging into a wild 'busyness'. He had his own private plans about Gatchina. He wrote to Paris, Vienna and Berlin for architects and engineers and for experts in ballistics and hydraulics. Enormous barracks and equally vast parade grounds soon neighboured the palace. By 1788 Paul had five companies known as his Imperial Highness's battalion, officered by men either cashiered or otherwise dismissed from Catherine's army. Everything at Gatchina, the uniform included, was in strict accordance with the Berlin pattern, Paul having himself translated the Prussian Army Regulations into Russian. The Empress shrugged at it all.

'There is no harm in his aping his father if it pleases him,' she remarked to her intimates, but her private intention was formed already: to disinherit Paul and to declare his eldest son, Alexander, her successor. Catherine told herself that she must not hurry over so important a measure, and she did not know that Paul had long since suspected it.

In bald truth, both mother and son were at fault. Neither seems to have made the least effort to recognize the other's true signature. Catherine never made allowance for Paul's odd upbringing, and all too often the mother vanished in the autocrat unwilling to hear even a single dissenting voice at her Council table. On Paul's side there always remained the horror of Ropsha and the obduracy with which he denied any virtue in Catherine's manner of governing. It was a climate of mutual misunderstanding, suspicion, falseness, and lack of sensibility.

But he could breathe freely at Gatchina where presently he had six battalions of infantry, four cavalry regiments, and two batteries of twenty-six guns each. A high brick wall stood between the palace and the barracks, but even meals and entertainment came second to the demands of the drum and trumpet.

As has been told earlier, the events of 1789 shattered the remnants of Catherine's liberalism. Paul saw the French revolution in terms of an immediate challenge. Where lay the sense of trying to drive the Turk out of Europe when France was being torn asunder 'by bestial violence and poisonous ideas'? He begged the Empress to send an army to France, and she refused, telling him that 'ideas could not be crushed by guns'. She was certainly right but such a reply served to deepen Paul's sense of frustration until a strangely coloured idea took possession of his mind. He told Marie that if ever power came to him, he would be the instrument 'of establishing eternal peace in the world by crushing the seven-headed hydra in France and putting a permanent check on all the intrigues of the British.'

'My country,' the Grand-Duke told his wife, 'would then be in a position to safeguard the peace of the whole world. Once all the turmoils are past, I would see to it that my people were kept immune from any poisonous contagion.'

Little by little, Paul began envisaging the Empire as a gigantic building, all its doors bolted and barred and no views from its windows, a place vast enough to house millions and millions of uniformed automata, all of them breathing, working and moving as his sovereign will directed them.

It is not easy to gauge the true reasons which prompted Catherine to send her two grandsons to Gatchina there to receive their military training. By that time both Alexander and Constantine were naturally aware of the cleavage between the two courts, and the Empress may have thought that the absurdities of Gatchina would influence Alexander in the right direction. He would see his father constantly fussing about such minutiae as the number of buttons on a musketeer's gaiter and so unstable in his moods as to be hardly fit to govern his own little 'Potsdam', let alone an empire.

If such were Catherine's thoughts, her judgment lay sadly at fault. Neither of Paul's sons was revolted by the bleak climate of Gatchina. And there was more. Their arrival so heartened Paul that at the beginning, at least, they saw their father's 'true self', as his mistress, Nelidowa, called it. They saw him courteous, amiable, tolerant and generous. Paul talked to Alexander about the iniquities of the Polish partitions. He discussed his plan for a grandiose crusade against the Jacobins, and he condemned Catherine's expansionist policy, arguing ably enough that the Russian conquest of the Straits would end in a conflict with Britain and thus plunge the whole of Europe into an unnecessary war. Paul told his son that the administration of the Empire made an Augean stable look tidy by comparison. The Grand-Duke's eloquence compelled and convinced Alexander, but the Empress never knew it.

The idea of disinheriting Paul was at last put by her at a meeting of the Council of State, Bezborodko's being the only dissenting voice. When the news reached Gatchina, Paul all but decided to flee at once – so terrified was he of being either imprisoned or murdered. But the Empress did nothing. She died in November 1796, and Paul was Emperor.

The fantastic curve and coil of the reign show that Paul's accession shattered what little mental poise remained to him. The idea that the sceptre would never reach his hand had been his companion for many years. Now he was Emperor. He suggested a man born blind, who, sight being accorded to him by a miracle, remained unable to tell colour from colour. From now on, Paul's ideas and actions, whether good or bad, would either be governed by unreasonable reasons, or else spring from moods shaped by the trivial, the un-expected and the grotesque.

Yet that brief chronicle affords some few proofs of what, given an adequate training and different circumstances, the man night have been. There come gestures of true nobility, great generosity, urges to do good for its own sake, sincere longings for a pure crusading climate, and delicate touches of childlike *naïveté*. Paul's 'best self', so passionately believed in by his wife and his mistress, was not an identity fondly imagined by two devoted women. Yet, as the brief reign went on, the evidences of that best self came more and more rarely until at last thick darkness engulfed them.

Within a few weeks Russia was transformed. The Gatchina bat-talions took precedence not only of the line regiments but of the Guards, and Prussian uniforms became *de rigueur* for all. All the government departments were ordered to start work at six in the morning. Prussian Army Regulations, clumsily modified, were intro-duced even into the navy, and civilians did not escape the iron discipline fallen to the lot of soldiers and sailors. Everybody was told what they might or might not wear. All tailors, hatters and shoe-makers in the Empire were commanded to apply for permitted patterns to the Gatchina quartermasters. Civilians' leisure was strictly regulated. Rules appeared about private dances, concerts, weddings and funerals. Anyone wishing to give a party had to report to the local police station, and a uniformed '*kvartálny*' had to be present, his duty being to report on 'the least deviations from loyalty, propriety and sobriety'. Even the number of courses at private dinners was included in the regulations. Parents were no longer free to choose schools and careers for their children. Nobility and gentry were no longer exempt from corporal punishment. Men trained at Gatchina, indifferent to human values, and totally un-acquainted with the ways and customs of life in the country, were at once sent to replace Catherine's provincial governors since, in Paul's opinion, no civilian could be entrusted with the administration of a province. So many, so varied and urgent were his *'ukazes'* that all the printing presses in the capital had to work day and night, Sundays and feast-days included, to keep pace with the ever-swelling stream of manuscript matter from the Emperor's Private Chancery.

Yet he freed Kosciuzko and all the other Polish prisoners, and told them how bitterly he regretted his inability to undo the great wrong done to their country. The Poles wished to go to America; Paul not only met their travelling expenses but he gave every man a sum adequate for a worry-free start in a foreign country. He also invited Stanislaus Poniatovsky, the ex-King of Poland, to come to Russia as 'my permanent guest', and settled a generous pension on him. Many men convicted of liberalism during the latter years of Catherine's reign were given their freedom together with 'compensation for their unmerited sufferings'. When individual cases of distress came to Paul's knowledge, his help came speedily and graciously. Thousands upon thousands of his subjects were groaning under his tyranny. Yet there were millions scattered up and down the vast breast of his Empire who thought that the harsh and mostly incomprehensible orders issued in his name were framed without his knowledge. Many privates permanently crippled in the Turkish wars had good cause to bless the Tsar's 'golden heart', and many peasant widows, their distress eased by him, did not stint themselves in singing his praises.

From the first day of his reign Paul resolved not to follow his mother's foreign policy. The war with Persia came to an immediate end, and all the ambassadors in St Petersburg received rather laboured pacific assurances from the Emperor. Yet not a few among the diplomats asked themselves searching questions as they watched the bewildering evidences of the dichotomy between Paul's protestations and the warlike footing of daily life forced upon his civilian subjects. And Europe wondered what Catherine's successor meant to do about France. Catherine having persistently refused to join the coalition against the French, Britain and Austria were hoping that Paul would prove himself consistent and repudiate his mother's policy in that most important particular. But he refused to commit himself, and his début in diplomacy was a dishonourable blunder.

At the beginning of 1796 Prussia had rather furtively guaranteed her neutrality to France, not a single chancellery in Europe knowing anything about it. On Paul's accession, King Frederick-William, well aware of his friend's resolve to keep 'an inviolable neutrality,' confided the secret to him. But Paul, enraged at what he called 'a friend's duplicity', betrayed the Prussian secret to the Austrian ambassador, with the result that Vienna cursed Paris, Paris raved against Berlin, Berlin was furious with Vienna, and all three together were indignant with the Emperor of Russia who calmly declared that he had never made any promises of secrecy to King Frederick-William.

In the end, Paul's pacific intentions lasted less than two years. When in August 1798 Malta was surrendered to the French by the Grand-Master of the Maltese Order, Paul declared that neutrality was a poor investment on occasions. So furious and far-flung were his reactions that in the end the Grand-Master was deposed from office, and a delegation from the Knights' chapter came to St Petersburg to ask the Emperor to accept the dignity. It was grotesque for a Russian sovereign, the self-styled head of a Church separated from Rome since the middle of the eleventh century, and a married man, to become head of a religious order subject to the Pope's authority and demanding celibacy from its members. But no incongruities, however glaring, ever troubled Paul. He did not become a Roman Catholic, he did not separate himself from his Empress, or relinquish his mistress. But he became the Grand-Master, established the Knights in his capital, attended services in their chapel, and carried out all his duties with the greatest attention to detail. He was as pleased as a child with the important robes he wore on those occasions.

There were more surprises in store for Europe. Before the end of 1798 the pacific Emperor signed a defensive treaty with Turkey. For the first time in history a Russian fleet entered Turkish waters, its guns fired in salute. Next Russia and Turkey joined the coalition, and Suvorov, the aged Field-marshal, was recalled from exile and ordered to lead the Russian armies into Italy.

The Russian adherence to the coalition was brief-lived. Soon enough Suvorov and the Austrians were at loggerheads. The Field-marshal's reports with their complaints about the poor Austrian co-operation made Paul call his ally 'a bedraggled hen' (*'Mokráya kourítza*'), an epithet which could not please the Austrian ambassador in St Petersburg.

The coalition also had an enemy at Paul's court, a man alleged to be in Napoleon's pay, one Grüber of the Society of Jesus – befriended by Catherine after its dissolution in 1773. Little by little Grüber, having won the Emperor's confidence, began paving the way towards a rapprochement with France. Grüber said that 'impious revolutionary ideas' would not be tolerated there for long. The information he had received was proof of a new breath coming into the French climate. Paul retorted that he would have no dealings with any republican régime, but Grüber kept assuring him that monarchy was about to be restored in France, and Paul ended by believing him.

So the Russian troops were recalled from Italy, and the British occupation of Malta decided Paul to break with England. All British ships in Russian ports were seized and their cargoes impounded. All trade with England came to a standstill which inevitably led to the grievous detriment of Russian mercantile health. Having quarrelled with Britain and Austria, Paul tried to woo Scandinavia and Prussia, but all his efforts fell on stony soil. His diplomatic somersaults had put even the lesser Powers on their guard. Paul, attributing the failure to 'British intrigues', poured venom on England. Her King was a madman and Parliament was composed of fools. Britain's stand against Napoleon and her seizure of Malta were but pegs for Paul's odium. The real root of his enmity must be sought elsewhere. The entire weave of his daily '*ukazes*' and his private correspondence point at a monstrous disregard for individual worth, an implacable denial of the rights of man, and a resolve to turn the Empire into an eighteenth-century equivalent of a concentration camp. It was precisely in the constitutional pattern evolved by England that the Emperor saw a challenge to his conception of state.

Meanwhile, Marengo came and went, and Paul showed himself utterly unmoved by the defeat of a former ally. Austria, crushed to the bone, was known to be contemplating a separate treaty with Napoleon. Old alliances were crumbling like a slice of a stale loaf scattered to birds on a winter's morning. Paul's representatives were on their way to Paris, and in Russia the French émigrés were imprisoned for being 'undesirable aliens' and that in a country which had once poured oil and wine over their wounds. Louis XVIII, who had been given a princely pension and a castle in Courland, was told that all his emoluments were to be stopped, and literally turned out of doors into the arms of a blizzard. The Emperor of Russia had no further use for the Bourbons. He was busily drafting his first letter to Napoleon.

'. . . and I suggest that you and I come together to put an end to all the miseries and disasters now ravaging Europe. . . . I am ready to listen to you. . . . I invite you to join me in establishing a general peace which will quieten the world. . . .' That correspondence, starting towards the end of 1800, was necessarily of brief duration, and the two men never met.

When Georgia asked to be taken under Russian protection, Paul's mind left Europe for Asia. He decided to conquer India. He sent detailed instructions to General Orlov, the then hetman of the Don Cossacks. 'I know that the British are going to attack us. . . . Therefore they must be attacked from the least expected point. . . . India is the best objective. . . . It is a four months' march from your head-quarters. Make straight for Orenburg with all your guns . . . all the riches of India will be your reward, and you and your Don Cossacks will be covered with glory. I enclose the only map I could find here.' There followed a lengthy postscript: 'I see that the map goes no further than Khiva. It will be your business to find the required information. . . . All the mercantile houses in India which belong to the British must be taken over as soon as you arrive, and all the natives are to be treated kindly and brought to Russia where they will enjoy as much independence as they do under the British rule. Remember that the entire trade of India must be diverted to Russia. . . .'

The very next day the Emperor sent another letter to the banks of the Don. 'I am now sending you a new and fully detailed map of India. Remember that your business is solely against the British and that you must deal peaceably with all the natives, and you must assure them of Russia's friendly dispositions towards them. . . . Make straight for the Indus and the Ganges. . . . See to it that the Chinese do not attack Bokhara. . . .'

Unhappily, General Orlov's private reaction to the imperial commands has not been recorded. In early February of 1801, at the very threshold of the most treacherous season of the year, twenty thousand Cossacks with forty thousand horses and twenty-four guns left the banks of the Don for what must surely remain the most fantastic expedition in the whole of Russian history. General Orlov did not proceed very far. Spring floods together with the virtual absence of proper victualling arrangements brought the venture to a speedy end. Not all the twenty thousand Cossacks ever saw their native Don again.

In spite of all the imperial injunctions of 'absolute secrecy', the story leaked out. General Orlov's force could never have threatened India, but England was annoyed. The Scandinavian mood hardened, and Austria had good cause to wonder if a continued alliance with Russia might not bring her into deeper jeopardy. Apart from the problematic good will of Napoleon and the personal interest of Pope Pius VIII in a schismatic sovereign who had started a vague flirtation with the project of reunion, Russia could count on no support in the West. In their private dispatches diplomats accredited to Paul's court no longer hesitated to speak of his insanity. In St Petersburg, society men and women repeated, their voices prudently lowered, a remark made by Paul's second son, Grand-Duke Constantine: 'My father has declared war on common sense with the firm resolve of never concluding a truce.'

At the Winter Palace, the deserted wife and the discarded mistress formed a curious alliance of their own. In the past, both of them had been able to suggest, to warn, and even to counsel. Now the Empress Marie knew she would never hold him again and Mademoiselle Nelidova's sun had set never to rise again. The Emperor was enjoying the favours of a younger and much less demanding mistress, though the charms of '*la belle Lopukhina*' had not enough substance to wean him from sombre moods. So the Empress wrote sadly to a trusted intimate: 'Our life is not very gay. The dear Emperor smiles so seldom.' 'The dear Emperor' hardly smiled at all. From his wife down to the youngest page at the Winter Palace he suspected conspiracies and attempts on his life. He ate and drank nothing that came up from the palace kitchens. All the food was prepared by a trustworthy German cook, and even a bowl of ordinary salad would be closely guarded on its journey from the private imperial kitchen to the dining-hall.

Just about that time Paul's heir, Grand-Duke Alexander, himself suspected of high treason, succeeded in smuggling a letter to his old tutor, La Harpe, in Switzerland. 'My unhappy country is now in a state of chaos which cannot be described. Security is well-nigh destroyed, and I am encumbered with duties which might just as easily be discharged by any serjeant. . . . If and when my own turn comes, I shall have to dedicate myself to my country and never let it become again a toy in a madman's hands. . . .'

The ordinary atmosphere at the palace was aptly described by a courtier's remark to an admiral who, having most unjustly incurred Paul's displeasure, was summoned for a reprimand: 'We all know what you feel, but under this roof it is impossible to say anything except "yes, sir," and "very good, your Majesty".'

Paul's daily activities now increased by leaps and bounds. He cut his sleep down to a minimum and hurried over his meals. He gave fewer and fewer audiences. He never missed his morning ride up and down the streets of St Petersburg when ordinary passers-by were known to hide behind yard gates and palings to escape his notice. Otherwise, the Emperor's time was spent wholly in his study, all its doors guarded by 'reliable' men from the Gatchina battalions.

At the very beginning of his reign Paul had had his father re-interred with fantastic pomp. Now, Potemkin's memory becoming more hateful than ever, Paul ordered his body to be taken out of the tomb and buried in an unremarked grave, the splendid monument raised by Catherine to be razed to the ground. A chance visit to the Academy of Sciences gave Paul the idea that all foreign books were bad for his people's morale, and the only library in the Empire was forbidden to lend them to anyone. All further imports of books from abroad were banned because of 'likely injurious consequences to the national morality'. Soon afterwards all the printing-works in the country were closed, with the exception of the Holy Synod Press and that of the Academy of Sciences. Book shops were placed under a rigorous police supervision, and censors' work was complicated by the spate of directives from the Winter Palace, many of which contradicted one another. The historian Karamzin, who had just translated Cicero into Russian, received a harsh reprimand and was told never to forget that 'Cicero and many others were on the proscribed list because they were republicans and their writings could be of no value in an empire.' All correspondence with foreign countries fell under such strict censorship that even innocent allusions to a new opera in Vienna or the latest fashion in Paris were instantly interpreted as 'signs of culpable discontent'. Finally, all journeys abroad were prohibited.

Such, then, was the climate in Russia in 1800. In spite of it all, Paul's physician, Rogerson, spoke the truth when he wrote that it was impossible to blame the Emperor for all wrong done by him. 'He once possessed an inherent passion to do good . . . and [he] was robbed of the ability to distinguish between good and evil. . . . All done by him [is] directed either by the weakness or the violence of false combinations (*"combinaisons fausses"*). . . .' The last two words strike a keynote in that they explain – in as much as anything could explain – that scrambled-egg condition of a mind where, so to speak, black could be white, or red, or grey, when a smile on his wife's face might be either pleasant or menacing, or a son's suddenly averted face furnish a proof of high treason. In certain moods, it was enough for Paul to see a footman hurry across a courtyard to conclude that the man was being used as a messenger by some undetected conspirator under the palace roof.

Yet Russia was not just the Winter Palace or the capital. Millions of illiterate people had their own image of the Emperor, and that image was painted in bright and happy colours. They all knew that he had lessened the privileges of nobility and gentry; he had marked his coronation by a manifesto, one of its clauses exempting peasants from Sunday labour, and he had travelled in the interior, scattering tokens of his benevolence wherever he went. To the masses, the angry light flashing about the throne did not exist. No peasant had ever witnessed these outbursts of blind and bestial fury which made Paul's household shake in their boots. To the masses, all the harsh administrative measures of the day were carried out without Paul's knowledge. They prayed for him fervently and called him 'their little golden heart'.

Early in 1801 the Emperor left the Winter Palace which he hated since every room carried the imprint of his mother's reign. He moved to the newly built St Michael's Castle, whose foundations had been laid in 1798, a monster of a building which offered grim evidence of Paul's mental condition. A massive jumble of grey stone, it was surrounded by a deep moat, and there were five drawbridges manned day and night by sentries chosen from among the men of the old Gatchina contingent.

Paul spent much care on planning his own five rooms on the first floor, a short passage linking them to the apartments of the Empress. A beautifully furnished ante-room led into a library. To the left a door led to a room for those in immediate attendance by day-time. At night, a valet and two sentries slept there, and beyond lay the Emperor's private kitchen. The second library door led to the bedroom, with an exquisite study of an angel by Guido Reni hanging over a camp bed behind a screen of Florentine work. In the middle of the room stood Paul's writing-table made of a rare East Indian wood and inlaid with ivory. A few odds and ends of jasper, rock-crystal and malachite, Paul's inkstand, standish, blotter and suchlike were arranged with the utmost precision on the table. There was also a heavy oblong malachite paperweight which was to find its way into history. All the doors had most intricate locks made for them, and a secret staircase led from the staff room. Paul's private refuge would have been perfect were it not for the mildew which appeared on the walls all too soon. St Michael's Castle was built very shoddily, no proper safeguards having been taken to protect the walls from the inevitable damp caused by the moat. But Paul did not seem to be in the least distressed by the discomfort. He told '*la belle Lopukhina*' that he felt 'marvellously safe' in his new home.

By the end of 1800 a conspiracy had been formed. The then Governor-General of St Petersburg, Count Pahlen, stood at its head. Its apparent aim was to make the Emperor abdicate in favour of Grand-Duke Alexander.

Pahlen's career had been rather of the see-saw variety. A member of the Baltic nobility, he had not reached any remarkable height until 1798. Then his roots went in swiftly and deeply. His post involved heavy responsibilities, the Emperor's safety being one of them. Pahlen's administrative methods soon enough won Paul's favour. The incidence of crime fell appreciably. The discipline among the police left nothing to be desired, and all the endless rules governing citizens' private lives seemed to be observed to the letter. 'I can rely on you absolutely,' said the Emperor to Pahlen.

The Governor-General was a man of matchless sagacity and prudence. 'All brain and no heart', said his enemies behind carefully locked doors. The task of acquainting Alexander with 'the abdication plan' fell to Pahlen's share and so brilliant were his arguments that he succeeded in persuading the Grand-Duke that the good of the country demanded that the Emperor's reign should end with the least delay possible. 'But my father's life must not be endangered,' said the Grand-Duke, 'Can you swear that it will be so?' And Pahlen gave a solemn oath that Paul's life would stand in no peril at all.

He began recruiting conspirators with the greatest caution, all the men being officers of the Semenovsky Guards Regiment wholly devoted to Grand-Duke Alexander. To all the conspirators in turn, beginning with General Talytzin commanding the regiment, Pahlen explained that their aim was to secure Paul's immediate abdication. He took care to add that he had sworn most solemnly that the Emperor's life would be spared.

In spite of all the precautions, a rumour did not fail to reach the Emperor. He challenged Pahlen about it. Though taken completely by surprise, the Governor-General kept cool and answered that he knew all about the conspiracy and he had himself joined it so as to gather all the threads in his hands the better to protect the Emperor's sacred person from all manner of peril. Paul, his face very pale and his hands shaking, commanded that all the names should be given him, and Pahlen promised to furnish the list as soon as he could. Then the Emperor screamed:

'Don't lose time! My father was murdered in 1762.'

Pahlen, his calm immovable, replied that there could be no comparison between 1762 and 1801. Peter III had hated Russia and her people. Paul was devoted to the country and the peasants loved him. Peter III was never crowned and the masses hardly knew him. In 1801 they were blessing the Tsar's name for all the benefits he had conferred on them. Peter III had neglected religious practices, and Paul observed them all with great devotion. Pahlen might well have added that the Empress Marie was not a Catherine but he was wise enough not to say so. He left the Emperor's private apartments convinced that no time was to be lost.

March the 10th that year fell on a Sunday. In the evening Pahlen told the Emperor that the conspirators' names would be given to him on the following Tuesday. That done, the Governor left St Michael's Castle for the house of Madame Zherebzova where all the conspirators were waiting for him. Any private meetings were at that time under strict police surveillance, but it was not the business of the police to keep watch over a house frequented by the

Governor-General, and the conspirators knew they were perfectly safe. Pahlen told them that since it was one of his duties to arrange for the guard at St Michael's Castle, he had decided that men of the Semenovsky Guards Regiment would be sent there the following evening. Then, his manner almost as casual as though he were discussing the weather, Pahlen issued his final instructions. All the conspirators were to meet for supper at General Talytzin's house; he, Pahlen, and a few others would later make for the Semenovsky barracks and bring a battalion with them to St Michael's Castle. He then named the seven men who were to make for the castle on their own and enter the Emperor's rooms: Platon Zubov, Benningsen, Prince Yashvil, Prince Wiazemsky, Skariatin, Gordanov and Tatarinov. When someone asked what they were to say on entering the room, Pahlen made no reply. He said instead that the reign must end by next evening and that the Emperor, strongly guarded, must be taken to the Fortress of SS Peter and Paul on the north bank of the Neva. Gordanov asked what they were to do if the Emperor resisted arrest. Pahlen kept silent.

On Monday evening nineteen people sat down to supper in St Michael's Castle. At the beginning of the meal the Emperor's mood was almost gay. He drew everybody's attention to the new dinner service of Copenhagen porcelain, views of his new home being painted on every plate and dish. He noticed that his eldest son barely touched his food and suggested that the Grand-Duke should see his physician that evening. He spoke graciously to his daughters-in-law.

But the mood did not last. The meal over, the officer commanding the guard came with his usual report and saw that the Emperor's face was distorted with fury. He shouted that he knew the men of the Semenovsky Guards Regiment were all revolutionaries at heart and that the Governor-General had no business to send them to St Michael's Castle.

'I have just signed an order for them to leave the capital. See that they are on the march by six in the morning, and the guard here must be changed at four.' Then Paul went to his private rooms and rang for his valet.

Meanwhile, at General Talytzin's house, an ordinary supper was ending in anything but an ordinary orgy. The host, earlier instructed by Pahlen, did not spare the wine. In the end, quite a number of the conspirators were far too drunk to be of any use to the leaders. That did not trouble Pahlen at all. As the clock struck eleven, he and a few others left for the Semenovsky barracks to bring the first battalion to St Michael's Castle.

A little later the seven men named by Pahlen made for the Castle. Prince Yashvil, Prince Wiazemsky and Skariatin were so drunk that, the first drawbridge crossed, Benningsen and Zubov decided to leave the three men together with Gordanov and Tatarinov at some distance from the main courtyard. Alone, Zubov and Benningsen made their way towards the secret staircase leading to the Emperor's rooms. The two sentries and the valet were overpowered without much trouble except that Zubov brought one man down with the flat of his sword. Then they crossed the library and opened the bedroom door. Paul was out of bed, his feet bare, a flannel jacket over his nightgown and a cotton night-cap on his head. Candles were burning brightly enough in the library and they saw his face clearly. His eyes were glazed with terror.

Benningsen came forward and said that he was arrested by order of the Emperor Alexander and that no harm would come to him if he did not resist. Benningsen never mentioned abdication. Paul understood nothing at all, and indeed how could he when they spoke of his son as Emperor whilst he was still alive? He just stood and stared. At that moment, a noise broke out somewhere below, and Zubov rushed out of the room. Benningsen remained and went on mouthing platitudes. The Emperor kept quite still. A door just behind him opened into a passage leading to the Empress's apartments. But he did not move. Two swords hung within reach, but he did not try to defend himself. He stood as though he were conscious that the nightmare which had haunted him for many years were there and that nothing mattered any more.

Zubov did not return. After an intolerable pause, the other five, led by Prince Yashvil, rushed into the room, and one of them knocked down the lantern Zubov had left by the door. Nothing but pale flickers of candlelight came in from the library when the five men bore down on Paul, and Benningsen at once slipped out to fetch a candle, as he said.

Paul managed to avoid the onrush and began running round and round the writing-table until something tripped him and he fell. Someone's hands groped and found a silken scarf lying on the floor and began tying a knot. Paul struggled and said in French: 'Gentlemen, in heaven's name spare me. . . . Give me time to say my prayers.'

Those were his last words. Time was not accorded, but in their drunken clumsiness and haste the five men botched their business. The silk scarf rasped plaintively and came apart. Then someone's hands began fumbling up and down the writing-table. In the end, the malachite paperweight was found, and someone, stooping, pressed it harder and harder against Paul's throat. Only when the last twitches and gasps were over did Benningsen come back, a lighted candle held high in his hand. He saw and turned his eyes away. The others hurried out of the room.

It fell to Pahlen to break the news to Alexander. A little later, the young Emperor's wife came to comfort him. Presently, dawn broke over the capital, and the people learned that the Emperor Paul had died of apoplexy in the forty-seventh year of his life and the fifth year of his reign. The fiction was maintained in Russia for more than a century.

Certainly, the country had to be relieved of the tyranny, but the means taken to achieve the end remains repellent down to this day. To begin with, the very shaping of the conspiracy was based on a fraud. Pahlen must have known – none better – that Paul would never consent to abdicate. There is not a particle of evidence that the necessary instrument had ever been drafted, let alone drawn up.

Again, for all the precautions taken by the conspirators, their own accounts of that night do not suggest that they had much to fear. Pahlen, being the head of all the police forces, saw to it that the way lay clear. They were not heroes who made their way to St Michael's Castle on that March night in 1801. They went with one resolve uppermost in their minds, and so it proved a murder most foul, five drunken giants against one small unarmed and cornered man, and one of those five bore the ancient and hitherto honourable name of Wiazemsky.

Alexander's share in the guilt cannot be denied. A pledge about safeguarding his father's life had indeed been asked by him and given by Pahlen, but how much sincerity was there in the asking, still less in the giving of it? Both the Grand-Duke and Pahlen knew that Paul would never abdicate of his free will, and what could have been done with a dethroned monarch? Paul was no Ivan VI to be hidden in some prison for the rest of his life, and a revolt on a major scale might well have broken out throughout the country, peasants ready to defend their 'little golden heart' with pitchforks, axes and hatchets. It is more than doubtful that any country abroad would have offered him shelter.

Catherine must bear a vicarious share of the guilt. It would be unjust to say that she was wholly responsible for Paul's unfitness to rule. Far too many complicated causes are here knotted together to arrive even at an approximate apportioning of individual responsibility. But to more than one intimate did Catherine admit that she was resolved not to have her son succeed her. Juridically, she was within her rights to name Alexander her heir. Unfortunately, dilatoriness played into the hands of Fate. She died, no manifesto embodying her intention. It is possible to conjecture that Paul might not have died in March 1801 if Alexander had become emperor in November 1796.

It is a sombre and pitiful chapter of Russian history, though it affords one or two redeeming flashes. All his insane '*ukazes*' and the rest notwithstanding, Paul may be considered the first Romanov to have had practical regard for the masses, and the official account of his death was proof that the day's government, however relieved at the ending of a yoke, were well aware of the reaction likely to break out among the people if they knew the truth.

All through that short reign the grim clutch of Fate lay upon the fortunes of the dynasty. At Gatchina, its spirit wholly at variance with the national moods and aspirations, the thorny past and the still thornier future seemed to reach a marriage-bed.

VIII

Alexander the Blessed

*Alexander I, eldest son of the Emperor Paul I and
his wife, Marie, née Princess Sophia-Augusta-
Dorothea of Württemberg. Born in December 1777,
succeeded in March 1801, died in November 1825*

FEW BOYS of blood royal in the eighteenth century had as happy
a childhood as Alexander. Brought up by the Empress Catherine,
who, though she had failed as a mother, proved herself an exemplary
grandmother, nursed by a sensible Englishwoman, early accustomed
to regular hours, his curiosity satisfied and his interests encouraged,
whether they concerned antique cameos or modern paper-making,
what more could there be at the beginning to foretell a no less
fortunate maturity? Alexander's affectionate nature, innate courtesy,
and more than average intelligence certainly promised well for the
future. Nor was his a lonely childhood: he had a playmate, his
brother Constantine, born in 1779.

None the less, those apparently carefree early years carried the
seeds of sharp future misery. We cannot tell at what age Alexander
first learned of the cleavage between his grandmother and his
parents. The English nurse was certainly wise and discreet but
though her authority came first in the nurseries, it could not altogether prevent her numerous Russian underlings from repeating the
gossip heard on the palace backstairs.

In 1784 Alexander's education was entrusted to La Harpe, a
brilliant Swiss scholar of undisguised republican principles. The
appointment caused a great stir at the Empress's court and provoked
Grand-Duke Paul to anger, but in 1784 Catherine had not quite
turned away from liberalism. La Harpe had been recommended to
her by Melchior Grimm, one of her greatest friends, whose judg-

ment she trusted and, her son's protests notwithstanding, Catherine stood firm in her choice of a tutor.

La Harpe succeeded in teaching his pupil that the varied modes of government could all be considered under a humanist's lens and that even autocracy could be instrumental in promoting the good of a nation so long as that autocracy did not sink to the level of tyranny, with the demands and urges of an uninhibited self enthroned above all else. La Harpe's lessons sank deep, and in later years Alexander would acknowledge the great debt he owed to his tutor. '*Je vous dois tout hormis le jour.*'

But La Harpe could do nothing to lighten the stifling and shadowy atmosphere of the family background. Direct interference was out of the question for anyone in his position. A man of unstained integrity, he held that his pupil owed 'duty and affection' both to the grandmother and to his parents, and he certainly tried to instil that idea in Alexander's mind. But the development of the idea led to consequences La Harpe could never have foreseen.

When in 1790 Catherine wrote to Grimm that her grandson 'was a bundle of contradictions', she used the words without giving herself a clear account of their true meaning. Alexander lived at the Winter Palace and at Tsarskoe Selo but neither he nor his brother were prevented from paying occasional visits to Gatchina. In St Petersburg and at Tsarskoe, members of the household permitted themselves to mock at 'the Grand-Duke's Prussian vagaries', such mockery never being expressed in the presence of the Empress. At Gatchina, nobody took the least trouble to hide their condemnation of Catherine, her foreign policy, her home reforms, her private life. Early enough Alexander understood that acquiescence with the opinions at each of the two courts was the wisest policy. He did so by assuming a mask he should never have worn at so early an age. He preferred his grandmother's court to Gatchina where nobody praised him very much. In St Petersburg he was certainly a success. The court could not say enough about his good looks, his charm and grace. In his mid-teens he grew rather preoccupied with wardrobe matters and became the most elegant dandy in the capital. To La Harpe's anguish, his pupil began neglecting his studies. At the same time, certain unpleasing qualities came to the foreground – vanity, cunning and a readiness to keep all disagreeable matters at a distance.

Catherine could not have chosen a better tutor than La Harpe. Unfortunately, he was not permitted to bring his task to the end and to have his pupil thoroughly trained in statesmanship. The Empress, already determined to have Alexander succeed her, began thinking of the dynastic future at too early a date. In the autumn of 1792, before the Grand-Duke was fifteen, she had two Baden princesses brought to St Petersburg 'on approval'. 'I did not attract [him]: he looked at me in a very hostile manner,' recorded Princess Louise after their first meeting. None the less, the young people were formally betrothed in May 1793, the Empress blandly remarking that 'the dear children looked as happy as angels'. By that time, Alexander was certainly attracted to the youthful and lovely Grand-Duchess Elizabeth – Louise's name on being received into the Orthodox Church – but the Empress's urgency greatly damaged her grandson. Alexander, married before his sixteenth birthday, would suffer much from the premature ending of the schoolroom routine. La Harpe had given him much and was prepared to give more, but married life and social responsibilities left scant leisure for regular studies. Lessons continued for a time, but in a sorrily patchy fashion.

Alexander's further enlightenment followed a wholly different course. He had several friends, a few among them slightly older than himself. Prince Alexander Golytzin, Kotchubey, Novossiltzev, Strogonov and the brothers Czartorizsky were the Grand-Duke's closest intimates. All of them were passionately committed to a liberal profession. Freedom of thought, word and creed was hardly a safe subject for open discussion during the last years of Catherine's reign, but such were the themes closest to the young people's hearts and minds, and Alexander did not escape the contagion.

Before he reached his seventeenth birthday, he ceased to cherish the image of a benevolent and affectionate grandmother and a wise sovereign. Catherine became a tyrant, her foreign policy exhausting and impoverishing the nation. Such were Alexander's conclusions shared with none except his young wife and his intimates. In certain moods he toyed with the idea of surrendering all his rights and vanishing into a commoner's obscurity somewhere abroad.

Neither then nor later did the Empress suspect such a change in her favourite grandson. He had learned to wear a mask only too well. 'The bundle of contradictions' expressed itself in several selves, some of which complemented and others fought one another. The family cleavage, which had led to much insincerity in childhood, was now accepted as a permanent condition. Alexander's way of accepting it should have disturbed those who prided themselves on knowing him best. It did not do so.

At the Winter Palace he remained an affectionate and courteous grandson. On his visits to Gatchina he proved himself a submissive son. A good friend to the few who were permitted to enjoy his friendship, an adoring husband, a popular dandy in the capital and its environs, his simple courtesy and charm winning anyone after a few minutes' talk, what contemporary could have guessed that the boy of seventeen was an accomplished diplomat, his true reactions and feelings known to none but himself?

Alexander's departure for Gatchina at the end of 1794, a move expressly desired by his grandmother, meant far more than an initiation into military sciences, though it is true that his passion for '*le soldatesque*' dated from that period. First of all, he began seeing his parents in a wholly different light, and little by little fell under his mother's influence, which would continue all through his life. Again, the strictly objective criticism of Catherine's personality and her way of governing gave way to starkly personal hostility. There were qualities in Paul, earlier unguessed at, which moved Alexander deeply. When the father grew fierily eloquent over the iniquities of the Polish partitions, the son was surprised by joy that Paul should share his own most cherished opinions. The matter of 'a crucified Poland' and of the Empire's territorial expansion, derided by them both, linked father and son together. And at the beginning Paul showed himself kindly, affectionate and tolerant. His conversation was evocative. His grasp of many problems of state seemed firm and original. Alexander grew indignant that such a man should never have been allowed a voice at Catherine's Council table. Soon enough affection for a parent began mingling with compassion for a Grand-Duke condemned to years of frustration. Yet Alexander was such a consummate actor that when he left Gatchina for a brief stay in St Petersburg or at Tsarskoe Selo, the Empress never suspected the change.

That halycon interlude, however, did not last. Gatchina was not just a palace where leisurely discussions could flow uninterrupted by any outside encroachment. Gatchina was primarily a barracks, and the two brothers were there to learn the art of war. The day's routine, once holidays were over, absorbed Constantine. Alexander, too, was affected by it, but in a different way. His sensitivity shrank from the daily display of his father's ruthlessness on the parade ground. When on duty, Paul made no difference between his sons and any private in the Gatchina miniature army. Many were the occasions when a certain gunner, promoted by Paul to a colonel's rank, served as buffer between an irate father and a terrified son. The gunner's name was Arakcheev, and Alexander came to owe him a debt never to be forgotten.

His intimates were not invited to Gatchina. The regimented day left no leisure for study, and the resolve to relinquish all his rights grew and deepened in Alexander's mind. Grand-Duchess Elizabeth, herself not particularly happy with her parents-in-law, shared his secret and wholly approved it. She told him there were many remote corners in the German states and in Switzerland where they could lead a commoner's life under a cottage roof, their wants whittled down to a minimum. 'We need not have servants,' said Elizabeth, 'I can easily learn how to cook and do my hair. There must be ample shelf-room for books in the cottage, and we could manage a small garden ourselves.' That fondly imagined idyll became a roseate corner of an otherwise sullenly grey horizon.

One day in October 1796 Alexander was summoned to the Winter Palace. The Empress remained closeted with him for several hours, and the affectionate grandson gave her his whole attention. No one else was present in Catherine's study, but Alexander's subsequent letter to her makes it obvious that his consent had been asked and not withheld in a matter of paramount importance.

In less than a month she was dead, and within a few days court life was put on a barracks footing, the spirit of Gatchina having invaded the capital. Alexander and Constantine, notwithstanding their officers' rank, were virtually reduced to the status of serjeants. All the maddening, soul-killing littleness of guard-room and parade ground filled their days from dawn till midnight. Week succeeded week, one month slipped into another, and despair engreyed Alexander's mind. True that he and his wife became all in all to each other through those years of Paul's reign, but they had very little time to spend together, Alexander's duties frequently keeping him up all through the night. In the end, tormented and baffled by all the evidences of insane autocracy round about him, the Grand-Duke fell victim to insomnia.

The pattern was made no easier by the father's suspicions of conspiracies evolved by the son. One by one, Alexander's friends vanished from court. Some were exiled into the country, others escaped abroad. Even Arakcheev fell from favour for trying to fight the Grand-Duke's battles for him. Alexander now had no time to spare for the sittings of the Senate or Council of State. Dwarfed to the condition of a mere cog in the vast state machine, the heir to the throne, supposed to receive ambassadors in audience, did not dare to say even a few words to diplomats met at court functions: Paul's presence paralysed Alexander into terror.

All of it certainly damaged him. It also matured him. He no longer considered a future eased by the undemanding pattern of a commoner's life. Such dreams were gone never to come back. By the end of 1797 Alexander was convinced that it would be his duty to steer the ship of state into calmer waters once he found himself called to the helm.

The masses barely knew him, but in St Petersburg and its neighbourhood he was popular. That unsought-for popularity now increased his peril because the Emperor refused to believe that he was doing nothing to win it. And, again unfortunately, Alexander was all but worshipped by the guards regiments where the resentment against 'the Gatchina scum' burned more and more fiercely with each new humiliation imposed on Catherine's 'eagles' by the whim of Catherine's son.

The harm done to such a nature as Alexander's by a climate where a mere breath of suspicion was enough for brutal arraignment, could hardly be exaggerated. His words to Pahlen 'I consent to the demand for my father's abdication on condition that his life be spared' could not have been spoken except by a man whose ability to distinguish truth from fiction had fallen temporarily asleep. When on that fateful night in March 1801 Pahlen came to announce that he, Alexander, was Emperor, he broke down and told Elizabeth that he was unfit to reign. Nothing but her own calm, resourcefulness and courage kept Alexander away from the abyss, but Elizabeth was sadly prophetic when she wrote to her mother that '(his) soul will remain wounded for ever. . . .'

In the end, the regicides, whose names were all known to Alexander, went unpunished. The official fable about Paul's death need not have been maintained for more than a century, but at the time it was a grim necessity to prevent a revolt on a national scale.

Through the months that followed, husband and wife were closer to each other than ever before, and much of the glory to come to Russia during the reign was due to the devotion and faith of a twenty-year-old Empress who, truly carrying her husband's burden, lightened it for him. Within less than a week the young Emperor was hard at work. All the *ukazes* limiting a subject's personal liberty in so grotesque a fashion were instantly repealed, and 'the sun shone bright over St Petersburg,' recorded a contemporary. At a meeting of the Council of State, a decree was passed forbidding the sale of serfs without the land. 'As your Majesty pleases,' remarked Bezborodko to be answered by Alexander: 'Yes, I am an autocrat, but autocracy is under the law.'

The men exiled by Paul were recalled immediately, Vice-Chancellor Panin and Arakcheev among them, but Alexander mistrusted Panin and Arakcheev was no statesman, and the Emperor found himself unable to make major changes in the administration and had to remain content with those who had once served Catherine. Still, his young friends were coming back, Kotchubey and Novossiltzev hurrying home from abroad and the others leaving their enforced exile in the country.

Little by little, vision and fever stirred in the young Emperor, but he had no clear programme in his mind and no men of proven experience and in sympathy with his views to offer him counsel. The nation's wounds were many and the repeal of restrictive measures could not heal them, but Alexander could not think of any positive remedies. Reforms seemed as necessary as air, but where was he to begin? Moreover, moods of despondency, mingled with the mordant remorse for his share in his father's murder, gripped him all too often.

The background and Alexander's mental condition considered, it is a matter of wonder that anything at all came to be planned during the first months of the reign. In May 1801 Alexander convened a Private Committee ('*Neglássny Komitét*'), its four members being Prince Adam Czartorizsky, Count Kotchubey, Count Strogonov and Novossiltzev, all young men of most telling promise. The very formation of such a committee was an excitingly novel departure in the history of Russian administration. The terms of reference had no limits set to them: the four members were to gather all the available data about the conditions in the country, their reports to be discussed at the meetings convened by Alexander. They met quite informally at the Winter Palace, dined with the Emperor and Empress, then withdrew into an adjoining room for their deliberations, the host joining them a little later.

In factual terms, the committee did not cover a very large distance. Serfdom being the predominant problem, its discussion came first and, after a number of meetings, it ended in a dead heat between the Scylla of the landowners' privileges and the Charybdis of the peasants' rights once emancipation became fact. Peasants could not be freed without land, their chief means of livelihood, and where was the land to come from except from the private estates of those people who would certainly feel most sharply the economic effect of emancipation. The Act of 1803 which enabled landowners to free their serfs proved more or less a dead letter because it bristled with far too many red-tape formalities. None the less, the act remained the first concrete expression given to a dream deeply cherished by the best minds of the day, and the findings of the committee were to come into use sixty years later.

At Alexander's accession, Russian foreign policy suggested a rudderless boat driven here and there by the will of a storm. There was not a country in Europe ready to approach Russia, with the sole exception of France. Durocq, sent by Napoleon, reported that France could hope for nothing since the young Emperor was entirely absorbed by home matters. Panin, re-installed in the Vice-Chancellor's office, urged a rapprochement with Great Britain, but Alexander said that he had no desire to form any hurried alliances with anyone. 'They usually lead to misunderstandings, ending in an open conflict. We must have peace. The Empire is in no need of further conquests.'

Yet, in spite of those words, he concluded an alliance with Prussia within a bare two years. In 1804, following the murder of the Duc d'Enghien, Russia broke off relations with France.

It should be noted here that quite a few seeds of the reign's darkened end lay in Alexander's beginnings. His exasperatingly sentimental attitude to Prussia and his often incomprehensible handling of Polish matters are good examples of it.

Not for nothing was Gatchina called 'little Potsdam'; Paul's worship of Frederick the Great and his literal rendering of the Berlin gospel into Russian were there for all to see in terms of homage paid to the memory of Peter III. Alexander's friendship with King Frederick William, his tenderness for Queen Louise, and the indulgence shown towards several Prussian breaches of good faith, were no more and no less than so many efforts to do honour to the memory of a father for whose murder Alexander held himself responsible to the end. Those efforts seldom ran in accord with Russia's own weal, but that to Alexander seemed of trivial consequence when compared with the debt he could never repay and with the reproaches of a conscience never to be stilled. Yet there was a difference between the Prusso-mania of father and son. Paul could cherish Peter III's memory, no sense of guilt darkening his homage. Alexander was never free of that burden.

In what concerned Poland, Paul's passionate condemnation of its dismemberment never ceased to colour Alexander's attitude to that country, an attitude which again and again bewildered and irritated his own people.

✳

By the spring of 1805, Russia stood definitely committed against Napoleon. Prince Adam Czartorizsky was appointed Alexander's foreign secretary – to the great displeasure of everybody, since no Pole was ever trusted by the Russians. And a beautiful and brazen Polish woman, whose manners belied her princely origins, became the Emperor's mistress. When an uneasy rumour became a disturbing fact, Alexander's popularity certainly tottered. It would have been shaken far more if the people were better acquainted with the young Empress. Elizabeth, however, preferred to leave the foreground to her imperious mother-in-law and led so retired a life that few knew her quality and still fewer realized the depth of the wound her husband inflicted on her.

The hurriedly made alliances contributed to the general disappointment. What good could be expected from either Sweden or Austria, people asked one another. The Emperor's sudden friendship with Prussia promised nothing but unfortunate and costly involvements in Prussian troubles. Alexander's Empire found itself at the threshold of a war it did not desire or expect, and could not afford. People blamed the new foreign secretary, Queen Louise of

Prussia and the Emperor's mistress. Kutuzov's armies were sent to Moravia to help the Emperor Francis I. The Russians had no stomach for the Austrians. Too many veterans remembered Suvorov's Italian campaign and its fruitless ending caused by an ally's ineptitude. 'The bedraggled hens will let us down again' the men kept muttering, 'they are good for nothing else.'

Kutuzov, aware that his men were worn out after a strenuous march, wanted them to rest. The Emperor Francis retorted there was no time for rest because the disaster of Ulm must be avenged immediately. So he told Alexander. Kutuzov, on being summoned to his sovereign, said that he was the Tsar's loyal servant and waited for his orders. Alexander gave them at once and they proved disastrous. The day of Austerlitz offered a grim proof that lack of synchronization was tantamount to suicide. The first mistake came out of an unexpected movement of Austrian cavalry cutting right across a road crowded by the advancing Russian infantry.

The battle lasted two hours. It ended in a complete rout of the allies, both Emperors fleeing for their lives, but the Russian regiments did not shame their oath even in flight: they were flung into a battle which should never have been fought at that place and at that time.

On the field of Austerlitz Alexander's youth was ended. That evening his tears were genuine enough. The senseless carnage and the appalling rout lay at his door. He should have listened to Kutuzov's counsels and not to Francis's persuasion. That night, as Alexander lay in a peasant hut, fever gripped him and his doctors were anxious. But it was not the Emperor's body that suffered most.

His friends in Berlin offered no help. Shortly after Austerlitz, King Frederick William made an alliance with Napoleon. The situation had no historical precedent: Prussia was at once joined to France against Russia and allied to Russia against France. It made no sense even to those least acquainted with the diplomatic map. Alexander's family and government begged him to sever all links with Berlin. He did not listen to anyone. 'King Frederick William is my friend,' he kept repeating.

The situation was resolved by the arrogance and stupidity of King Frederick William. Not at all certain of Napoleon's assistance and assured of Alexander's friendship, the King sent a senseless ultimatum to France demanding the immediate withdrawal of French troops from Prussia. Napoleon could afford to call his bluff. The Prussians were virtually annihilated at Jena and Auerstädt. In Russia hopes for a break with Prussia leapt high indeed, but the Emperor had no such intentions. He went to the rescue as energetically as though his own Empire were in jeopardy. For the second time his troops met the French forces. Kutuzov was not there. The Russian army was led by Benningsen, whose alien beginnings and poor reputation could not inspirit the men. Preussisch-Eylau and Friedland placed the whole of Prussia into Napoleon's hands. No more could be done on any battlefield, and generals retreated to give place to diplomats.

Tilsit suggests a comedy with a Ruritanian setting. Alexander wrote to his sister, Grand-Duchess Catherine, that God had saved them and they had gained time. '. . . But imagine me passing all these days with Bonaparte . . . whole hours *tête-à-tête* with him . . . the man is certainly very vain. . . .' But Alexander's private gamble irritated and shamed his people who were in no mood for comedies. Savary, sent by Napoleon to St Petersburg, found all the doors in society closed against him. A bare six years after Alexander's accession, people began talking about his successor, whose identity nobody could yet determine. The Emperor had no children. Grand-Duke Constantine, deserted by his wife, was living quite openly with a mistress who could never be crowned Empress. Alexander's younger brothers, Nicholas and Michael, were still in the schoolroom. There were vague hints about Grand-Duchess Catherine, his favourite sister, but those hints carried as much weight as a gossamer thread.

The ugly mood in Russia can be understood once it is realized that for generations the country had looked on war in strictly expansionist terms. The only deviation from the familiar course – Suvorov's Italian campaign under Paul I – had ended in a fiasco. Alexander's people considered that they had no business to meddle in European affairs. All the lost battles were regarded as costly and futile sacrifices on behalf of an ally at once disliked and despised in the country. It would not be too much to say that Alexander's obstinacy in clinging to the broken Prussian reed might well have lost him the crown if there had been a suitable successor. Court and society mocked at a war *'faite pour le roi de Prusse'*. Discontent brooded over the army and the masses were bewildered into sullen silence. The Emperor's apprenticeship in foreign policy was certainly not bought in a cheap market. He could not afford to be as frank with his ministers as he was with his sister. To explain Tilsit from his own point of view would have been, as he saw it, an admission of his unpreparedness to face vast issues. And there was more. Tilsit happened because of Prussia, and in the matter of Prussia Alexander admitted nobody into his confidence.

Such, then, was the situation at the beginning of 1808. The nation, having expected reforms, grew weary of waiting for them. They had hoped for brightly coloured changes, and there was no evidence of them to please the public eye. Few people knew that the findings of the Private Committee disbanded in 1803 were by no means stillborn and that men like Kiselev and Malinovsky had begun working on drafts for emancipation. All the people could see was the Dead Sea fruit of unprofitable alliances. Everybody hated Bonaparte but King Frederick William was detested with no less vigour.

'We cannot understand the Emperor,' people said one to another. And who could? Neither his contemporaries nor those who came after were able to decipher Alexander's character. Even his private life offered too many bewildering proofs of some inner division of heart and mind in the man. There was the wife to whom he was bound by the closest of ties, a woman who had enabled him to endure all the nightmares of his father's reign, and who had inspired and encouraged him all through the thorny beginnings of his rule. Yet within two years of his accession Alexander was capable of forsaking Elizabeth for Marie Naryshkina, as vulgar as she was beautiful, whose horizons went no further than the pleasures of bed and board, who deceived her imperial lover from the very beginning of their liaison, and was capable of boasting about her pregnancy at a court function in the presence of her lover's wife. Yet Alexander continued to be loyal to his mistress until incontrovertible proofs of her unfaithfulness came to him.

If '*la belle Naryshkina*' had not been born a Polish princess, the general feeling would have been far less bitter. As things were, people took keen pleasure in airing their discontent, a liberty which would have been undreamt of during the reign of Paul.

Yet, in spite of the Emperor's preoccupation with foreign matters, administrative affairs were by no means at a standstill. Two men were rapidly gaining ascendancy at the Council table – Arakcheev and Speransky, who hated each other lustily and who were both indispensable to the Emperor. Arakcheev was entrusted with the reorganization of the army. Speransky was asked to submit a detailed report on administrative and judiciary reforms. Little by little, the work of all the Ministries, except that of War, came to be supervised by Speransky. The report took him more than two years to complete, and much of it was in full accord with the Emperor's ideas, in particular Speransky's views on autocracy.

'. . . Absolute power in one man's hands argues against the well-being of the State . . . no Government should be recognized unless the will of the whole nation accords the recognition . . . the power of the Government should be counter-balanced by the power of the people. . . . Today there are two estates in Russia: slaves of the Crown and slaves of the landowners, and the former are free only in relation to the latter. . . . In reality, nobody is free with the exception of vagrants . . . [and] all national energies are being atrophied by the inter-relationship of the two estates. . . . Emancipation will be a very difficult task, but the public conscience should be made to acknowledge . . . that serfdom is a condition warring against commonsense, to say the least.'

The report was never published. Gradually Speransky's 'omnipotence' became a most rewarding weapon in his enemies' hands. His undisguised approval of French policy and his personal feeling for Napoleon brought about his downfall. In March 1812 Speransky was relieved of all his offices and sent into exile. The Emperor was deeply distressed but the public acclaimed it as the first victory over the French.

The treaty of Tilsit was an uneasily shaped contrivance and as such had a brief lease of life. Alexander's war with Sweden undertaken at Napoleon's instigation and the subsequent annexation of Finland left an unpleasant taste in the Russian mouth. 'No further conquests?' people said 'And here we are adding Finland to the Empire! Is it fitting for the Tsar to dance to Bonaparte's music?'

The Duchy of Warsaw was governed by the King of Saxony, an unpleasant sycophant, who would not have dared to go against Napoleon's wishes even in the choice of a supper dish. Napoleon's invasion of the Iberian Peninsula added to all the other shocks. As the French interference in Polish affairs grew more and more ominous, Alexander decided to meet Napoleon once again, but the atmosphere at Erfurt in 1808 had nothing in common with Tilsit. Napoleon lost his temper and Alexander, all his illusions gone, kept an even manner all through the most difficult interviews. 'We shall watch his fall calmly enough.' So he wrote from Erfurt to Grand-Duchess Catherine.

The two sovereigns parted, each aware that the hour of pretended friendship lay far behind them. The invasion of the Netherlands and Napoleon's seizure of the Duchy of Oldenburg came almost as an anticlimax. Nobody knew where, when or how the flame would break out, but everybody felt certain that it would. Arakcheev was given his orders, and ordnance works all over Russia were now busy day and night. By the end of 1811, the shabbiest stallholder in a St Petersburg market would say as he weighed out his apples or carrots, 'The Tsar is in his right mind again, bless him! Our fellows will teach the French toads a lesson they will never forget.'

Eighteen-twelve meant thousands of different things to millions of people. To the forefront of them all stood a vehemently reborn loyalty to and love for the Emperor both as person and as sovereign.

Arakcheev had worked prodigiously hard and the country had enough military potential to face the emergency, but not even the most experienced secret agent could have discovered Napoleon's immediate plans. It was generally assumed that he would either march through Prussia and attack the Baltic Provinces, or else accentuate the French interference in Polish affairs to such an extent as to leave Alexander with no alternative but that of action. At the beginning of 1812 nobody imagined the possibility of the French invasion of Russia proper. All that the army hoped for was that they should not be ordered to fight again side by side with 'the Austrian hens'. The men's morale was not particularly heightened on learning that General Barclay was appointed Commander-in-Chief. Barclay, a German from the Baltic Provinces, was an excellent Minister of War. He had no gifts as a leader, and the choice was most unfortunate, but the Emperor did not see any alternative. There was

Field-marshal Kutuzov, but Alexander disliked him intensely. In late spring 1812 the imperial headquarters were at Wilno. It was known that Napoleon was in Saxony with an army, its strength then beyond anyone's computation.

On a June morning the news of *La Grande Armée* crossing the Niemen fell like a proverbial bombshell. The tumult at the headquarters was indescribable: nobody had imagined that Bonaparte would invade Russia. Alexander's anxiety did not prevent him from keeping calm. He sent General Balashev to Bonaparte with the finest and most dignified letter ever written by a Romanov. In it Alexander linked the French crossing of the frontier with a trivial diplomatic misunderstanding and he promised to regard the incident as closed once the French army was gone from Russian territory. 'It now depends entirely on your Majesty to avoid the calamities of yet another war.'

Bonaparte sent an abrupt refusal. So quick was the progress of *La Grande Armée* that Wilno had to be evacuated and the headquarters moved farther north. The Emperor had hoped to stay with his army, but he was persuaded of his duty to go to Moscow and there to inform his people that a national war was begun. Alexander went, his heart heavy, but all the belfries of Moscow put an immediate end to his sombre mood. The bells were ringing not to announce a calamity but to tell the people of the city's pride and joy that he had come to it. Those days in Moscow made the Emperor realize that he and his people stood shoulder to shoulder in the struggle. It was Alexander's first high moment, and he did not shame it. From a nobleman to the most tattered peasant, he won them all by his dignified eloquence, his calm, his resolve not to give in, and his faith that they would not be broken by the disaster fallen on them. So they called him '*Blagoslovénny*', 'The Blessed One', firmly convinced as they were that he was the man to lead them to a triumph unprecedented in their history.

But the news from the west brought little comfort. Barclay kept on retreating, and the enemy plunged deeper and deeper into the heart of Russia. Witebsk fell. After the surrender of Smolensk, the nation clamoured for Barclay's resignation. They wanted Kutuzov.

The Emperor was back in St Petersburg. Away from his army, with the uplift of the Moscow experience growing thinner and thinner in his memory, he fell prey to remorse, doubt, and misgivings about the future. He disliked the old Field-marshal, whose very name spoke of a past Alexander wished to forget. To him Kutuzov, his brilliant apprenticeship served in Catherine's Turkish campaigns, was the very last person to direct a national war.

Kutuzov was nearly seventy at the time. The army called him 'Rodimy' for that indefinable quality which created a oneness between him and the men he led. Never wasting his breath on flamboyant speeches, never looking for danger or turning away from it, that fat old man embodied an ideal the soldiers worshipped and had no name for. Kutuzov laughed at patriotic gestures and would have made a rude reply if told that he *was* Russia in 1812.

He accepted the supreme command and was big enough to follow in his predecessor's steps. *La Grandé Armée* kept advancing deeper and deeper into the country, and Kutuzov kept retreating, his genius enabling him to see far beyond the apparently shameful evidence of a withdrawal. On 5th September 1812 his two hundred thousand men were encamped in the fields in the neighbourhood of four obscure little villages, one of which was called Borodino. At dawn of the 7th, they met the vastly superior French forces face to face, and the battle lasted all day.

Borodino came to be idealized by painter, composer, novelist and poet. In reality it was brutal carnage. By sunset, fifty-eight thousand Russian corpses lay in the fields, General Bagration, Kutuzov's most brilliant pupil, being among the fallen. Seven hundred Russians were taken prisoners. Yet Borodino cost Napoleon over fifty thousand men, forty-seven of his best generals being among them. Each side claimed a victory. As a battle, it was more or less a stalemate, and nobody then imagined that a beginning had been made towards Paris, Elba, Waterloo and St Helena. After a tumultuous council of war at Fili, a village some few miles north of Borodino, Kutuzov again retreated. He led his army right through Moscow, struck south-east towards Riazan, and then went to earth, confounding his own sovereign and Napoleon.

The news of the surrender and the fire of Moscow stunned Alexander at first. Then he took heart and his resolve stayed un-broken. 'Napoleon or I – we cannot reign together. I know him now. He shall never deceive me again. My people and I stand together.' Those were bold words, but Alexander had earned the right to speak them.

Kutuzov's army was resting. The old man knew what would happen. By the end of November 1812, *La Grande Armée* had ceased to exist, and just a few thousand starved, tattered and panic-stricken Frenchmen crossed the Niemen. Alexander's vow was fulfilled to the letter – not a single enemy remained on Russian soil. Meeting the Emperor at Wilno, Kutuzov supposed the war to be finished.

'Peace terms,' Alexander answered him, 'are to be arranged in Paris.'

It happened in the very heart of the most ruthless winter in living memory. The country was deeply scarred, and several provinces had lost their harvests. Many towns and innumerable villages were burned to the ground, Smolensk being nothing but a huddle of blackened ruins. People were weary beyond weariness and the men who stood closest to the Emperor were against a continued campaign. Future historians would echo such opinions and blame Alexander for 'an unnecessary war carried on for the purpose of helping Prussia'.

The judgment is at once shallow and unjust.

No Romanov either before or after Alexander stood on such a height. He knew that peace must be arranged in Paris and that not only for the sake of quietening Europe. He was jealous of Russian interests and honour with a heightened jealousy. He had no illusions about Napoleon, whose attempt to enslave Russia had been frustrated at a gigantic cost. Another titanic effort was now necessary to prove that Alexander's country had earned the right – and that not by virtue of conquest – to a voice in the councils of Europe. The 1813–14 campaign can hardly be seen in any other light. The Russians did not fight at Waterloo, but it was Leipzig which paved the way to Waterloo.

Alexander stood virtually alone at the time. A substantial loan had indeed been promised by Great Britain, but gold as such was not enough, and what allies had he except for a ravaged, vacillating Prussia and an enfeebled, equally untrustworthy Austria? *La Grande Armée* was indeed gone, but Napoleon's name had not lost its magic. He was back in France where a choral *'vive L'Empereur'* spoke with an ominous clarity of his hold over the people.

'Peace terms must be arranged in Paris.' It was at once a desperate gamble and an act of perfect faith. Alexander had no false ideas about the ultimate issue, and he knew that failure would cost him his throne and lead to chaos in his country. 'So I must not fail,' he wrote to his mother.

Yet failure brushed against him during the first stages of the campaign. Criticism of Alexander's resolve to continue the war rose to a peak when Napoleon's freshly gathered forces routed the allies at Lützen in April 1813. The Austrian commanders began clamouring for a truce. The King of Prussia burst into tears and exclaimed: 'God in Heaven, does it mean that I must return to Memel?'

'I beg you to remember that we are nearer Paris than we were a month ago,' was Alexander's reply to his disheartened allies.

And he was proved right. Lützen was a Pyrrhic victory for Napoleon. Always well informed about the bitter dissensions in the allied camp, he thought that he could spend the summer in inactivity. In the autumn he flung his entire strength into the battle of Leipzig, an engagement which lasted for three days.

Its beginning promised little for the allies. On the very first day the Austrian lines were broken by the fierce French attack. That proved Alexander's brilliant moment. He gave orders to the Cossacks to check the French onslaught, and Barclay was told to throw in all the artillery reserves. His orders given, Alexander, leaving Frederick William and Francis I to tell each other how miserable they were, galloped away into the very thick of the battle, his presence among the men worth more than a hundred batteries.

Two days later, with Napoleon's forces fleeing for their lives, Alexander rode into Leipzig. When the last Frenchman had fled across the Rhine, the Emperor of Austria and the King of Prussia decided that there was nothing left to fight for. 'Peace must be signed in Paris and Bonaparte must be dethroned,' said Alexander, and in January 1814 his men were crossing the French border.

Shoddy backstage diplomacy vitiated those fine hours for Alexander. Prussian intrigues mattered little enough, however deeply wounded he felt by Prussian ingratitude, but Metternich's adroit moves to exaggerate the Austrian share in the campaign were not altogether barren; Castlereagh reported to Lord Liverpool that 'nothing seemed to foretell so much danger for the future as the Russian Emperor's chivalry.' Castlereagh wondered if Alexander could be trusted in the matter of his repeated protestations that he wanted nothing for his own country. Was it not a cloak thrown over the Russian hunger for territorial expansion? Unjust as those words were in relation to Alexander, Castlereagh had something of a case. The record of the earlier Romanovs, in particular that of Catherine the Great, was only too well remembered in Europe. And how was Castlereagh to know that Alexander hated his grandmother's foreign policy? He had accomplished all by him resolved, he had carried the war to the very gates of Paris and Paris would acclaim him as a liberator. To a politician of Castlereagh's colour there was enough ground for suspicion.

But neither he not Metternich realized that the Emperor of Russia was living in the future. To him the past had no other significance than a certain night in March 1801. At the least sign of mistrust or recoil, he found himself assaulted by a conscience which, leaping across the boundaries of logic, brought him back to the hour when he knew that his father's death must be laid at his door.

Yet those were hardly matters for diplomats or soldiers to probe into.

The war in France lasted about two months. On 31st March 1814 the Emperor entered Paris – not as a conqueror but 'as a denizen of spring'. One goal was achieved with Napoleon's abdication. There remained the task of 'gathering up the nations into the palace of abiding concord, well away from the muddy waters of politics'. To Alexander, all of it seemed at once simple and terrible: the will of God for Europe at that particular moment. And in Vienna he was certainly the arbiter of Europe, and that in spite of the failure of the Congress to serve all the interested parties. Prussia complained because Saxony was not ceded to her, and Austria wasted many a sitting on airing her own grievances. Talleyrand considered it his duty to sow as many seeds of dissension as he could think of. The constitution granted to Russian Poland greatly displeased Alexander's own people. None the less, he amply justified Madame de Staël's words that he alone of all the sovereigns of the day walked his way 'dans le sens de la postérité'.

The basic idea of the Holy Alliance was not original. Charlemagne's imperial concept had been shaped to the same design, to quote no later examples. What was novel in 1815 lay in Alexander's passionate conviction that the idea and the moment accorded with each other as never before and that, with Napoleon gone, Europe was ready to become a federal union, its policy based on mutual confidence and justice. What was novel, too, lay in Alexander's attempt to bring the urges of conscience into the business of governing. He invited the heads of states 'to publish their firm determination that they would take for their sole guide the precepts of the holy religion, of justice, Christian charity and peace . . . such a declaration cannot but have an immediate influence on the councils of princes.'

The Emperor himself drafted the Act of the Holy Alliance. Needless to say, it remained an inaccessible ideal. To begin with, the particular moment was no more and no less propitious than any other moment in history. It was true that the guns were silenced after several years of incessant turmoil, but seeds of wars to come were hidden in economic ravages, not to mention other causes. Again, the divisions in Christendom, which said nothing to Alexander, said much to others. 'Holy religion' meant one thing in Prussia and quite another in Austria.

In the end Prussia alone approved the Act wholeheartedly and signed it. Metternich's acquiescence was a mockery, and Great Britain ignored it altogether. Not until the end of 1815 was a formal treaty of alliance signed, all allusions to Alexander's document being studiedly avoided.

For all the irony its publication received, the Act remains one of the finest memorials of Alexander's reign. Not a clause is there but it mirrors his magnanimity, modesty and sense of justice. To quote Sorel, in 1815 Alexander '*vit de haut, il vit clair, il vit loin, et il agit avec autant de simplicité et de droiture que d'energie et d'habileté.*'

And who could have imagined that the events of 1815 rang at once a triumphant clarion and a knell for the arbiter of Europe?

In 1816, back in St Petersburg, the Emperor wrote a letter to his ambassador in London. It carried a startling reference to 'the spirit of evil . . . [now] making fresh efforts to overcome the good. . . .' At that time, the period usually called Alexander's twilight was still some two years distant, but the long dormant seed was already stirring into life.

The end of the Napoleonic wars opened vast new horizons in the European consciousness. Liberalism became a temple much frequented by many among the generation grown to maturity by way of a prolonged Calvary. The champions of civic liberties borrowed little enough from the past but looked steadfastly towards a future when the voice of the people would be interpreted as an imperative defining the needs of a whole nation and not the whims of a few individuals, their authority either inherited or bestowed by the will of one man. 1789 had been but a threshold leading into vast halls, their doors still locked. New and ample breaths were stirring all over Europe, and thousands of Alexander's officers had their own vision clarified by the comparisons their experiences abroad enabled them to make between the conditions in the West and those in their own country. They returned to Russia deeply athirst for reforms, in particular for the end to all mental and bodily enslavement, and the more impatient among them formed secret societies, one in the north and another in the south. The former dreamt of a constitution. The latter planned in terms of a republic.

The Emperor understood none of it. The inexorable flux of History seemed to say nothing to him after the Vienna Congress. His own dreams of a liberal national horizon were now entombed, and he refused to make any allowances for the irrevocably altered European outlook. Each fresh evidence of liberalism at work was to him but another manifestation of 'the spirit of evil'. His mind, leaping from peaks of enthusiasm into the abyss of melancholia, was just about to take a perilous plunge into other-worldly waters for the sole purpose of quietening his own ravaged conscience.

Such a plunge demands a lengthy and most careful preparation and a total dedication. Alexander had had none of the former and the latter lay wholly beyond him, burdened as he was with numberless cares of state. There was nobody to warn him that the authentic spirit of evil could use an unprepared soul for its own purposes. An uninformed neophyte, the Emperor would soon be running headlong down a path where he should have deliberated over each step. The fanatical religiosity of his friend, Prince Alexander Golytzin, a feverish study of the Bible, the events of 1812 now seen through the lens of pseudo-mysticism, the ephemeral but none the less baneful influence of Baroness Krüdener, the apocalyptic frenzy of the monk Photius, all of it together made a devastating impact on Alexander, and by 1819 his twilight had set in. At Aix-la-Chapelle, at Troppau and at Verona, 'the arbiter of Europe' was little more than a figurehead. Gradually, all his utterances came to be shaped in accordance with Metternich's counsels. To the Austrian, 'the spirit of evil' was little more than a phrase and it is doubtful if matters of conscience ever troubled him, but his indictment of liberalism and his unwearying defence of reactionary policies accorded but too well with the Emperor's own views.

The sudden death of his favourite sister, Grand-Duchess Catherine, the ever-present problem of succession made all the more acute by Grand-Duke Constantine's marriage with a commoner, and his own longings to be rid of all monarchical burdens – such were some of Alexander's torments. His subjects were nearing the end of their patience; the long delayed reforms were altogether shelved, and Arakcheev's iron hand lay upon the entire administration, but the Emperor seemed no longer to care. At forty-two, he looked an old man; his deafness increased, the leg injured in a riding accident gave cause for sharp anxiety, and his eyes were the eyes of a man who could not escape phantoms either by daylight or in the dark.

At the Troppau Congress in 1819 the original aims of the Holy Alliance were wholly forgotten. The revolution in Naples made Alexander direct all his remaining energies towards a struggle as futile as it was sad. It looked as though he, conscious of having once been Satan's accomplice, now felt it his paramount duty to fight 'evil' wherever he imagined it to exist. The plan of creating a European police corps fell on stony ground, but a mutiny in one of his own Guards regiments was punished by Alexander with a cruelty recalling the days of Paul I. So diseased was his thought that he imagined 'the spirit of evil' in a corporal's disobedience to a trivial order as being 'stronger and more dangerous than Napoleon's tyranny'.

When in 1821 Alexander refused to help the Greeks and blamed France for inciting them 'to rebel against lawful authority', the best minds in Russia felt that the national humiliation could scarcely plumb any deeper, but the Emperor considered himself 'an unworthy instrument of the All-Highest'.

Month by month, the shadows thickened. No longer able to concentrate on issues of moment, listening to Photius's dark prophecies, lulled by Arakcheev's assurances that all was well in the country, and using ignoble puppets of Magnitzky's kidney to crush the liberties of the mind, Alexander lived with futile remorse as his constant companion.

A few lances of light broke across the darkness of those last years: the Emperor's reconciliation with his wife, his heroism during the terrible flood in St Petersburg at the end of 1824, and his reply to General Wassilchikov's report about the secret societies' plans for a constitutional monarchy, if not a republic. The Emperor listened to the report, sadness deepening in his eyes. Then he said very slowly: 'My dear General, I used to share and to encourage precisely the same ideas in my youth, and it is not for me to punish these men.'

In the summer of 1825 the Empress's health worsened sharply, and her physicians recommended a long stay in a warmer southern climate, the Emperor at once deciding to accompany her. Some two years earlier he had signed a manifesto naming his younger brother, Grand-Duke Nicholas, his successor. Very few knew about its contents. The papers were sealed by Alexander and marked in his own hand – 'To be opened immediately on my death.' The manifesto as such was kept in absolute secrecy, but he had discussed the possibility of his abdication so often that most extravagant rumours were floating about some time before he left the capital for the south. Alexander's reign lay in the past, and none knew it better than himself.

But he never abdicated.

He and the Empress, lovers once again, reached Taganrog on the shores of the Azov Sea. There, Elizabeth's health slightly improved, but Alexander fell ill and died at the end of November 1825. The masses, knowing nothing about 'the twilight', mourned for him, their 'Blessed One', a Tsar who had shared their misery and their triumph together. Taganrog was isolated from the rest of the Empire, and couriers had to travel across endless steppes to bring the news of Alexander's death into urban areas. Many people refused to believe that he had died. Years later a mysterious hermit, living in Siberia, was alleged to be 'the Blessed', and the legend of Fedor Kuzmich struck deep roots in the national consciousness, but legitimate history cannot build its conclusions out of legendary tissue.

Those sadly twilit years cannot be excluded from Alexander's story. Nor can they be accepted as his abiding memorial. That, begun in 1812, maintained its radiance and its strength until the end of 1815. It brought his country's record to a height but rarely gained in its history and it redeemed many a dynastic misdeed.

IX

The Crowned Policeman

Nicholas I, third son of the Emperor Paul I.
Born in 1796, succeeded in 1825,
died in 1855

OF NICHOLAS'S early years there is little to record. Not quite five years old at the time of his father's assassination, he remained wholly under his mother's care. He had a playmate, Michael, his brother, about two years younger than himself. He was a noisy and clumsy child, given to easy tears and ugly temper, and possessing very little physical courage. The portrait does not gain much colour when Nicholas leaves the nursery for the schoolroom. The Dowager did not ask anyone's counsel when choosing the head tutor for her two younger sons, and her choice could hardly have been more unfortunate. General Lamsdorff was a passionately convinced militarist. He trained the little Grand-Dukes for the barracks, the parade ground and the manoeuvre field, and he certainly made an exceptional horseman of Nicholas. Some other tutors were invited to work under Lamsdorff's direction but, languages apart, Nicholas reached his mid-teens with his mind more meagrely furnished than that of an eight-year-old boy.

Nearly twenty years lay between him and his eldest brother, Alexander I. The heir-presumptive, Grand-Duke Constantine, had long since been trying to divorce his wife, Grand-Duchess Anna, who had deserted him soon after Paul I's murder. It was an open secret in the family and at court that, since the Emperor had no children and Constantine's matrimonial tangles – apart from his determination never to reign – would eventually be a bar to his accession, there was no one else to succeed except Nicholas. Yet nobody seems to have considered the task of teaching the boy even the rudiments of statesmanship.

His first journey abroad should have added to his education. He travelled through the states of Germany, Switzerland and the whole of eastern France. Neither people nor nature, still less any historical monuments, made the least impression on the young Grand-Duke. Parades, manoeuvres, foreign uniforms, discipline and horsemanship – nothing else attracted him. His father certainly would have been pleased, but even General Lamsdorff, for all he was a dedicated soldier, was slightly surprised.

Nicholas's return to Russia, however, was broken by a brief romantic interlude. At Potsdam he found himself betrothed to the beautiful Princess Charlotte of Prussia, Queen Louise's daughter, the Emperor Alexander having arranged the alliance and the Dowager Empress having warmly approved it. For all the formalities leading up to the engagement, it proved a genuine love match. Charlotte was swept off her feet by Nicholas's physical beauty.

'The most handsome prince in Europe,' they said in Prussia, and it was not flattery. Nicholas was certainly the best-looking Romanov of his generation, and he would bequeath his looks to all the male members of the dynasty who came after him. Tall and splendidly made, with a sculptured head and a most exquisite profile, Nicholas certainly inherited his mother's looks. He appeared at his best in the family circle, always gay, easy-going, courteous as a Frenchman at the court of Louis XV. '*Mon chevalier si bien aimé,*' his enraptured fiancée called him. But, once away from the intimacies of the palace, the Grand-Duke became a different man, no light or laughter in his blue-grey eyes which looked 'cold and leaden', his mouth pursed, his manner abrupt and arrogant.

It was common knowledge that all the officers and men under his command hated him for his rigidity, harshness, cruelty and meanness. However well trained in military discipline, Nicholas was not above making an occasional mistake, but those mistakes were never brought to his own door: always some junior officer would have to bear the blame. The Grand-Duke, perfectly aware of it, accepted it all without comment. His own mother had once hoped that soldiering would not make that favourite son of hers, 'my handsome Niki', either brutal or harsh. The Dowager Empress's hopes were not answered. When on duty, Nicholas was every inch his father's son. Alexander's charm with the men was never his and he lacked the salty humour of his brother Constantine. It was said that Nicholas could not see a joke even when its point was explained to him twice over.

As early as 1817 people in Russia and abroad referred to him as the future ruler of the Empire. His own brother-in-law and closest friend, Prince Frederick-William of Prussia, seems to have known of Alexander's plans for the succession. In the spring of 1818, after the birth of her first child, Grand-Duchess Alexandra, as Princess Charlotte was called after her marriage, wrote of the baby in her diary: 'How sad to think that this helpless little infant will one day be the Emperor of Russia. . . .' In 1819 Alexander I broached the possibility of his own abdication to Nicholas and his wife, and mentioned that he meant his younger brother to succeed him. Less than two years later Grand-Duke Constantine's divorce of Grand-Duchess Anna and his subsequent marriage to his Polish mistress made it obvious to anyone at all enlightened about Russian conditions that he would never reign. It is true that the official manifesto, naming Nicholas as the heir, was kept secret from all but a very few, but those standing closest to Alexander, including his mother and his wife, knew all about his intentions. In a letter to the Margravine of Baden, the Empress Elizabeth spoke of Nicholas as having but one idea in his head – '*celle de régner*'.

And yet when the crucial moment arrived, Nicholas behaved as though he knew nothing at all of Alexander's intentions. Two reasons may be offered to explain his otherwise inexplicable behaviour. In the first place, it flattered his vanity to be able to speak 'of the most honourable action in my life', i.e. his refusal to accept Constantine's refusal of the crown. Secondly, and this author thinks much more importantly, Nicholas's behaviour was moulded by his fear of a possible hostile reaction. For all his several limitations, he was no fool. In 1825 the nation at large did not know him at all. The army knew him only too well and hated him, and Constantine's popularity stood high in military circles.

All through those critical days in December 1825, Nicholas's patently contrived self-effacement was most carefully calculated, his eye very much on the mood of the army. At the time, he did not seem to know anything about the two secret societies. Indeed, it cannot be said that he knew much about conditions in the interior of the Empire. He had passed his twenty-ninth birthday, his world still encompassed by the family and by his military duties.

They were all in the Palace chapel when the courier arrived with the news of Alexander I's death at Taganrog. The Empress Marie fainted. Nicholas lost his head. Leaving his mother and wife to the care of their ladies, he hurried up the altar steps, made a priest bring out a cross and a book of the Gospels, and then and there swore allegiance to Constantine, compelling all the other men present to do the same. But his mother recovered from her faint rather rapidly, and her first words lent a well-nigh burlesque colour to the moment: 'Niki, what have you done? You knew you were our angel's heir. . . .'

But, that most solemn of all oaths once taken, it was too late for Nicholas to speak the truth, and he took refuge in a spate of ambiguities. He had no absolutely clear idea of Alexander's intentions and nothing at all had been made public. Nicholas kept repeating that the crown belonged to Constantine 'unless my brother chooses to abdicate', a statement soon to be shattered by Constantine's letter to St Petersburg in which he said that, having never been Emperor, the question of his abdication could not arise.

Nicholas, having ordered all the administrative bodies to swear allegiance to his brother, now declared that 'all the other matters' must wait till his brother's arrival from Warsaw. 'I expect him to leave Poland at once.' But there was nothing for Constantine to do in St Petersburg, and he never left Warsaw. Again at Nicholas's feverishly given orders, all the state papers were sent to Warsaw, the sealed envelopes addressed to 'His Imperial Majesty', but the couriers returned to St Petersburg, the packets unopened. Clergy in the capital received hurriedly printed sheets of liturgical changes in the prayers for 'their right sovereign Lord and Emperor Constantine', but 'the right sovereign Lord' kept saying that the crown could never be his. In the meantime, the very few who had knowledge of Alexander's intentions kept silent for reasons best known to themselves.

Constantine's letters to his mother and to Nicholas are rather pleasant to read in that they offer the only sensible evidence of those clouded three weeks. Those letters were brief, straightforward and strictly factual. His divorce and subsequent marriage to a commoner put the sceptre out of his reach, he said. His late brother's plans were quite clear. 'Let us get away from fantasies and come down to facts,' said Constantine, but Nicholas was in no mood to accept facts, however incontrovertible they were. A hysterical element crept into his replies. In justice to him, it should be noted that at the time Nicholas could not have known what he was letting loose upon the country.

The tragic muddle by him created lasted for three weeks.

The horrors of the December mutiny cannot wholly be laid at Nicholas's door. None the less, he must bear a large share of the responsibility. Whilst weary couriers kept galloping between St Petersburg and Warsaw and back again, all kinds of fantastic rumours came to their flowering in the capital. Alexander I was not dead, said some. He had either abdicated or been kidnapped by the Turks. Other variants had it that Alexander was dead and Constantine poisoned. The feverish mood spread all over the city until herring-women and pedlars of rags asserted that there was no Tsar in Russia and that the end of the world was certainly round the corner.

At last, after three weeks of a perfectly unnecessary interregnum, Nicholas went to a meeting of the Council of State. His eyes sombre and leaden, his voice robbed of all colour and warmth, he declared himself 'forced' to accept the crown because of his brother's repeated refusals to reign.

By the end of the third week of the interregnum, Nicholas had learned of 'a serious conspiracy', and he convinced himself – and that not without reason – that his life was in danger. Later in the same day, addressing an assembly of Guards officers, Nicholas announced that '. . . should I be emperor for one hour only, I shall prove myself worthy of the honour' – words which in the circumstances revealed a braggart's vanity rather than the Romanov pride of race. In the morning of 14th December the Senate and all other administrative bodies swore their allegiance to him, and Nicholas wrote to one of his sisters that he looked upon himself as 'a victim of God's will and Constantine's. He has refused the allegiance I owe to him and, being his subject, I must obey' – thus adding still another lie to all the others since Constantine had not been his sovereign even for the space of an hour.

All that time members of the Northern Secret Society had not been idle, though their activities lacked cohesion. In broad terms, they relied on Nicholas's unpopularity with the army and they meant to proclaim a National Assembly. The conspirators were all fiery and determined, most of them young. The goal they were striving for was a splendour indeed, but leadership was lamentably absent among them, nor did they see that they had fixed their eyes upon noontide long before the breaking of dawn. A few of them knew, however, that their chances of success were indeed thin. Ryleev, the poet, ended the last meeting with the words: 'If we fail, our very failure will certainly inspire those who come after us.'

The revolt broke out later that very morning of 14th December, several of the regiments stationed in the capital refusing to swear allegiance to Nicholas and clamouring for Constantine.

Now, with the breath of a grave crisis in his face, Nicholas proved his courage. 'His eyes colder than ice,' he left the Winter Palace and made for Senate Square there to face an enormous crowd of soldiers and civilians. Unhurriedly, he gave orders for the deployment of such regiments as had remained loyal, and then addressed the crowd more than once, telling them to disperse and not to listen to mischief-mongers. They listened to him in grim silence. They did not disperse.

General Miloradovich, one of the 1812 heroes, had already been killed by the insurgents, and Nicholas's own life was certainly imperilled. Those hours on Senate Square, when he rode up and down as unconcerned as though he were on a parade ground, turned a braggart's boast into a proud man's truth. Had he been killed that morning, he would have died with his honour unsmirched.

The shot which brought down General Miloradovich had been an earlier and isolated incident. The brief winter day was drawing to its close before Nicholas allowed the loyal artillery to come into action. The very first shots resulted in a complete rout of the rebels and the onlookers together. Two cavalry units chased them right across the Neva. The angrily crimson sun set over a shaken city, and the exact number of victims was never made public. 14th December 1825 graved a landmark in Russian history: for the first time a sovereign and the spirit of revolution had met face to face.

Still apparently unshaken, the Emperor wheeled his horse round and rode back to the Winter Palace. Those who knew him best could see that the stony courage displayed on Senate Square had not followed him home. The jerky movements, the nervous speech, the spurts of flaming anger when some of his orders were not instantly understood, and a twitching eyelid, all spoke of fear. For something like a couple of hours Nicholas resembled his father, Paul I. He kept telling everybody that the danger remained and that it was for him to grind it to dust.

He proceeded to do so the same evening. His wife's pleas did not persuade him to go to bed that night. Nicholas spent its hours personally interrogating the prisoners, brought to the Winter Palace at his command. His mood kept changing from calmness to fury, from curiosity to contempt, from paternal benevolence to a jailer's cruelty. Nicholas never knew that he was committing the first major blunder of his reign; such an interrogation should never have been carried out by the monarch.

Having begun, he could not stop, and was absorbed in the business for several weeks. It ended by leaving a disastrous sediment in his mind. The majority of the men brought into his presence, all tattered, handcuffed and bearing signs of having already been manhandled by the soldiery, came from the highest families of the Empire. The method Nicholas employed during the interrogation would lead to a cleavage between him and the only social stratum he knew, a cleavage which would create awkward and painful repercussions all through his reign. In 1825 there was nothing to assure Nicholas that the masses he did not know would presently come to love him.

Not until June 1826 did a specially convened military court pronounce sentences on a shamefully prejudged case. Five of the conspirators were condemned to death. The rest, their number running into three figures, were sent to lifelong penal servitude in Siberia. At the time there was no hangman in Russia, and it was necessary to import one from abroad. The man came from Sweden. His Russian assistants had not had the time to learn their job: the ropes broke, and the victims' agony was prolonged most cruelly.

The sentences shook the Empire and revolted the West. Yet in the final reckoning Nicholas must be acquitted of the charge of wanton inhumanity. Foreign newspapers compared him with Caligula, Nero, Louis XI and Ivan the Terrible. Yet what other choice was there before Nicholas? None among the Decembrists could have led the Empire towards freedom. The ideals they believed in were based on all they had seen in the West after 1812 and on dry academic studies. Such ideals would have said nothing to the peasant, but the unceasing hardships of his yearly round certainly predisposed him to rebellion. He would fight 'for his rights' without even a glimmer of any idea about those rights, all because his distrust and hatred of uniformed authority came from a centuries-old bourne. The Decembrists had certainly done some work among the military. They had never tried to approach the masses.

Had that mutiny been allowed to spread into the countryside, the consequences might well have equalled, if not surpassed, the horrors of the Pougachev revolt in the eighteenth century. The peasants had all but worshipped 'The Blessed One'. His younger brother was not even a name to many of them in 1825.

Nicholas was an affectionate son, a devoted husband and father, and a conscientious soldier. Of the intricacies of governing he knew nothing. He came to the throne in a hardly propitious manner. All the more can one wonder that his very first administrative measures should have assured the nation of brighter days to come.

Yet such proved the case. The summary dismissal of 'the tyrant Arakcheev' and the subsequent closure of his concentration camps, known as 'military settlements', heartened all the liberal-minded people in the Empire and disturbed the reactionaries. Men like Magnitzky and Runich, whose educational 'reforms' had led to a mental stagnation in schools and colleges, were likewise relieved of their posts. Speransky was recalled from his thirteen years' exile, the young Emperor telling him that juridical reforms were the most urgent business of the day. Pushkin's exile, too, came to an end. 'I need you,' Nicholas said to him. 'A poet is the Empire's best ambassador, and I beg you not to trouble about censorship. I, your Tsar, shall be your censor.'

It seemed indeed a dawn of promise, and Nicholas's personal dedication to the task spoke well for the future. Up sometimes before dawn, he spent hours mastering the business of governing. Diplomats accredited to his court were enchanted by his courtesy, his simplicity and his obvious desire to stand well with the Great Powers. His family life stood beyond reproach. After eight years of marriage, he and his wife were still bridegroom and bride to each other. People were not quite so sure of the young Empress. She was distant and haughty and, for all her prowess in the native tongue, Alexandra remained very much a tight-lipped and buttoned-up German, and nobody had very much use for anyone from Prussia. Still, she was known to be a good wife and mother, and it seemed pleasant to observe the warm relations between her and the Dowager-Empress.

Yet, even through that first apparently unclouded period, Nicholas was unable to conceal the tyrant in him. Shockingly educated and intellectually limited, he could not understand autocracy except in its literal sense. 'I cannot permit anyone to defy my wishes once they are made known,' was one of his early utterances at a meeting of the Council of State. 'Since I am autocrat (*'samodér-zhetz'*), my will is law,' he said on another occasion, all unaware that he was but echoing the words once spoken by his father.

And soon enough the country became acquainted with other evidences of Nicholas's affinity with Paul I. Embodied in official documents, those evidences resulted in endless irritations up and down the bureaucratic ladder. The Emperor declared it to be his wish that all civil servants, professors and university students should wear a uniform 'designed by authority'. All civil servants, whatever their rank, must be clean-shaven. Beards were permitted only to clergy, merchants and peasants. The army were ordered to shave their chins and to wear moustaches, which had to be black – dye was used when necessary. All of it irritated a good many people. It also led to much mockery. 'I have decided to open a shoe-shop on the Nevsky,' laughed a university professor, 'and safeguard my beard.' The minor clerks in the civil service were worried whether the cost of newly decreed uniforms could be met out of their meagre pay. 'The coat must have a velvet collar,' they complained, 'and velvet cannot be bought for a copper.' Then they remembered the unceasing flow of palm-oil, and took heart.

Peculation grew and spread faster than weeds in a neglected garden. The government fought it but half-heartedly since graft in one form or another had taken deep roots throughout the entire administration. The Emperor did not forget the civil service but his chief absorption was with the army. Hours and hours of his working day were devoted to studying reports from the War Ministry and from heads of regiments. To Nicholas, that pattern looked gratefully clear. It had no ambiguities and made few demands on his thinking faculties. Orders were given and were obeyed. There was no more to it. Authority followed by instant obedience meant perfection. Again all military exercises gave Nicholas intense personal pleasure and caressed his vanity. He knew he looked his best on horseback and he also knew that his best was excellent indeed.

There were occasions when some instinct within him told Nicholas that his vanity should be reined in. But modesty proved a very hard virtue to master and often enough vanity refused to be bridled.

'I have an example to follow in Peter the Great', the Tsar would say to ministers and to diplomats, and such imperial remarks could not be received with a derisive smile.

The first Emperor of the dynasty rode his immense bronze horse in the middle of Senate Square. That gigantic monument, raised to the first Peter by the second Catherine (*Petro Primo-Caterina Secunda*, ran the brief inscription), was at once inspiration and anxiety to Nicholas. Peter's was not an example to emulate, still less to surpass, except by a greater giant. 'But I must surpass it, and I can,' Nicholas said to himself. From the windows of his study he could see the magnificent waterfront girdled by Finnish granite. The first Peter had created his capital out of a gloomy swamp and had laboured hard to win an outlet to the sea. The freedom of the Baltic and of the Black Sea now belonged to Russia, but the Black Sea waters ran into the Bosphorus, a barrier even Catherine the Great could not conquer. Whenever Nicholas thought of her Turkish campaigns, a great name kept teasing him, the name of Chesmé Bay on that summer day in 1769 when the sun set on a total destruction of the Turkish navy.

'And what of my own ships?' the Emperor asked himself.

There was little enough to please him about the navy. Naval matters had been neglected for several years. At Nicholas's orders, heightened activity began throbbing in the shipyards. So many keels were laid that Europe had cause to feel disturbed. What plans were being made by the young Emperor? Most certainly he was no dreamer as his elder brother had been. Was he getting ready to follow in his grandmother's steps and threaten Turkey again so as to win his way through the Straits and fulfil her own unfulfilled hopes? Nobody could tell, and the young Emperor, his manner more suave than ever, kept assuring the diplomats that he meant his country to stay at peace for many years. At the very threshold of his reign Nicholas was certainly sincere in his protestations.

But circumstances he could not control made pitiful dust of such intentions. The Persian invasion of the Caucasus in 1826 led to the first military clash of the reign. That war, however, would never have lasted for a whole year if the Russian military potential had not been suffering from an incredible lack of synchronization. All the difficulties and setbacks of that campaign, even though it ended most advantageously for the Empire, should have proved to Nicholas that the spirit which had once repulsed Napoleon was now little more than a memory. On the contrary, the felicitous ending of the Persian adventure spurred him on. When the Sultan's government showed themselves intransigent about various litigious matters, Nicholas replied by sending his army to occupy the Danubian Principalities. In spite of the limping commissariat, epidemics and constant dissensions among the generals, the Russians kept advancing, reached Varna, took it, and laid siege to Adrianople. With the fall of the latter, the way to Constantinople lay open. Turkey asked for a truce, and to the grief of his generals, Nicholas agreed.

'I wish for no further conquests,' he told King George's ambassador.

All through the winter of 1829–30, gaiety trod a heightened measure in Russia. Balls, routs and concerts succeeded one another in both capitals. Even in the deep country peasants spent their scant leisure in merry-making, so glad did everybody feel that a war which might have ended disastrously had brought such a triumph. 'I like my people to amuse themselves,' remarked the Emperor. 'It certainly keeps them out of mischief.' He made one or two journeys into the interior, and was received with tumultuous cheers everywhere. 'What a happy nation!' Nicholas observed blandly to an equerry.

Public opinion certainly shared his view that quieter days lay ahead. A grave conspiracy had been quelled, two wars had ended victoriously, men like Speransky were working at the most urgent reforms, and the hateful Arakcheev no longer darkened the national landscape. Grand-Duke Constantine, still Viceroy of Russian Poland, kept peace in Warsaw where everybody seemed satisfied with the privileges granted by Alexander I – the Diet, the Constitution, the army and so forth. St Petersburg and Moscow went on dancing until the coming of Lent in 1830 put the customary stop to all merry-making.

Neither the Emperor nor his government and certainly not the public at large knew much about the real conditions in Russian Poland. They did not know that the Viceroy was absorbed in army matters to the exclusion of all other problems. The greatly vaunted Constitution granted by Alexander I was hardly observed. The activities of the Diet were hedged about by numberless restrictions, particularly in the field of education. On the very rare occasions when Grand-Duke Constantine remembered the existence of the Diet, he mocked at its 'posturings'. Pilgrimages to national shrines were either banned altogether or else subjected to rigorous police surveillance. The mere appearance of a Russian official in any Polish village would sometimes drive the inhabitants into the neighbouring woods. Taxation was turning the well-to-do into paupers.

When a report on those conditions was sent to the Emperor by General Benckendorff, Nicholas refused to believe it. 'My brother tells me nothing of such things and I trust him.' His own feeling towards the Poles was profoundly contemptuous. Poland had asked for all the calamities fallen on her in the past, he argued, thus dissociating himself from his two predecessors.

The police remained on watch. But they were not vigilant enough. Nobody in the imperial administration knew about the slowly swelling ranks of 'Patriots'. The July Revolution – however vicariously – provided them with a chance to stand up in an effort to win back all the forfeited liberties.

The accession of Louis-Philippe infuriated Nicholas. 'I suppose the French felt they had to be rid of Charles X, but the Duc de Bordeaux should have succeeded his father. France has violated the dynastic principle,' he kept telling everybody. Soon enough Europe had the first glimpse of Nicholas's 'policeman' mind. When the first breath of revolt reached the Netherlands, he told Grand-Duke Constantine to organize an immediate conscription in Poland, the recruits to be sent into the Low Countries to help quell the rebellion. At once, the 'Patriots' came out in Warsaw and declared their refusal to trample anyone's liberty underfoot. Within a few days, the Viceroy had to go into hiding. The 'Patriots', having killed a number of the most hated Russian officials, proceeded to muster adherents all over the country. By early October 1830 the whole of Russian Poland was up in arms against the Empire, and the whereabouts of the Viceroy were not known.

In public the Emperor remained unperturbed, but his orders to General Diebitch revealed the measure of his panic. Diebitch was instructed to lay siege to Warsaw 'even if the rebels are not there . . . let famine take its course. . . .' There was no accurate information about the mutineers' forces, but eighty thousand men were to go into Poland. In December, the Diet declared Nicholas to be 'an usurper of the Polish crown', proclaimed independence, and established a republic with Prince Adam Czartorizsky as president. Each new report angered Nicholas more and more, and Diebitch's tactics proved lamentably dilatory. Not until 1831 did he cross the Polish frontier, having repeatedly assured his sovereign that 'the whole matter would not take more than a few weeks to settle'.

He had eighty thousand men under him. The Patriots scarcely numbered fifty thousand, but they fought not merely at their commanders' orders but at the compulsion of their hearts. Diebitch's army was thrown back again and again, and he kept retreating until cholera claimed him at the very height of summer, the rebellion raging more furiously than before. In his turn, Grand-Duke Constantine died of cholera, in a peasant hut, forsaken by all except his wife. Nicholas, out of conceit with Diebitch, was not particularly grieved at his death. The Grand-Duke became 'a martyr to the sacred cause of authority', though Constantine's share in quelling the revolt was not very remarkable. His flight from Warsaw was officially explained as 'an expediency'. General Paskiewicz was commanded to go and rally the demoralized Russian forces.

All in all, it proved a long and bloody business, its rights and wrongs so tangled up that no outsider could gauge them. Europe, remembering the December days of 1825, watched narrowly. There was much indignation in England and French monies were known to be smuggled into the rebels' camp. Austria and Prussia, both actuated by anxiety for their own Polish possessions, alone approved Nicholas's policy.

Unluckily for Poland, the Patriot leaders lacked solidarity; men and funds were wantonly wasted, plans were made and dropped on the spur of the moment, and the rank and file of the mutineers began losing heart. Paskiewicz stormed his way into Warsaw in December 1831.

Nicholas's vengeance fell on the guilty and the innocent alike. In the opinion of Europe, seldom if ever had a victor been so inhuman towards the vanquished. Within a couple of months not only were all the Polish privileges forfeited but the last traces of the national identity were wiped out. Paskiewicz and his fellow-commanders did not sit in judgment: they pronounced sentences, and gallows became a familiar feature of the Polish landscape. Monasteries and convents, schools and colleges were closed. The use of Polish was banned. The least important administrative post was now occupied by a Russian. Those Poles whose lives were spared went in their thousands to work in the Siberian mines.

Yet in the end Nicholas's vengeance proved a boomerang. Great numbers of Poles, having escaped both the hangman and Siberia, found refuge, comfort and means of sustenance abroad. From now on, the Emperor would hold those émigrés responsible for every setback his policy suffered. The blood spilled so freely by Paskiewicz alienated Britain and France. Angry with the European reaction, Nicholas maintained that he was being misjudged by those who knew nothing of history. But he should have remembered his own father's views about the iniquity of Polish partitions, and the complaint about the foreign ignorance of Russian history lost all weight when Nicholas began reiterating that Lithuania had always been 'an inalienable possession of Russia'.

The turmoil was over. His conscience untroubled by any phantoms, the Emperor felt that he could devote himself again to home matters.

He and indolence never spoke to each other. At the Winter Palace, surrounded by the oriental splendour of state apartments, the Emperor would leave his straw pallet and leather pillow, have a cold tub, and settle down at his desk long before anyone else began stirring under that roof. He called illness 'an indulgence best left to women' and mere indisposition was nonsense to him. Abstemious in food and drink, Nicholas never wasted time at table. For recreative occasions he liked paying surprise visits to various ministries and institutions where an unshaven chin, the wrong cut of a collar, or a disorderly scatter of papers on a desk caused imperial anger to break over the culprit's head.

None the less 'the Northern Nero' had moments of warmth when he would pay a widow's debts, give a dowry to a priest's daughter, or enable an obscure civil servant, stricken by tuberculosis, to go for treatment to some German spa. An inpoverished landowner once petitioned him to grant free education to his son. The man, having spent his whole life among woods and fields, had no idea how to begin such a petition but, having heard of the Tsar being called 'August sovereign', he decided that, as he was writing in the autumn, he must begin by 'September Sovereign'. Nicholas's marginal comment ran: 'Have the boy admitted into the Artillery School, otherwise he may become as much of a fool as his father is.' In 1833, a Polish rebel was arrested after two years spent in hiding. The man's wife petitioned the Emperor for clemency. He marked the letter with three terse words: 'Pardon impossible, execute'. (*Prostít nielziá, kaznít'*), and misplaced the comma. When the Minister of Justice drew his attention to it, Nicholas stared at the paper and sighed. 'Yes, I meant the man to be hanged. But the mistake is mine and I must abide by it. Let him go free.'

After a day's labours, a rout or some such function meant an effort to him. He preferred to belong to his family in the evenings, and then Nicholas was at his best, relaxing in an armchair in his wife's drawing-room, ready to listen to music or to his children's daily chronicles, or even to admire the Empress's embroidery. She, who worshipped him, remained a Prussian princess all her life. Her memory was like a drawer which must be frequently pulled out. She never forgot the humiliations undergone at the hands of the French in her youth, and would not allow the language to be spoken in her presence. She remained virtually unknown to the masses. What little individuality she may have had was wholly sunk in her husband's. Were Nicholas to tell her that two and two made five, Alexandra would not have questioned it. In her eyes, he stood as '*un chevalier sans peur et sans reproche*'. His least decision was endorsed by her immediately. In her native Prussia, her menfolk smoked pipes incessantly. Nicholas hated tobacco. Smoking was forbidden not only at the palace but even in the streets.

'It is such a dirty habit and has such a vile smell,' Alexandra would say, curling her upper lip, 'and it is an indulgence of the lower classes'. Nobody would have dared to remind her that her own royal father had been addicted to the 'dirty habit' all his life.

The Empress never interfered with state matters. She bore seven children and did not neglect them. Beautiful and haughty, she faithfully discharged her duties within the orbit of the court. She never learned much about the great Empire ruled by her husband, nor did he expect her to do so. Sincerely devoted to her and loving the faithful echo that she became, Nicholas could not be called an ideal husband, and his feeling for Alexandra began getting frayed some time before his relations with Prussia came to a straining point. Indulgent enough with his daughters, Nicholas was stern with his sons. A personality like his could not shed despotism even within the family circle, and the soldier in him hardly slumbered at all.

The leaden drifts of the reign considered, the Emperor's unquestioned popularity with the masses is a matter for wonder. His looks, his voice, his appearance, all meant magic to the common folk. His courage made them feel as though they were sheltered by a rock. When a cholera epidemic smote St Petersburg, a mutiny broke out. A mob, imagining that doctors and nurses were responsible for the spread of the scourge, rushed to the Obukhov Hospital, murdered a few of them, and wrecked several chemists' shops for 'poisoning their victims with the Devil's concoctions'. Without the least escort, Nicholas ordered his coachman to drive him in an open carriage to the great Sennaya Square and there faced a savage crowd just about to rush to another hospital. Standing up in the carriage, the Emperor wasted no time on a laboured speech. His few words scourged them into shame, and within a few instants the savage mob became a crowd on their knees.

There were many other occasions away from the capital when the common folk would be magnetized both by the man himself and by all he stood for. Nicholas could allay their anxieties by telling them that all would go well if they did what he told them to do. He had the power to make them aware that he, their Tsar, and they stood together within a vastly important national idea. He certainly invited both hatred and contempt, but neither came from the masses.

Meanwhile, St. Petersburg was stirred by many whispers about imperial '*affaires*'. There were innumerable stories, and some won credence because the Empress was known to be 'cold'. Nicholas's surprise visits to girls' boarding schools and to the Imperial Ballet School certainly yielded material for gossip-mongers, but he was neither an Alexander I nor a Paul I and never dragged any adventures into daylight. Fire as well as marble and ice formed part of his personality, and he may well have had liaisons of which no record has survived, but only two names were definitely linked with his. The rest was gossamer gossip all the more unfounded when it is remembered that Nicholas had no time for idle philandering.

When he looked at Europe, he realized that, with the exception of Prussia and Austria, no other country shared his views, and he was often at a loss about his own diplomacy. He never learned statesmanship thoroughly and the lacunae in his education remained evident to the end. In Nicholas's mind, whatever could not be simplified was *ipso facto* subversive, and alien to his own needs and those of his Empire. Here, Nicholas's vanity proved disastrous: he considered his own judgments infallible, and to his dying day he could not grasp the true nature of an argument. Nor did he ever realize that he, an autocrat 'by the grace of God', was in pitiful reality slave of a bureaucracy, the logical consequence of absolute power.

Under him, that bureaucracy was rotten all through. Saltykov's *History of a City* did not exaggerate the sombre colours of provincial administration where influences and bribes rather than ability led to promotion and promotion paved the road to tyranny. On the lower administrative levels, salaries were meagre, and the least important clerk soon learned to consider his post as a gate into the delectable garden of graft. Even verdicts in provincial courts were governed by a discreet use of palm-oil.

No less than his predecessors, Nicholas knew of the evil web. No less than they, he fought it all through his reign but, infinitely less far-sighted than, say, Peter the Great or Catherine, Nicholas refused to see it as a losing fight, and not even Speransky was permitted the luxury of arguing with the sovereign. Moreover, Speransky, Kankrin and Bludov were the only ministers of intellect and vision during the whole of Nicholas's reign. The rest were pallid mediocrities appointed to administer the will of a crowned mediocrity.

Under Alexander I some attempt had been made to find a way towards emancipation. Nicholas began trying to fight serfdom in 1833 when peasant risings leapt to a disturbing peak. He chose an avowed liberal, Count Kisselev, to prepare a draft of the emancipation programme, and the work took nine years. But at least on three occasions, lack of support among the landowners brought matters to a bleak stalemate, and in the end the Emperor lost heart. He pretended that the country was not ready for such a step, but to one or two intimates he admitted defeat 'because of the untoward circumstances'. In plainer language, aristocracy and bureaucracy between them proved stronger than the sovereign's will.

Nesselrode, a man of peace, was his Prime Minister, but Nicholas's own views did not always run along the same course. Early on in his reign he is supposed to have said to an ambassador that he had no intentions of interfering either in Spain or in Portugal but that Turkey was pre-eminently his business. That, Nicholas maintained, formed part of his heritage. His first steps in that direction were prudent enough to astonish Europe. He checked his army's advance to Constantinople and declared that he had no intention of incorporating the Danubian Principalities into the Empire – and Turkey, for all she was defeated, felt gratified. The Emperor went even further. When in 1833 trouble broke out between Turkey and Egypt, he promptly answered the Sultan's appeal for help. Little by little, such cordiality came to be woven between two ancient enemies that the Black Sea, according to Nicholas, became 'one of our lakes', an incautious remark unlikely to please either London or Paris.

The Emperor was convinced that every hostile breath from the West was inspired by the intrigues of the Polish émigrés. Moreover, even old enmities did not grow pale in his memory. One year it gave him pleasure to celebrate the Borodino anniversary by issuing a most provocative manifesto which spoke about the triumph 'over the insolent enemy hordes'. Nicholas must have forgotten his brother's words that the quarrel had been with Napoleon alone and not with the French nation. Those occasional excursions into unmannerly burlesque were rather reminiscent of the days of Peter III and Paul I.

And Nicholas proved sadly inconsistent. He provoked one country after another and he kept wooing them all in turn. He needed allies for a scheme he had nursed since his accession, and what allies had he? He stood bound to Prussia by former treaties and by family ties, but Prussia was weak and lukewarm, her policy often disenchanting. There was Austria where something of an accord came to be shaped, but even Nicholas's poor statesmanship was enough to make him see that Metternich's ideas of treaties were such that any advantages born of a signature were rather like a peeled apple, the whole of the fruit falling to Austria's share, the peel alone reaching the ally. 'I always remember sulphur and brimstone when I have dealings with Metternich,' Nicholas once said to his wife.

There was also England for him to woo. In 1839 Nicholas sent his eldest son there and incurred Vienna's sharp displeasure by so doing. The plan of a dismemberment of Turkey had begun creeping into secret dispatches from St Petersburg. 'The guardianship of the Bosphorus to be mine, and the Dardanelles had best be British,' decided the Emperor, but the idea perforce accepted by his cabinet would hardly have been welcomed in a country like England where public opinion remained stonily hostile to Russia.

So in 1844 the Emperor went himself to England. Socially he proved a great success. The drawing-rooms in London were enchanted by his looks, his courtesy, his gallantry. Not so Queen Victoria, whose relief at the Emperor's departure found outlet in her letters to the King of the Belgians. '. . . the expression of the eyes is formidable. . . . He gives the impression of a man who is not happy, and on whom the weight of his power . . . weighs heavily and painfully. . . . He seldom smiles. . . .' Melbourne stressed the importance of the visit, but Nicholas's allusions 'to the coming death of Turkey' met with non-committal replies. Not content to talk to the Queen's ministers, Nicholas discussed his 'plan' with the leaders of the Opposition, who thought among themselves that it was all 'humbug'.

Four years later, with revolutionary thunders all over the skies of Europe, the Emperor found himself in an isolation he had scarcely expected. The Austrian alliance suggested a frayed piece of string. King Frederick-William IV of Prussia became a stranger because of his flirtation with constitutional ideas. The greatly desired rapprochement with Westminster was shrivelled in the bud, and Nicholas's comments on European events deepened the general mistrust of his policy. In blunt language he declared that the governments had brought the trouble upon themselves by their flirtation with liberal ideas. 'That danger will never knock at my door.'

In crude reality, the first crashes of 1848 terrified the Emperor, and the immediate measures decreed by him go far to reveal the extent of his panic. In April 1848 a Super Censorship Department was established in St Petersburg, and the iron gauntlet of police surveillance was clamped down on all schools and colleges. Professors lost their chairs – and sometimes their liberty as well – for reading prohibited books and lecturing on 'subversive' subjects, philosophy being considered one such. Works of Pushkin, Lermontov, Gogol and Turgenev vanished from bookshops, and foreign travel was forbidden. At the conclusion of the Petrashevsky case, twenty-one men, Dostoevsky among them, were condemned to death, to be reprieved at the foot of the gallows – one of the macabre gestures Nicholas sometimes delighted in. The men's guilt consisted in having read and discussed Saint-Simon, Schelling and a prohibited pamphlet by the critic Bielinsky. The reprieve did not restore liberty: the twenty-one were sent for life to the Siberian mines and they remained there until the amnesty granted by Nicholas's successor in 1855.

Obduracy and stupidity together prevented the Emperor from admitting how far his own Empire had travelled since 1825. Its working class had nearly trebled. It possessed a few railways and quite a number of roads. It had penetrated deeper and deeper into Central Asia and maintained a thriving trade with China. Its finances, ably directed by Kankrin, were healthier than ever before. And finally, and most importantly, the best minds in Russia had met their compeers in the West and been nourished on the ideas and hopes which were Europe's daily bread at the time. The all but cindered framework of officially approved education had ceased to satisfy. And Nicholas understood none of it.

In spite of the tightened censorship, in spite of Benckendorff and the strangling activities of the Third Department – so vilely recalling the days of the Empress Anna – it was a new Russia where ever-increasing numbers of people held that independent thought was as essential as breathing. The wonderful evidences of that sturdy newness were there in abundance, but Nicholas saw it all through curiously tinted glasses. His reign saw the birth of great Russian music and the flowering of the national literature. The Moscow University led the way in encouraging deeper studies of humanities as distinct from the frozen curriculum of the Ministry. The gag of censorship and the ban on foreign travel were belated and futile gestures. The mind of the nation would never again fall into deep slumbers. But university students were 'loathsome scum' to Nicholas, who, himself standing still, did not see why anyone should want to walk, let alone run.

And Europe to him was just a map of alliances and counter-alliances. There were also 'nurseries' and 'schoolrooms' where books were read and poetry and music written and where people talked about themes divorced from politics and war. That Europe was of no importance to the Emperor of Russia.

Revolutionary outbursts did not stir him into action until he learned that Polish help was being secretly accorded to the Hungarian rebels. Then he sent Paskiewicz to Austria's aid. The rebellion was crushed by the autumn of 1849.

A multitude of petty ecclesiastical dissensions formed a nebulous enough background to the Crimean affair, though Nicholas preferred to insist that the intrigues of the Polish émigrés had penetrated into Holy Land. In honest truth, the quarrels in Palestine accorded rather well with his own secret intention. Because by 1852 Nicholas was wholly possessed by a dream. Some of it was shaped by his desire to imitate Catherine the Great. Some of it recalled Paul I's oddly coiled foreign policy. Within that dream Nicholas convinced himself that he was not actuated by any selfish urges. Within that dream, therefore, the independence of the Balkan Peninsula – sharply divorced from Russian interests – became a *sine qua non* for the European equilibrium. Everybody professing the Christian faith must be freed from the Muslim yoke. The ultimate goal of it all lay in Nicholas's scheme to erase the name of Turkey from the European map. The embryo of some such project was communicated to the Great Powers and found no response anywhere. In 1853 Menshikov was sent on a mission to the Sultan. Ordered by Nicholas to confront the Sultan with a virtual ultimatum, Menshikov left Turkey to report his failure. A few months later, whilst the Emperor kept assuring Victoria's ambassador of his unfailingly peaceful intentions, he ordered his armies to occupy Moldavia and Wallachia. When Turkey demanded the immediate evacuation of the Principalities, the Emperor rather belatedly declared war, and in November a Turkish squadron was destroyed off Sinope. Great Britain and France went to the Sultan's aid.

'Palmerston – that perfidious pig of a man!' cried Nicholas.

Now he stood totally alone. Neither Prussia nor Austria offered any support. In the end, even Sardinia joined the allies. Reports of one defeat after another reached St Petersburg, and Nicholas could not understand why the whole of Europe seemed to be aligned against him in his struggle 'to crush the infidel'. No one in his immediate circle had enough courage to tell him that his loudly asseverated intentions to free the Balkans were considered as so much humbug by the least enlightened Western statesmen, from whose point of view an ultimate defeat of Turkey would have meant the carrying of Russian expansion farther than the Sea of Marmora and the Dardanelles.

'I did not really start the war. It was provoked by British and Polish intrigues,' the Emperor said.

At the end of 1854 he went to Gatchina all by himself there to spend a few weeks in futile restrospection. The sombre landscape of palace and park answered his mood. The world he had once believed in now seemed an illusion. Phantoms crept out of the shadows, and their whispers brought nothing for his comfort. The Autocrat of All the Russias was like a child lost and forgotten in an unfamiliar darkened room. At Gatchina, his solitude unbroken by the least intrusion from the outside world, his gentlemen and his valets performing their duties like so many automata, Nicholas may well have seen his true self, and such an experience would certainly have deepened his despair. Conventional piety forbade suicide. A re-awakened sense of duty made him return to St Petersburg and to the wormwood and gall of the daily reports from the Crimea.

One day in February 1855 the capital, having known nothing of the Emperor's illness, learned of his death. Was it an illness? Was it suicide? Or poison? . . . The physicians declared that the end had come because of grave pulmonary trouble. The physicians may have been right. . . .

'Why need you cry so?' the Empress Alexandra is supposed to have said to Grand-Duchess Marie. 'God has taken your father to himself, and he will be spared a terrible future.'

The reign began with a hysterical outburst and ended in despair. The record is woven of a great many contradictory threads. But the man himself, within his limitations, was something of a minor paradox. That he meant to do good is evident by his efforts to end serfdom, but the will to achieve any lasting good was hampered by the inborn inability to face obstacles, by a streak of moral cowardice and – in the end – by a total mental paralysis. Drunk with the heady wine of power, his conception of his own abilities swollen to the point of fantasy, honest and deceitful in turn, generous and mean, Nicholas would deserve pity were it not for the fact that his unceasing vagaries, to call them by no harsher name, darkened the skies for so many and for so long. All things considered, Nicholas was too small a man to wear imperial purple. As a commoner, he would have been a great nuisance to his neighbours – and no more. Fate had seldom been as unkind to the Romanov dynasty as when it denied a son to Alexander I.

X

The Liberator

Alexander II, eldest son of the Emperor Nicholas I.
Born in April 1818, succeeded in February 1855,
murdered in March 1881

IT WAS a most happily coloured augury that two poets, Zhukovsky and Tiutchev, should have welcomed Alexander's arrival at the Kremlin in Moscow that Easter week of 1818. The parents were overjoyed, though the sentimental Prussian mother confessed to a melancholy feeling when she wrote in her diary about her first-born child, 'such a tiny helpless thing', having one day to ascend the imperial throne. In 1818, Grand-Duke Constantine was still heir-presumptive, but he had long since made up his mind to marry his Polish mistress, and people best qualified to judge of dynastic matters knew that he would never reign.

The most important child in the Empire, soon joined by a younger brother, grew in most Spartan surroundings where strawberries for dessert were a luxury and where the prince must make his own bed. As a child Alexander never appeared at any court functions. When the French ambassador wondered if he would be accorded an audience in the Grand-Ducal apartments at the Winter Palace, the Emperor replied that, invited to Tsarskoe Selo, he would certainly meet his children in the park. 'For my little son to be giving audience in the Grand-Ducal apartments at the Winter Palace, the vanity.' Nicholas proved his commonsense again in choosing the first tutor for Alexander. Colonel Moerder was sensibly kind and sensibly strict, and he did not wrap unpleasant facts in tinfoil. To quote from one of his first reports, '. . . well-mannered and un-selfish . . . quick at lessons . . . but his Imperial Highness is apt to be lazy, rather given to tears, and is too quickly defeated by obstacles. . .'

Colonel Moerder was a man of high integrity, but as a tutor he had his limitations. The Empress Alexandra had her ambitions. One of them was realized in 1825 when she became Empress. Her first-born being the heir must have the very best tuition in the land. The young Empress did not know Russia at all well, but she had had the good fortune to be taught the language by a poet. She could not always understand the poetry he wrote, but Zhukovsky's personality, his genius, modesty, gentleness and intellectual attainments had attracted her from the first, and she told her husband that she wished the poet to be their son's tutor-in-chief. Alexandra argued that there was no better man in the country to prepare Alexander for the throne, and it is rather extraordinary that she should have done so. She was not clever. In this case she proved herself wise. She left no more than a pallid streak across the dynastic tapestry. She was sentimental and yet cold; she lived for her husband and children, and large national issues said nothing to her. One of her most pro-nounced traits was her loathing for France and all things French. She would not allow the language to be spoken in her presence and she resented her children having to learn it. It irked her that it was the *lingua franca* of diplomacy. She pretended to an incredible ignorance of French history and literature. Yet in her choice of Zhukovsky as Alexander's mentor, the Empress came very near to redeeming her several absurdities.

The poet had been at court for many years. He had won no popularity there because he refused to be linked to any of the existing factions. His appointment led to ripples of discontent and jealousy soon to be replaced by shocked amazement: Zhukovsky did not leap at the high honour. He hesitated to accept it.

In the end, he wrote to the Emperor and said that, with God's help, he felt he could prepare the young Grand-Duke for the throne but not for the army. Nicholas left the letter unanswered and re-proached his wife for having made him take so 'imprudent a step'. 'Our eldest son must be a soldier,' he argued. Alexandra pointed out that there remained Colonel Moerder and his assistants to see to that side of the boy's upbringing. The Emperor still hesitated, and Zhukovsky was warned that 'his Majesty is most particular about [soldiering], and he has already remarked on the Grand-Duke's lack of interest in military matters. . . .' Zhukovsky did not reply to the warning and left for abroad there to await Nicholas's final judg-ment. That came in time in the shape of consent to the appointment.

The words about Alexander's lack of interest in military matters were true, and Nicholas felt troubled. From his early childhood, the science of war bored and frightened Alexander in turn. Uniforms, discipline, drill, the art of strategy, parades and manoeuvres, the whole world of '*le soldatesque*' which delighted, sustained and inspired the father, said nothing at all to the son. It symbolized a purpose and a way of life he could not understand. His grandfather, Paul I, would have despaired of him. 'People go to war to kill,' argued the boy, 'and all killing is murder. We are Christians, and we are forbidden to do murder.'

Once at Tsarskoe Selo the little Grand-Duke cried bitterly over a transplanted tree which, not taking to its new habitation, withered at the root. He could not express himself at all clearly, but he felt that all life was a precious and holy mystery – in man, beast, bird, tree and flower. War cut right across the heart of that mystery and destroyed it. Therefore war must be evil. A manoeuvre was but a threshold to a battle where life, God's most precious gift, could be destroyed by a cut of a sabre, a bullet, a cannon ball. Colonel Moerder, Napoleonic wars being part of his experience, could not help his pupil very much. 'Some wars are inevitable,' he said rather lamely. 'Why should they be?' rejoined Alexander. 'We believe in Christ and not in Mars.'

In his own turn, Zhukovsky, a man of deep peace, considered war to be a barbaric occupation fit for none but backward nations, though he was prudent enough not to voice too many of his opinions at court. Of course, they were well known, and Nicholas's hesitation about the appointment can well be understood.

But he gave in, and it proved a rewardingly new departure. No other Romanov – not even Alexander I – was as well prepared for the throne as Alexander II. His uncle had had a humanist for a tutor, but La Harpe was also a fiery republican. Zhukovsky was a humanist with no political leaven in him. In preparing his pupil for the throne, the poet never limited the future to sovereignty alone; the paramount task was to fashion Alexander into a man able to discharge his responsibilities to his own kind.

Nicholas, himself wholly untrained for his high office, kept complaining about his son's lukewarm attitude to his military duties. The Empress supported Zhukovsky with an energy nobody would have expected of her. But the poet had no easy time of it, his position made all the more uncomfortable by the endless intrigues of court sycophants who for a time succeeded in making Zhukovsky lose the imperial favour altogether. Yet he retained his post, and he never lost his faith and his patience. Alexander proved no easy pupil, spurts of idleness and rather exaggerated diffidence hampering him at every turn. One of the poet's many notes, written when the Grand-Duke was still in the schoolroom, crystallizes Zhukovsky's ideas about a prince's education:

'You will one day walk into History. That is inevitable by sheer accident of birth. History will pass its judgment on you before the whole world . . . and [it] will remain long after you and I have left the earth. . . . To be respected by one's contemporaries is the most difficult and yet the most essential thing for any man. . . . You must begin winning that respect whilst you are still in your boyhood. . . .'

Little by little, idleness was conquered, though some diffidence remained. At nineteen Alexander would have been welcomed at the most demanding university in Europe, though it is doubtful that he would have won distinction on a battlefield. The Emperor, for once agreeing with Zhukovsky that the Grand-Duke should be getting acquainted with his country, decided to send him travelling all over the Empire, Siberia included. But Nicholas chose to draw up the programme of the journey himself. It was hardly digestible for a young mind. Precisely thirty provinces were to be visited in exactly seven months. The details of every visit had been worked out by Nicholas. It was a whirlwind of a journey, the several appointed halts involving great expenditure of physical energy. One province vied with another in the splendour of the festivities. Moreover, factories, hospitals, jails, barracks, town halls, cathedrals and monasteries must all be visited by the Tsar's son. 'He cannot possibly have seen much of Russia in such a hurry,' Zhukovsky, himself worn out, complained in a letter to a friend. 'Hours crowded with sightseeing almost every day. . . . And on top of all else, all those banquets and endless speeches. . . .'

But that breathless, fatiguing journey would bear good fruit in the years to come. For the first time Alexander met the people he would rule. Often he chose to wreck the imperially detailed schedule by leaving the high road for some obscure village, its humped roofs seen from a distance. Zhukovsky was pleased. The coachmen were relieved. The Grand-Duke's equerries dared not protest. Thus some of the time which should have been devoted to a governor-general's reception was spent by Alexander in learning at least some of the outline of the hard peasant pattern. In those out-of-the-way hamlets nothing had been furbished up in his honour; evidences of penury, dirt and disease were there for him to observe, and Alexander reached conclusions he shared with none at the time, though Zhukovsky's sensitivity enabled him to guess that his pupil's capacity for compassion was moved to the very depths.

He returned to the north, and his parents decided it was time to get him married. For that purpose they sent him abroad, giving him liberty of choice, provided the girl were of blood royal and not a Roman Catholic. The Emperor and his wife were hoping that their son's choice would fall on a Baden princess. They were disappointed. A mere chance led the Grand-Duke to Darmstadt where he met and fell in love with Princess Marie of Hesse-Darmstadt. Zhukovsky was enchanted, but the parents objected. For the first time Alexander asserted himself. He said he would remain a bachelor if he could not marry Marie. There were his three brothers, Constantine, Nicholas and Michael, to carry on the dynasty. Alexander won in the end, and enjoyed some idyllic years with his wife, who did not change her Christian name on becoming a Russian Grand-Duchess. She proved a great helpmeet to her young husband.

Zhukovsky saw to it that his pupil reached a statesman's threshold with his mind well furnished, but the books Alexander had read and the friendships he had made ended by weaving some estrangement between his father and himself. Conditions in the country made the Grand-Duke wonder if such an Augean stable could ever be cleaned. the lengthy catalogue of evils started with serfdom. The Emperor's own attempts were wrecked partly by the opposition of the nobility and partly by his own ineptitude, but the Grand-Duke, brought up by a passionate humanist, felt that no obstacles should have interfered with reform, which, as he believed, could alone raise the Empire to a civilized level. The dignity of the individual, whatever his background and origins, was the cornerstone of a healthy society, and that dignity was trampled into dust by cruelty, contempt and a juridical machinery all too often set in motion by graft.

Alexander could not discuss such things openly with his father, but there was the young wife who wholly shared her husband's ideas and encouraged them. There were many occasions when Alexander, despair clutching him, confessed that he would not know what to do when he became Tsar.

'Of course, you would,' Marie replied and to his question how 'an impossibility' was to be achieved, she said: 'By believing in God and in man since God created man.'

When Turgenev's 'Sportsman's Sketches' began appearing in the *Sovremennik* ('The Contemporary'), husband and wife read them together and discussed them far into the night. What a rich lode lay in the peasant mind, they said to each other, what detachment, enabling them to carry their several hardihoods in the manner of Stoics, what a refreshing lack of sugared sentimentality. They could be tender. Also they could be bestially cruel as was witnessed by the treatment they meted out to inhuman landlords and tax collectors during the all too frequent peasant riots. 'But they would not be what they are if their patience did not break sometimes,' said the Grand-Duke.

His innate gentleness and his passionate liberalism considered, the change which swept over Alexander in 1848 remains a painful enigma. Zhukovsky, a very old and ailing man, was then living abroad. Having witnessed some of the excesses carried out by the revolutionaries, the poet somersaulted into reaction, but that sad metamorphosis cannot explain the change in the Grand-Duke. Zhukovsky's letters had not reached him by the time his own views swung to the reactionaries' camp to such an extent that he called the Hungarian rebels 'a bunch of impious criminals', and applauded the Emperor's decision to send Paskiewicz into Hungary to help Francis-Joseph's army in crushing the rebellion. The Grand-Duke no longer read Turgenev and Gogol; he subscribed to every repressive measure commanded by the Emperor, and he even wrote to his Prussian relations that all universities in the German states should be closed because they were being turned 'into nursery-beds for sedition'.

Such a violent conversion cannot be explained except by a certain halvedness in Alexander's character, its flickers discernible in his childhood. The attitude adopted by him in 1848 did not last long, but it left a sad enough sediment.

Nicholas's fantastic Eastern policy helped to reawaken Alexander's better self. He openly disclaimed his father's optimism about British neutrality, and opposed the war as much as he could. Yet, being Nicholas's heir, the Grand-Duke did not fail in outward expressions of loyalty when talking to the ambassadors at the Emperor's court. Only Grand-Duchess Marie and a few intimates knew that Alexander considered the Russian occupation of the Danubian Principalities as the first step towards an abyss. A few days before the Emperor's death, the Grand-Duke, by the authority given to him at Nicholas's departure for Gatchina, replaced the inept Menshikov by another and much less vacillating commander. Later, whispers ran about the capital that it was precisely Menshikov's dismissal that caused Nicholas's death by sending him into a fury his weak heart could not afford. The story, however, was never proved.

Sebastopol was in the fifth month of the siege when Alexander became Emperor. He had not begun the senseless carnage in the south, but he was powerless to stop it at the time. In September 1855, he went to the south to visit the army, and despair clutched hard at him. The men were worn out. Their unbroken morale shamed their Tsar all the more when he saw that the victualling arrangements were chaotic. Orderlies from the Medical Corps were known to steal the baptismal crosses from the wounded and the dead. Doctors complained that surgical and other supplies allocated in St Petersburg and Moscow were either delayed or never reached them at all. The poison of graft seeped everywhere. Clerks in the Civil Service were carrying on a busy traffic in army boots. Thousands of recruits had bast sandals issued to them. But the men did not complain, and their morale, though it shamed the young Emperor, was the only plank for him to rest on. Most likely, his would be the only heart in Russia to thank God for the Treaty of Paris.

Yet, in spite of the Crimean shadow, the reign had started in most promising sunshine. Strangers would stop one another in the street and thank heaven for 'the deliverance from the iron heel'. The ban on foreign travel was immediately lifted, censorship relaxed, and the activities of the dreaded Third Department pared down. Books forbidden since 1848 again appeared in the shops. Professors deprived of their chairs were recalled to the universities. For all the mournful reports from the south, people began taking pride in the endurance of the Sebastopol defenders. Ideas and hopes, shelved for so many years, began stirring again, and everybody wished the young Emperor well in the gigantic undertaking he mentioned within the very first weeks of his reign – the total abolition of serfdom.

✲

There were several drafts of the great reform in existence, but ordered activity was slow in coming, and the Crimean campaign was not entirely responsible for the delay. Alexander did not lack vision, energy or faith, but at the beginning only his wife, his brother, Constantine, and his aunt, Grand-Duchess Elena, widow of Grand-Duke Michael, were his immediate supporters. Among the statesmen there was nobody except Kisselev to confirm the sovereign's hopes. Nicholas's long reign had not been exactly conducive to the development of healthy statesmanship. The programme followed by his ministers had been shaped by the imperial will on one side and by blind obedience on the other. Broadly speaking, Nicholas's servants had all but turned into bureaucratic robots. So one of Alexander's first tasks was to search for men capable of interpreting his desires in the manner of those who were unafraid of argument. He had found a few such men with the help of his brother and his aunt who, Grand-Duchess though she was, excluded nobody of 'genuine merit' from her palace. By the summer of 1855 both administration and society, the reactionary leaven thick in their thought, began murmuring about 'the upstarts' near the throne.

Jacob Rostovtzev was chosen to carry out all the preliminary work for emancipation. Lanskoy, another 'newcomer', was appointed to the Ministry of the Interior to replace a puppet of Nicholas's. And there were others whose names gladdened the liberals. In March 1856 the Emperor went to Moscow there to address an assembly of nobility and gentry. '. . . serfdom [must be] destroyed from above and not from below. . . .' He stressed his firm resolve to abolish the evil with all possible speed, informed them of the measures already taken, and asked for their co-operation. 'I ask you to consider my words carefully and to carry them back into the country.'

It will be remembered here that on three occasions Alexander's father had failed chiefly because of his fear lest the obduracy of the nobility were to result in a public shock to the autocratic power. The great assembly addressed by Alexander heard him in reverent silence. To make suggestions to, still less to argue with, a Tsar, was utterly alien to their mentality, but the young Emperor was conscious of a reluctance the gathering had not dared to voice.

On his return to St Petersburg, he said to his brother Constantine: 'I could not escape the feeling that they were all against me.'

'But many more are for you,' replied the Grand-Duke.

In August 1856 the Emperor came to Moscow again, for his coronation. By then all the shame and despair of the Crimean war were forgotten. The splendours of the occasion were insurpassable, and few people knew that the Treasury, sadly depleted by the expenses of the war and by the indemnity, had not been asked to defray any costs, the Emperor's private means meeting everything down to all the free meals and beer for the population of Moscow.

The Coronation High Prayer, '. . . enlighten and guide me in the high and hard service . . .' and the customary Manifesto were in most fortunate accord. The Manifesto carried more than thirty amnesty clauses. All the Decembrists and other 'political' prisoners, together with the Poles condemned to lifelong penal servitude in Siberian mines, were freed. The long and tiring ceremony in the Assumption Cathedral coming to its end, the Emperor could hardly get across the Red Square to reach the palace, his family and a meal. The immense crowds mobbed him. They wept, laughed, clapped, cheered and sang. They clutched at his knees and elbows. They kissed his hands and his purple mantle. They called him 'our little sun', 'our little father', and 'our very own' since he was born in Moscow. He stood to them for a symbol. He was also a man with a heart which, as they guessed, would soon answer all their needs and assuage their anguish.

Contemporaries recorded that Alexander was weeping when at last he reached the Granovity Hall there to eat the traditional Coronation dinner, alone with his Empress.

The Coronation Manifesto was a bombshell to the reactionaries. 'The Emperor has opened the way to sheer lawlessness . . .' they whispered on every side. 'The Decembrists alone are certain to plan his downfall. Did they not clamour for a republic in 1825? And all the other "politicals" are known to be against the monarchy. The Emperor has signed a death-warrant for the dynasty. . . .' The amnesty granted to the Poles gave rise to differently coloured apprehensions. 'They will leave for abroad and poison the Western mind

against Russia. Who could have advised the Emperor in the matter?'
Many of the reactionaries, still occupying high posts at court and in
the administration, did not scruple to share their misgivings with
distinguished foreigners come to Russia for the coronation, and the
West came to the conclusion that the reforms contemplated by the
young Emperor – emancipation in particular – were certain to pave
the way to a revolution in the Russian Empire.

At that time Prussia, 'the weakest of the weak', was about the only
friend Alexander had in the West. The habitual Russo-phobia in
England was heightened by the Russian successes in the Caucasus
and the penetration into Central Asia. Relations with France and
Austria were anything but friendly, and the Treaty of Paris had
not turned the Sultan into a friend. There was not a government in
Europe which believed that in Alexander II they had a ruler who
regarded all war as an evil, who was wholly committed to gigantic
labours at home, and who, above all, was a man of honour. They all
regarded him first and foremost as a Romanov, and the dynasty's
expansionist policy was known to them all.

Alexander was aware of all the suspicions, but he brushed them
aside. There was so much to do at home, and emancipation stood in
the forefront of all tasks. Its realization took more than four years
to accomplish. The first appeal made by the Emperor to nobility and
gentry might have been spoken in a desert for all the response he
received. None the less, the landowners could not wholly be blamed
for the inertia. Emancipation having been put before them as a goal,
there were no signposts erected to enable them to reach that goal. A
number of drafts having been drawn up, there was as yet no definite
plan to follow, and not until January 1857 did Rostovtzev submit
one. By that time the murmurs of reactionaries had reached the
Emperor. 'Let some of them get down to work on the programme
instead of complaining,' he said, and the Special Committee he summoned was composed almost wholly of diehards who went to work
with a will, wasting one session after another in discussing futilities.
'If the sty should belong to the landowner and the pig it shelters to
the peasant, which of them should have the lien on the litter?' They
found themselves facing the triangle of landowners, peasants and
land, and they could not solve the problem since from their point
of view any land taken from the gentry would lead to the ruin of the
country.

Presently, Grand-Duke Constantine, Lanskoy and Milutin came to support Rostovtzev on the committee. They brought great draughts of fresh air, much energy and occasional anger to the sittings. But the anti-reformers continued fighting their own battle and were pleased to find an ally in the hierarchy, since a few of the forty million serfs belonged to the Church.

Alexander's patience came to an end, and early in 1858 he decided to take the matter to the country. Emancipation Committees started work in all the provinces. In London Herzen wrote in his *Bell*, '[his name] now belongs to History. It would not matter if his reign were to end tomorrow. The work of liberation has started in earnest. . . .'

In January 1861 the Reform Bill was brought before the Council of State, and the Emperor declared that the matter was to be settled in a fortnight. Being chairman at that meeting, he 'won immortality' by a stirring speech. Not a single note before him, he sketched the development of serfdom through the centuries, spoke of its appalling influence on the spirit of the nation and the horror of such a total negation of man's dignity. Every sentence of the speech was informed by deep feeling. Even some among the anti-reformers were forced to admit that the Emperor's arguments were not built of straw.

'As we listened,' wrote one of those present to his wife, 'we knew that the Tsar must have ached and burned for many years with the resolve to put an end to slavery. It was far more than an administrative measure. All he said echoed a true love for freedom. . . .'

On the first Sunday in March 1861 the Manifesto was read throughout the Empire, the inhabitants of every hamlet having been instructed to go to their nearest village, there to hear it read by the parish priest.

Serfdom died a juridical death. The Emperor's words to his daughter on returning from the solemn Te Deum at the Kazan Cathedral in St Petersburg were true enough: 'This is the happiest day of my life'. But the publication of the Manifesto led to consequences all too gleefully welcomed by anti-reformers. The Emancipation Committees in the country had done their work in the most slovenly manner imaginable. Of all the provinces Kaluga was the only one where the foresight of the authorities had really prepared the peasant population for the great change. Elsewhere, the several clauses explaining the conditions of land tenure to be granted to them were wholly misunderstood by the peasants. 'The Tsar has given us liberty together with the land. . . . Stands to reason we must have land or else we starve. . . . And now the Tsar's clerks are out to rob us. . . .' There followed a great many outbreaks of violence and arson. In one province disorders reached such a pitch that the governor had to call on the military for help. 1861, begun in so radiant a climate, ended gloomily.

And none felt it as sharply as the Emperor. But he refused to give in to despair and the reforming work continued, although Rostovtzev was dead by that time. Tremendous changes were introduced into the field of judicature where the principle of defence and trial by jury were introduced for the first time. Justice was to be 'swift, merciful, and equal for all', in Alexander's own words, embodied in the instruction given to Bludov. The use of the word 'equal' meant a revolutionary departure, and the great army reform, carried out some years later, was informed with the same spirit. That, at least, was a singular triumph over the reactionaries and became the Emperor's finest memorial. Military service, its hideous penal aspect destroyed for ever, became 'equal' for all. In the past, landowners had the right to have their serfs recruited as a punishment and to enter their own sons almost at birth as officers in the best regiments. Now military service made no distinction of wealth or rank, and included every male on reaching the age of eighteen, only sons alone being exempt. Now a prince's son and a docker's had to start in the ranks. That reform of Alexander's was the first breach in the hitherto impregnable fortress of privilege. Corporal punishments were abolished, and the service term reduced from twenty-five years to seven.

The reforming process continued, but the unclouded morning of the reign was over. Incessant work began fraying Alexander's energy. His asthma worsened. His sparrings with those who were still committed to the archaic pattern led to occasional outbursts of temper. Finally, his relations with the Empress Marie had already begun to follow the usual matrimonial course of all Romanov husbands to whom fidelity appeared as a counsel of perfection. Finally, he was perplexed by the complaints reaching him from every corner of the Empire. Few appeared satisfied with the results of the reforms.

Doubts began crowding into the Emperor's mind. How could evil have come out of good? Yet it seemed obvious that the economic consequences of the abolition had worsened, if anything, the peasant's condition. Again his educational reforms had carried elementary enlightenment into the villages and done away with the police surveillance of the universities, but unrest brooded among the students. In Moscow and elsewhere they clashed with the police, and violence held the stage again and again, and the Emperor had to sanction measures of a severity out of all accord with his nature.

What he failed to grasp was that all the separate lesser freedoms by him sanctioned and encouraged had inevitably led to a thirst for absolute freedom, that new ideas had caught at the imagination and made it hunger for activities wholly alien from those pursued by bureaucracy, Constitution had ceased to be a tempting word. It became an imperative among all intelligent people. Some, yearning for it, stayed passive. But great numbers were teaching and preaching their varied evangels. They longed to draw closer to the masses, to win universal franchise, to have a voice in an assembly free of all bureaucratic supervision. The Emperor kept shuffling and re-shuffling the cabinet; he censured provincial governors for cruelty and yet himself signed warrants for exile and penal servitude, but the young refused to wear the tattered raiment of the past, and any new idea was grist to their mill, and crumbs picked up from the Socialist table in the West kept sustaining their efforts. The reading of 'prohibited' books and day-dreaming satisfied them no longer. Groups were formed, only to be tracked down by the police. With the leaders exiled, new cells came on the national scene. Many of those expressions were puerile, chiefly because the intelligentsia knew nothing about the people. But the sum total of all those movements could be put under the common heading of inevitability.

The Polish mutiny under Alexander II was the bloodiest outburst of an ancient racial quarrel born of a hunger never truly uprooted from the hearts of those who were bred to pray that they might see their country return to her past: 'Poland from the Baltic to the Black Sea, Queen among the Slavs.' The partitions of the eighteenth century pushed such a prayer into the domain of fantasy: a Polish victory in the Russian Poland could never have led to a resurrection of the whole country since neither Prussia nor Austria would have surrendered their respective Polish possessions, and 'the White Eagle patriots' could never have mustered a force strong enough to defeat the three Great Powers together.

In the matter of Poland, Alexander did not at first follow in his father's steps. He appointed Grand-Duke Constantine Viceroy and empowered him to restore a great many privileges forfeited in 1831. He also included all the exiled Poles in Siberia in his coronation amnesty. But he understood the Polish problem no better than Nicholas had done, and his words, 'we are all Slavs and brothers together', did not really accord with his knowledge of history: the mutual hatred of Russian and Pole stretched back for centuries, and 'brotherhood' speeches were derided by both.

The revolt broke out at the beginning of 1863 and lasted for fifteen months. The cause of Poland was received by the West with great sympathy, except in Berlin and Vienna. The rights and wrongs of the matter were not particularly clear either to the Polish or to the Russian rank and file, but the suppression of the mutiny by Berg and Mouraviev and the resultant cruelties meted out to the vanquished ended by establishing the Polish case very firmly in English and French eyes. The mutiny had a different and a very sad consequence: it turned Alexander towards a path once trodden by Nicholas I. Now those thousands of Poles who, having escaped gallows or prison, found sanctuary in England, France and Switzerland, became, in the Emperor's eyes, responsible for every check to Russian policy abroad and for every breath of unrest at home. Such a pathological attitude was still further deepened by Alexander's ill-health, by the early death of his heir, Grand-Duke Nicholas, and – much more incisively – by Karakozov's attempt at regicide. Alexander then escaped death by a miracle. A peasant, standing behind Karakozov, seized his elbow at the right moment. That shot, as the poet Tiutchev said, 'laid us all low in dust and shame'. The scenes in St Petersburg described by Clay, the American minister, were proof of the strong link between the sovereign and his people. '. . . thousands assembled at the Winter Palace and hurrahed till his Majesty showed himself again and again on the balcony . . . [then] they camped there all night and the next day. . . .'

Alexander had escaped death, but the country did not escape the consequences of the attempt. Censorship and police vigilance were heightened at once. Men known to have liberal views were dismissed from their posts, and creatures of Dimitry Tolstoy's kidney stepped into ministerial shoes. A contemporary wrote sadly in his journal: 'Our worst enemies are neither nihilists nor Poles but the so-called statesmen who turn people into nihilists and malcontents [and] try to undermine justice.' One repressive measure after another came to be signed by the Emperor, some among them all but cancelling the fair noontide of his reforms. 'Justice must be equal for all – and cases are no more to be heard in camera but in public so that our people may learn the way justice is administered in their land.' But now all 'political' prisoners were denied a trial by jury and there was to be no appeal from any court sentences passed upon them. A great many 'subversive' cells having been traced back to 'the culpable inactivity of local government authorities', the latter once again found themselves under the iron thumb of bureaucracy. Russian students at work in foreign universities were ordered to return home, and that particular measure ended in a tragic absurdity: those young men and women, having sat at the feet of Western socialists, came home with no other idea than to spread all they had learned. For every 'subversive' cell run to earth by the authorities, five new ones would be established.

Reactionaries, their thoughts turning back to the beginning of the reign, were darkly triumphant. What was it all but the natural outcome of imperial indulgence, they said. It greatly pleased them to remind their listeners that it would take more than a century for the country to assimilate the spirit of reforms in the right way. They quoted many a frayed tag such as 'a little learning is a dangerous thing', and hinted that the Emperor had not given enough thought before he plunged into the troubled waters of reform. Such people did not understand the mainspring of Alexander's motives. Feeling, not reason, governed all his actions. His nature was such that he hardly ever trod along a steadily level path. He either climbed to the top of a mountain or else fell into an abyss. Once the latter claimed him, all his negative qualities took command: a streak of harshness, vacillation, inability to face obstacles, and a peculiarly coloured bitterness which, gnawing hard, would not let him rest until he had slaked it by actions his better self would never have endorsed.

✳

It was just about then that a second sunrise broke over the Emperor's private life. He had been deeply in love with his wife, but the idyllic climate did not last very long after his accession. Marie's growing ill-health, her frequent absences abroad, constant demands for sympathy, and an earlier unsuspected penchant for criticism, all those and many more contributed to the first breaths of estrangement. She had been a wonder and a delight. Now he saw her as a habit he wished to be rid of, and his worst self came to the foreground in many unkind and egoistic gestures. To her own misfortune, the Empress never ceased to love him.

Alexander passed through some ephemeral affairs, his bodily hunger satisfied, his heart stonily untouched. In the mid-sixties he took for his mistress a girl who would hold him to the very end, Princess Catherine Dolgoruka, eighteen to his forty-six.

The liaison worked a painful cleavage in the family. Alexander's daughter and one of his younger sons, Grand-Duke Alexis, neither condoned nor condemned. All the other sons, most particularly the heir, Grand-Duke Alexander, did not conceal their indignation, felt all the more deeply because of some clumsy mistakes made by their father. The Emperor should never have bestowed a court rank on his mistress. It paved the way to endless humiliations for the Empress when she was in Russia. And later still Alexander's decision to install Catherine at the Winter Palace showed an unpardonable lack of taste, to say nothing about the cruelty to his wife who should have remembered her dignity and gone abroad for good. But she stayed on.

Yet such developments were still distant in 1866. For the time being, Catherine Dolgoruka, so hard for the Emperor to woo and to win, remained in a discreet background, proving herself her lover's good angel. Reactionaries felt angry because she inspired him to issue an order commanding all the factory owners to build hospitals and first-aid points for their workers. 'Pampering the scum,' grumbled the die-hards, 'it will be playrooms for their children next. . . .' and it greatly irked them that the newly appointed '*dame de la cour*' could not be detected in a single false step. She shunned publicity to the very utmost. And at the end of a few months, she won the respect of friend and foe by parting from the Emperor, and, at a relation's suggestion, leaving for abroad. Alexander did not protest, but he lived in a tortured twilight, not a hint of which found its way into his letters to Catherine. At the end of a year he could bear it no longer. She left her refuge in Italy and returned to him, and they stayed together to the end.

She seems to have been successful in one important particular: she instilled in her lover respect for womankind, a singular phenomenon for a man of the Romanov house. His predecessors' and ancestors' attitude to women had always been touched with an Oriental brush. Some among them had loved their brides genuinely enough at the beginning. Peter II was supposed to be devoted to his fiancée. Paul I and two of his sons were known to 'adore' their wives for a time, but the relationship between Alexander II and Catherine Dolgoruka was stamped with a different die. They were friends as well as lovers. Their feeling for their three children was of a kind which might have been found in any commoner's household, hardly in a palace. They respected each other's foibles and failings. The reverence paid by Alexander was all the more remarkable when it is remembered that Catherine never forgot the sovereign in him. She may indeed have given him counsel in private, but she was not a Marie Naryshkina who would flaunt her affair with Alexander I in all the drawing-rooms of the capital, not excluding those of the Winter Palace. Catherine Dolgoruka, created Princess Yurievska, effaced herself to the extent of not appearing at social functions unless he expressly wished her to do so. Nor did she ever allow a single sycophant to turn her into a carpet leading to the steps of the throne.

Psychologically and emotionally she was good for the Emperor.

Prussia remained about the only Western door wide open for Alexander's country. Reprisals after the Polish mutiny, odd ministerial appointments, unceasing reports of restrictive measures, the persecutions of university students, all of it together could not but harden the Russo-phobia in England and France. Alexander's neutrality in the Franco-Prussian war had been expected, but few people knew that such neutrality was the price asked for by Bismarck for the restoration of the Russian shipping rights in the Black Sea, rights which had been forfeited by the Treaty of Paris. The Prussian victory over 'the motherland of sedition and socialism' was wildly acclaimed by every reactionary in Russia. Bismarck's creation of a new empire was welcomed in the Russian press as 'the first step towards the stabilization of the balance of power in Europe – not for our generation only but in perpetuity.' The Dreikaiserbund, engineered by Bismarck, whereby Alexander, William I and Francis-Joseph pledged themselves to maintain 'the closest possible ties of friendship and confidence' was interpreted as a proud answer to the British hostility.

Bismarck, tranquilly watching the Russian advance into the fastnesses of Central Asia, said with a shrug: 'If the Russian bear chooses to annoy the British lion, what is that to us?' Between 1866 and 1873, the Russian bear had acquired Turkestan, Bokhara and Khiva.

But the German Chancellor did not really know the Emperor of Russia. He had hoped for Alexander's complaisance 'in all important matters of policy', yet within the next four years the horizon changed colour, and Russo-German relations entered an uncomfortable new phase.

In St Petersburg, the ageing Gorchakov was still at the helm in foreign affairs in spite of his having committed one blunder after another. He was about as well matched with Bismarck as a newly born puppy would have been with a grown tiger, but he clung to Bismarck's coat-tails tenaciously and never ceased to praise the creation of the Dreikaiserbund. All the more was Gorchakov disturbed by the change in his sovereign's outlook. The old man never tired of repeating that a strong and united Germany stood for a surety of European peace, and Alexander would reply: 'I suppose you are right, so long as she is not an aggressor. She is friendly enough with Austria today, but Sadowa should not be wholly forgotten, and I wonder if my uncle is not troubled sometimes by his Chancellor's advice. Bismarck is ruthless, my friend.'

Certainly, the German Chancellor felt uneasy about the possibility of an Anglo-Russian rapprochement after the marriage of the Duke of Edinburgh to Alexander's only daughter. In Bismarck's eyes, the policy of Germany was entirely Germany's business, but he preferred Russia and Austria to keep aloof from friendships outside the orbit of the Dreikaiserbund.

Hot upon it all came the crisis of 1875 when Berlin took violent exception to certain measures adopted by the French government to improve her military potential, and the German note to France was menacing enough to cause an explosion. Alexander neither listened to Gorchakov's entreaties to leave well alone nor wrote to Berlin. He went to see his old uncle and he wasted no time on polite ambiguities. 'I will not allow France to be attacked,' he told the Emperor William. 'Germany could not move unless we remained neutral, and I do not mean to stand aloof if an unhappy emergency should arise.'

'He is a traitor, sir,' said Bismarck to the old Emperor who, all his timidity notwithstanding, had the courage to reply that he knew his nephew was right.

It was one of many fine moments in Alexander's life. Bismarck withdrew. Victoria and her government praised the Emperor for 'sustaining the peace of Europe'. The delicate dalliance known as the Dreikaiserbund came to its end, and Alexander did not feel very troubled. He had clashed with Bismarck and come out victorious, and Europe was ready to listen to him. On his return from Germany he went at once to a house on the Palace Quay to see Catherine and their children, and her comment richly rewarded him for the weeks of strain and anxiety. 'You could have done no other. You were true to the very best there is and I am so proud.'

For twenty years Alexander's Empire stayed at peace in Europe. The ambition of Catherine the Great and of Nicholas I, that immemorial imperial longing for sovereignty in the Straits, was in their successor's eyes a mere tombstone in a forgotten churchyard. Once again the Russian flag had the freedom of the Black Sea, and Alexander asked for no more. He certainly cherished ideas of expansion, but his vision marched east and not south, and his policy was pre-eminently governed by economic urges. Trade with China and India was essential to Russian prosperity and the advances into Central Asia made it grow with every year. More and more railways were being built in European Russia, and the volume of her exports was increasing steadily.

The Balkans, all peopled by Southern Slavs with the exception of Bulgaria, were still held by Turkey. If Alexander had ever nursed dreams about a grandiose Slav brotherhood, those were shattered by the Polish mutiny. The luckless fate of Southern Slavs certainly stirred his compassion, but it never prompted him to contemplate a crusade for their liberation from the Turkish yoke.

The Balkan volcano began murmuring in 1875 when exceptionally bad harvests up and down the peninsula brought no easing of taxes demanded by the Turks. There followed risings in Bosnia and Herzegovina. They were put down most cruelly. Serbia and Montenegro began mustering their forces. A challenge was thrown at the Turks. Within a few months the Balkans were ablaze.

The Emperor went abroad in the spring of that year. At Darmstadt he said to Princess Alice, 'I am dead against war. It would be sheer madness for me to think about Constantinople. Please tell your mother.' She quoted his words in a letter to Queen Victoria, but in England few believed in the Emperor's sincerity.

In all fairness, the West had a case. Whilst the sovereign kept making protestations of his resolve to keep out of the Balkan trouble, his own country lost itself in hysteria. Volunteers in their thousands hurried down to the south. Not a city was there in the Empire but set up special funds for Balkan relief. When the government rather belatedly forbade all official gestures, gold started pouring in from private sources. And, whilst her husband was assuring every ambassador in turn that he meant to stand aloof, the Empress was sending ambulance trains to the Balkans, manned by Russian doctors and orderlies and equipped at her own expense. Up and down the country, Westerners linked arms with Slavophiles in pressing 'the start of the holy crusade'. The entire Russian press clamoured for Russia to join 'the holy war for the liberation of our brethren and for the honour of the Cross'. There were a few tranquil minds, but whatever was said by them came to be drowned in the hysterical uproar. Old Prince Peter Wiazemsky, the poet, wrote sadly to a friend about 'this typhoon of vapid sentimentality. . . . Our true Russian blood is all but denied . . . Slavomania holds the stage. . . . Unity of faith should not mean anything. . . . Far, far better to have an enfeebled Turkey for our neighbour than . . . a quarrelsome Slavonia [to whom] our own country is just a milch cow. . . . There will never be any peace in the Balkans. . . . Nor will they show any gratitude to us if we are foolish enough to stand by their side. . . .'

Meanwhile, the Emperor was trying one means after another to put a stop to the carnage, but the mad fever of his own people hampered every effort he made. In England, Russo-phobia was a rising crescendo. Shuvalov, Alexander's ambassador at St James's, assured the British government that his sovereign's purposes lay in conciliation, but Lord Derby replied that 'though everybody knew that his Majesty was against all belligerent policy, yet, unhappily, many things [in Russia] were happening not in accord with the Emperor's views'. Lord Derby might well have added that the Emperor's own sons were clamouring for action and that his Minister of Finance, Reutern, had told him that the Empire could not afford a war. 'Sir, we would be plunged into penury even if we were victorious and increased taxation would certainly play into the hands of the revolutionaries.'

Everybody's hand was against Alexander. Germany sent warning that he was not to expect any help if he joined the war. He had no intention of joining it and he refused to lose hope. But everything failed in the end. In March 1877 a sick and disillusioned man learned of Turkey's refusal to accept a protocol signed by the six Great Powers. Russia was triumphant. Her Tsar felt broken-hearted. 'At last,' cried the Empress, 'it is a Holy War.' 'That is blasphemy,' he shouted. 'All war is sin against God and man.'

The West said, 'he is going to fight after all. . . . What duplicity!' There had been no duplicity. Certainly, there had been weakness. The Emperor should have dismissed some of his ministers and taken firm measures to quieten the national hysteria. Censorship might have been used to check some of the more provocative articles in the press, and the stream of volunteers, supplies and money to the Balkans should have been stemmed.

That most sanguinary of all Russo-Turkish campaigns lasted nine months. Begun under the least favourable conditions for the Russians, it ended with Alexander's armies within a day's march from Constantinople. The Treaty of San Stefano assured the independence of the Balkans in perpetuity. Yet old Prince Wiazemsky's prophecy came true. The quarrelsome 'Slavonia' could not remain at peace even with the Turkish yoke taken off her shoulders. Serbs and Montenegrins were jealous of Bulgarians. In their turn, the latter complained about their unfairly traced boundaries. Away from the peninsula, its dissensions and grievances, the West once again remembered all the earlier Russian dreams about expansion. The altered map of Central Asia now spoke to them in accents which, as they thought, might well be echoed west of the Straits.

Alexander was furious, but the Great Powers had something of a case. The affair of the Crimea was still near enough for them to remember the deceitful policy of Nicholas I. Much earlier ambitions of the Romanovs once again occupied the attention of the West, and Gorchakov's truculence did not particularly advance the Russian cause at the Berlin Congress. In the end, very little remained of the provisions of San Stefano. The manifesto which rather belatedly published the Berlin Treaty began with a pompous preface about Russia having entered the war for no material advantages to herself. That certainly rang true where Alexander's own intentions were concerned, but the nation's silent acquiescence was big with anger and shame. And the silence was short-lived. Why, they asked, should Austria have received Bosnia and Herzegovina? Why did Eastern Rumelia remain under Turkish administration, subject to Western surveillance? A little later the national indignation burned fiercely on learning that Turkey had ceded Cyprus to England. 'The Englishwoman has again done the dirty on us' (*'Anglichánka opiát nam nagádila'*), they said up and down the country.

The general dissatisfaction was not hidden from the Emperor, but what wounded him most sharply was the attitude of the self-same countries which he had freed from the Turkish oppression. Wiasemsky's prophecy was fulfilled to the letter: the young, hot-tempered, irrational Slavonia had no use for gratitude. Freed from one yoke, she fell a slave to private jealousies.

1878 proved the darkest year of Alexander's reign. Outwardly again at peace, the Empire suggested a battlefield within, with her government, police and bureaucracy ranged on one side, and nihilists, anarchists and social-revolutionaries on the other. All the political assassinations of that year ended by pushing the ailing and weary Emperor back into the mood of 1848. He gave unbounded confidence to men who should never have held office, like Timashev, Dimitry Tolstoy and Grieg. He sanctioned repressive measures and approved penalties which would have revolted him at the beginning of his reign. Yet, whatever is thought of such a policy today, it must be admitted that Alexander II was not wholly wrong in seeing all manner of 'subversion' as a menace to the very foundations of the nation's health. The ideologists of his day knew very little about the masses, as was proved by the failure of the *naródniky* to win a hearing in the countryside. All of them thought in terms of their own particular political gospel. National needs as such did not come into their reckoning. The liberation they had in view was – in bald terms – little more than the exchange of one autocracy for another.

What the Emperor failed to see was that his own government, to say nothing of the lesser administrative fry, helped to create the very climate in which 'subversion' could increase its strength and make its appeal convincing to the intelligent minority.

By the mid-seventies, *'podpólnaya rábota'* (underground activity) had shifted from the countryside to the towns, and revolutionary cells of one colour or another were organized in most of the important urban centres. Savage murders were followed by even more savage reprisals which in their turn gave birth to more and more violence. In 1878, it was terror at its grimmest. By the beginning of 1879, the Social-Revolutionary Party formed a small secret cell, its name explaining its aim – 'The League of the Regicides'. In the first months of the year there were two unsuccessful attempts on the Emperor's life. The government was in a panic. One of Alexander's recorded comments was: 'Am I a wild beast that they should hound me to death?'

A little later a third attempt was made under his own roof. The explosion at the Winter Palace caused the death of some ten footmen and about twenty men of the Finnish Guards Regiment who were on duty at the palace. The Emperor, his guests and family escaped solely because the arrival of a visitor had made the Emperor postpone the dinner hour. The catastrophe afforded a shattering proof of the official ineptitude, to give it no sterner label.

Valuev, Makov and their brethren kept talking about 'the formidable enemy' they had to fight. The revolutionaries were anything but formidable. Their numbers were few, their influence, except in factories, negligible, and there was little solidarity among the various groups. They hid in towns because the countryside would have none of them. In no fewer than ten provinces, the peasantry, on hearing about a political murder in the neighbouring city, reacted by setting fire to the houses of 'intelligenstia' suspected of 'red' tendencies. The revolutionaries' strength came from the helplessness and the savagery of the government on one side and the shameful indifference of the educated minority on the other. As to the country as such, there the Emperor's name shone as brightly as ever. The feeling of the majority would be reflected in the grief and horror after his murder.

The catastrophe at the Winter Palace made it possible for an Armenian general, known for nothing except his genius in the field, to become a dictator in little. Within six months Loris-Melikov centralized every arm of the law to fight sedition, loosened censorship, invited and obtained the co-operation of the press, re-established the independence of local government, and won the confidence of every enlightened subject of the Emperor. Gradually, parcels of dynamite and loaded guns ceased to appear on the urban stage. People no longer heard about trains derailed by an explosion. It was again possible to walk in a street without encountering a surge of panic caused by a shot from round a corner.

Having achieved it all, Loris-Melikov remained at his post. He told Alexander that, with terrorism uprooted, it would be imperative to introduce people's representation. His idea was that the reform should begin with a reorganized Council of State, all the classes irrespective of rank and wealth invited to take part in the work. The Emperor agreed to the plan, and in the autumn of 1880 Loris-Melikov began working at the preliminary draft of the reform.

The country appeared calm. Yet Loris-Melikov still kept his finger on 'the subversive pulse'. Its beats were certainly fainter and fainter, but he was not wholly satisfied. A remnant of terrorists had so far escaped arrest. They were led by one Zheliabov and Perovskaya, his mistress, whose whereabouts were still unknown. At the end of the summer the Emperor left for the Crimea. A few days before his return to the north, packages of dynamite were discovered on the permanent way not far from Moscow, and Loris-Melikov's agents reported certain traces of underground activities in St Petersburg. The general begged Alexander to go either to Tsarskoe Selo or to Gatchina, but Alexander refused saying that he was too old to learn a new lesson – that of fleeing from danger.

The winter of 1880–81 brought no new horrors. Not a single outbreak of violence marred the calm. Alexander felt happy. Catherine, become his wife after the death of the Empress earlier that year, and her children and he were all together at the Winter Palace. Loris-Melikov was nearing the end of his work. And presently Zheliabov was arrested. Of all the leaders, Perovskaya alone eluded capture.

In February 1881 Loris-Melikov finished the draft of the proposed constitution, and the Emperor approved it. At the end of that month the official manifesto was drawn up. Loris-Melikov was to be received in audience on the evening of March 1st. 'And you will then see me sign the paper,' said Alexander. The publication of the Manifesto was fixed for March 2nd.

That year March 1st fell on a Sunday. All those who met the Emperor in the morning were struck by his high spirits. Years seemed to have fallen off his shoulders. He had the air of a man on his way to some great festival. Early in the afternoon he paid a call on his favourite cousin, Grand-Duchess Catherine. On the way back to the Winter Palace, a bomb was thrown at him. It shattered the carriage from end to end but left him unhurt, though it killed two cossacks of the escort, an errand boy passing by, and some of the horses, and wounded a few other people. Alexander, having seen to the wounded, was turning towards his equerry's carriage when a second bomb was thrown by a young man in the crowd. When the smoke had cleared away, about twenty people lay, their blood staining the snow, and the Emperor was among them. He was unconscious by the time they brought him to the Winter Palace and died within a few hours.

XI

The Dwarfed Titan

*Alexander III, second son of the Emperor
Alexander II. Born in March 1845, succeeded
in March 1881, died in November 1894*

THE TSAR-LIBERATOR had many virtues, but those of an ideal
husband and a wise parent did not belong to him. Together with
most of his predecessors, he carried on the Romanov tradition within
which duties, demands and delights of home life were seldom permitted to emerge into the foreground. Of Alexander II's six sons,
the eldest, Nicholas, being the heir, was the only one to receive an
education more or less in keeping with the future which awaited
him. The other five, Alexander, Wladimir, Alexis, Serge and Paul,
once the schoolroom years were behind them, had the choice of two
services offered them. Four of the Grand-Dukes entered the army,
and Alexis joined the navy.

A reign such as Alexander II's – shaken by reforms and mutinies,
and troubled by breaths new to the Russian mentality – would, so
one imagines, have stirred the dullest intellect out of phlegm and
indifference. There was also the tragic ending of a war and sharp
family tensions. Yet, until his elder brother's death in 1865, Alexander, one day to be the third Tsar of that name, had not given
much, if any, evidence of being aware of any stresses and challenges.
Of a massive build and a proportionate clumsiness, he was, as a
child, nicknamed '*bychók*' ('little bull') by the family. Pobedonostzev
was his tutor-in-chief, an unfortunate choice on the part of Alexander
II since the man was a devoted follower of every reactionary drift.
But the little '*bychók*' was primarily trained for a military career, and
even the most cursory study of statesmanship was considered unnecessary. Pobedonostzev, however, succeeded in imbuing the young
Grand-Duke with a patriotism bordering on pure chauvinism. Even

as a boy, he loved repeating 'Russia is for the Russians'. That deadening slogan, which ignored the splendid ethnological, credal and linguistic heterogeneity of the vast Empire, early enough entered Alexander's mind, and was never to be uprooted.

A smattering of rather pedestrian 'general knowledge' and a thorough grounding in three foreign languages summed up Alexander's equipment. French, English and German were necessary since it was essential for a Grand-Duke not to play the mute either at his father's court or on visits to the numerous foreign relations. He was voted an indifferent soldier chiefly because of his dislike of parades and very poor horsemanship. The tutors were not slow to notice a predisposition to self-indulgence and a reluctance to face any task which required serious mental effort. Alexander's manners were in striking accord with his physique. 'He glowered rather than looked, and had a habit of thrusting his head forward in a most menacing way whenever anything displeased him,' remembered an officer in the Grand-Duke's regiment. All in all, the great height and the heavy build, combined with a stony lack of grace in movement and demeanour, suggested a mysteriously animated monolith. In spite of the family nickname, Alexander resembled a bear more than a bull, his ursine quality not too far removed from Gogol's Sobakevich in *The Dead Souls*.

Yet he had two qualities which streaked even his earliest years with light; a big heart and a vehement honesty, its expressions all too often disconcerting to many members of his father's household and his own. Even a white lie would dampen an otherwise happy moment for him and send him into a fury. 'Conventions,' he once remarked, 'need not be observed at the expense of veracity.' His dancing might have been compared with the antics of a performing bear. Once at a ball at Wiesbaden, when a German cousin, strictly adhering to conventions, thanked him 'for the great pleasure of the dance,' Alexander cut her short: 'Why can't you be honest? It was just a duty neither of us could have relished. I have ruined your slippers and you have made me nearly sick with the scent you use. Also your glove has left a mark on my sleeve. Do you have your gloves cleaned with chalk or with flour?'

Such rugged manners, to say no more, would lead one to think that '*bychók*' could have no friends. But he had several – his mother, his elder brother, Nicholas, Pobedonostzev and many others. Once '*bychók*' found himself among them, the rock-hewn abruptness gave way to an almost incredible gentleness. His friends felt that they mattered greatly to him. There were other sources of happiness in '*bychók*'s early life, particularly at a carpenter's bench, his enormous hands extraordinarily deft with the tools, the uniform he usually wore replaced by a much more comfortable cotton blouse and linen breeches. '*Bychók*' had other equally innocent diversions, such as furtive visits to the palace kitchens for a plate of cabbage soup and a generous helping of '*grécha*' gruel – a kind of buckwheat, the staple food of the peasant, which the palace cooks had learned to prepare for the Grand-Duke and which he liked to eat in the privacy of the palace back premises. 'Table delicacies were invented by the damned French. A Russian stomach needs food, not silly titbits fit for a kitten to peck at,' he said once. Whenever he went shooting, a satchel would be slung over his right shoulder. The satchel contained chunks of rye bread, a couple of hard-boiled eggs or a pickled herring, and salt in a paper twist – the customary daily provender of any cabman in the capital.

There was yet another particular which must be recorded of him. His piety was never exaggerated and he indulged in no mystical excursions. He took his religion in an absolutely literal sense, Pobedonostzev's influence having moulded him in that respect. Incredible as it may seem in the case of a Romanov, sex to Alexander was a grievous sin outside marriage. The most zealous gossip-mongers in St Petersburg and Moscow failed to discover anything about his 'pleasures'. Not a single breath of any scandal ever brushed against his name.

Alexander's awakening did not come until 1865 when, his elder brother Nicholas dying of consumption, he became the heir and also fiancé of Princess Dagmar of Denmark who had already been betrothed to Nicholas. She entered the Russian Church, became Grand-Duchess Marie, and married the Grand-Duke in 1866. He was then in his twenty-second year, and his marriage might be said to be his initiation into reality. A life of perfect matrimonial concord, the constant companionship of a girl who had enough sense to help her young husband towards a clear realization of his future position, a happiness he had never dared to hope for, all of it metamorphosed Alexander. Apathy began flaking off his mind, and the awakened vitality was that of a giant.

There had not been much happiness for him at the Winter Palace. But now he had his own home. Anitchkov Palace on the Nevsky gradually became a centre for court and society to reckon with. Grand-Duchess Marie, herself far better educated than most of the princesses in her day, helped her husband at every turn. Certainly the Grand-Duchess could not improve Alexander's seat on horse-back or uproot his chauvinism, but she encouraged him to fill in the lacunae left by his education. So the Grand-Duke turned to history and other disciplines. It proved a steep hill for him to climb since his mind, unaccustomed to concentrated effort, moved at a snail's pace. To read 'a heavy book' was torture at first, but, constantly en-couraged by his young wife, the Grand-Duke refused to give up. Step by painful step he learned to decipher the lettering of the contemporary map.

One province alone remained closed to Grand-Duchess Marie, and that by her own choice. She wisely decided that matters of government were not for a consort to meddle with.

So, little by little, the Grand-Duke emerged into the foreground. He became known away from the narrow court circle. His charitable gestures could not escape notice since his own servants broadcast them over the capital. Alexander's Civil List was very large, but he would not spend a penny piece on personal indulgences. He helped hospitals, struggling private schools and almshouses, he was known to come to the rescue of many people whose impoverishment stemmed from circumstances beyond their control. The Grand-Duke gave without stint. He also learnt to refuse, and stories of fabled distress did not stand much of a chance with him.

Gradually people came to learn about Alexander's pronounced and occasionally grotesque antipathy towards foreigners, in particu-lar the Germans. His Grand-Duchess did not wear the national dress, and the rooms at the Anitchkov were not furnished in that slightly exaggerated 'Muscovite style' then coming into fashion, with peasant bast sandals hanging on the walls and painted wooden spoons arranged here and there for ornament. But the national impress was felt in every room at the Anitchkov. Unless 'aliens' were present, Russian, not French, was spoken. Russian poetry and music were offered for entertainment; gambling was discouraged, and lovers of tittle-tattle liked to hint that it was wise 'to satisfy the inner man' before leaving for a meal at the Anitchkov: the Grand-Ducal meals were patterns of austerity both in quality and quantity.

It is a curious fact that a pupil of Pobedonostzev's should have been a liberal in his early years, but his father's reforms had fired the Grand-Duke when he was still in his teens. None the less, the estrangement between father and son deepened every year after 1866. The Emperor's liaison with Catherine Dolgoruka, his inept ministerial appointments, and the trend of a foreign policy too much in accord with Berlin and Vienna, were among the causes. 'Austria,' the heir said, 'has never been anything but a broken reed to us, and Prussia wants to use us as a ladder for her to climb to the top, and heaven help Europe if she ever does get there.'

The gulf between the two Alexanders widened most alarmingly during the Franco-Prussian war. Both the Grand-Duke and his wife hated Prussia and he felt no great love for France, but the Te Deums ordered by his father to celebrate Moltke's victory sickened the younger man. Present at them he must be, since no feelings of his were ever permitted to interfere with an obvious duty, but his reaction in private spoke of deep anger, if not shame. 'My father will not see that Berlin is a menace,' he said. 'He and I both consider that all war is vile. That war was a crime.' He said so in one of his own drawing-rooms at the Anitchkov, in the presence of friends and of some few people who strove to win his friendship.

The words were imprudent. They annoyed the German relations. But 'bychók' did not greatly care.

'This is supposed to be a civilized age, but the wild beast is still alive in us. So we must go to war and snatch at a neighbour's territory, and cover it all up with excuses which would not be tolerated in a schoolboy. We are worse than cocks in a pit because we are supposed to have minds of our own. The world is in a mess as it is. Let every country keep an eye to its own business.'

So the Grand-Duke spoke in 1871. Those views would be vehemently changed by 1877.

All the enlightened minds in the country were heartened by the evidences of Alexander's liberal views. He chafed at the slowing down of reforms and at the reaction that had set in after Karakozov's attempt.

'And just look at some of the Ministries,' he said sombrely. 'Tolstoy alone will put the clock back for decades.'

Alexander called all war vile and wasteful, but his rabid Slavo-mania came to override his adherence to peace, and he became the leader of the war party in 1876, and converted one of his brothers, Grand-Duke Wladimir. Both were overjoyed that their mother shared their views. Wladimir was a soldier first and last, but Alexander saw the Balkan problem in rigidly racial terms, all to often forgetting that Bulgaria formed no part of the Slav brother-hood. In 1877 Alexander went south in the spirit of a dedicated crusader. There was nothing really distinguished in his service but at the headquarters they referred to the heir as the only com-mander who never caused them any trouble.

In 1878 he came back to his wife, his mind scarred by disillusion-ment.

The campaign left him with a reawakened and deepened horror of war and intensified horror of peculation. The Emperor's adminis-tration left plenty of room for graft to stalk about. Soldiers lacked boots, biscuits and bullets whilst speculators of every kind could build marble villas in the Crimea and buy diamonds and rubies for their mistresses. The canker had thrown its tentacles into most unexpected quarters. His own uncle, Grand-Duke Nicholas, was known to be hand in glove with the despoilers of national integrity. The heir clamoured for his dismissal from office.

'Deprive him of supreme command,' he said to his father. 'He is unfit for it.' But Alexander II replied that he could not be expected to bring dishonour upon the dynasty by revealing his own brother's misdeeds.

It is on record that the heir never spoke to his uncle again. The scandal never came into full daylight, but Grand-Duke Nicholas's greatly increased revenues were a gold-mine to every gossip-monger at court.

They were in 1878. In less than three years the Grand-Duke would be Emperor. To him those last three years of his father's reign were like so many centuries. The terror gripping the country, the govern-ment ambling from one blunder to another, and himself, though with a seat at the Council table, prevented from making any inde-pendent decision, all of it was gall and wormwood to the Grand-Duke. Finally, there was the humiliation of having his father's mistress lodged under the same roof with his father's wife, his own greatly beloved mother! Abhorring all strife and dissension, the Grand-Duke could not prevent the spread of a sharp cleavage between himself and some of his close relations, particularly his uncle, Grand-Duke Michael, who considered that 'an autocrat's private affairs should never be criticized by anyone, least of all by his own children.'

'An autocrat's private behaviour should stand above criticism,' replied Alexander.

His principles and his feelings were equally outraged. When Grand-Duke Michael remarked that 'all judgment had best be left to the Almighty', his nephew retorted that it was his duty to consider his mother.

All such stresses might easily have defeated him if it had not been for the harbour he found at home. Grand-Duchess Marie was wife and mother and mistress of the Anitchkov. She was also the last of the long line of foreign princesses to make the Romanov case her own. Year by year, she stitched most diligently at her intimate tapestry. The frequent illnesses and absences of the Empress Marie compelled the daughter-in-law to take up the tasks of the consort. The wife of the Emperor Paul I had founded innumerable educational and charitable institutions up and down the Empire, her personal interest in their development never flagging to the end. That vast field was now Marie's to cultivate, and there she worked untiringly. Except for the wholly private talks with her husband, she left all state matters alone. It was both joy and pride to Alexander to see her popularity grow from year to year.

There was little else for him to rejoice in during those last years as Grand-Duke. The outcome of the Berlin Congress shocked him deeply, and he blamed his father for sending Gorchakov to represent Russia. The antipathy for Germany swelled into an almost pathological odium. By far the best bakers in St Petersburg were German. Alexander ordered that not a single loaf was to be bought from them for the household use.

All too frequently unguarded in his speech, the Grand-Duke gave so many airings to his views that some of the ministers begged the Emperor not to allow his son the least share in the government. So Alexander lived at the Anitchkov or at Gatchina, carried out his none too onerous regimental duties and what social functions he could not escape, continued with his studies, and was more than ever affectionate towards his mother, whose death in the spring of 1880 was the second great grief in his life.

The Empress Marie died in May 1880. Less than two months later, whilst the Grand-Duke and his wife were on a visit to their Danish relations, Alexander II married Princess Yurievskaya. Now that she was no longer a mistress but a wife, every visit to the Winter Palace was a trial for the heir. The thorniness of the situation was felt all the more sharply because in his censure he stood virtually alone among his Romanov kin. His uncles, in particular Grand-Duke Michael, did not permit themselves to criticize the Emperor. All the younger members of the clan were enchanted by Princess Yurievskaya. To all of them alike the late Empress had been little more than a pallid, constantly ailing shadow, a woman foolish enough to continue loving a husband who had no further use for her. To Grand-Duke Alexander and his brothers she had been a deeply wronged mother. The heir never forgot how kindly she had been to his wife, disliked by Alexander II for her anti-German feelings. All in all, Marie had been a mainstay and a warmth, and he considered his father's hurried second marriage. a dishonour to her memory.

All those family difficulties came to be dissolved in a most violent manner that March afternoon in 1881 when the third Alexander ascended the throne.

The Empire and Europe waited for the first imperial pronouncements. They came soon enough. Terse and unequivocal, they were as rough-hewn as the new Tsar's body. They proved that the terror-flecked years had destroyed all liberal breath in him. He spoke of his firm faith 'in the strength and the justice of autocratic power', and declared that his foreign policy would be devoted to the preservation of peace. The constitutional manifesto which should have been signed by Alexander II in the evening of the day of his murder was just a paper nobody had any use for. Its architect knew that there would be nothing for him to do under the new dispensation, and he left for abroad soon enough. An ultimatum, most recklessly sent to the new sovereign by the committee of the Social-Revolutionary Party, was to have most tragic consequences.

They promised that they would refrain from further acts of violence if a National Assembly were convened without delay and full constitutional rights given to the entire nation. The paper reached Alexander III a mere few days before his father's funeral. Clumsily and hurriedly composed, the ultimatum ended with the words: 'Now it is for you to choose which of the two paths to take.'

The Social-Revolutionaries could not have committed a grosser blunder. His father's murder atoned for all his failings in Alexander's eyes, plunged the entire nation into sorrow, and shocked the West. The wording of the ultimatum showed plainly that its signatories were far more concerned about their particular ideology than with national feelings and the immediate interests of the country. The demand for the abolition of hereditary autocracy screened very thinly the ambition to introduce an autocracy shaped by chance. The demand for the immediate creation of a national assembly revealed the authors' abysmal ignorance of the conditions under which such a process could begin.

It would hardly be an exaggeration to say that the cruelly mistimed document was largely responsible for many a twilit moment in the thirteen years of Alexander III's reign, for the sharply intensified activity of the secret police, the tightened-up censorship, the heavy bureaucratic gyves clamped on all educational establishments, and the savage war against all 'subversive' thought, speech and deed. The European press would refer to 'the inhuman persecutions' and gasp about 'a reign of terror', but Alexander III, conscious of the national wrath at his father's murder, had a case where 'subversion' was concerned. Cruel he could be, and cruel he would be towards a minority pursuing a policy alien to the national understanding and needs, but 'the reign of terror' proved a most rewardingly peaceable spell for millions and millions of his people.

There was no alternative for him where the Social-Revolutionaries were concerned except to follow the pattern outlined in his Accession Manifesto, '. . . [therefore] we call upon all our loyal subjects to serve us and the state in truth and in justice and [to help us] to up-root the horrible sedition that now dishonours our Russian land . . . with faith in the strength and justice of the autocratic power we hold under God . . . [the same power] which has more than once succeeded in making our country overcome great trials . . . and [under which] Russia has grown in strength and in glory. . . .'

Those words were addressed to a people still half-paralysed by the shock of the Liberator's assassination. For a minority, magic had for some time since gone out of the monarchical concept, but a sovereign could not afford to think or plan in terms of a minority. To the masses, the purely personal character of the Tsar was all too often of less meaning than a leaf tossed by the wind. The Tsar's office, however dimly and even crudely apprehended, was a symbol of the national necessity.

That first manifesto of the new reign was supposed to be drafted by Pobedonostzev, but Alexander revised and enlarged it himself. His conception of autocracy was almost alarmingly simple: the word meant what it said, no more and no less. Giers became Alexander's Prime Minister, but Giers's office was soon shorn even of the small measure of independence enjoyed by a Nesselrode or a Gorchakov. The new Emperor preferred to be his own Chancellor. He lost no time in dismissing Dimitry Tolstoy, Timashev and a few others. When Bunge, then Minister of Finance, was at the point of tendering his resignation, he found himself summoned to the palace to be told by his sovereign: 'You seem to forget that in my country Ministers are appointed or dismissed. They do not resign.'

Such an iron attitude came to be somewhat softened with the years, and on the whole the Romanov 'bychók' showed a surprising ability in judging both character and merit. There was Witte, for one, and Richter, the Emperor's Private Secretary. Pobedonostzev, to the grief of many, remained at his post as Procurator of the Holy Synod, Alexander's attachment being rooted in personal reasons. It was from that ungainly and ungracious man that he had first learned the opening article of his private creed: 'Russia is for the Russians.'

From the very first days of his reign the Emperor plunged into work. The several splendours of his court must of course be kept up, but only when state occasions demanded it, and he saw to it that those occasions were to happen much less frequently than had been the case under any of his predecessors. He decided that the Winter Palace was to be kept open for formal state entertainment only, and he had little love for the Alexander Palace at Tsarskoe Selo. He preferred the familiar simplicities of the Anitchkov when he was in St

Petersburg and the even less formal climate of Gatchina where he could afford to wear a peasant's blouse and breeches and keep a table in the manner of a none too wealthy civil servant or merchant. Some of the Ministers, when summoned to Gatchina, were taken aback by the austerity of the meals. Witte, rather inordinately fond of 'la haute cuisine', complained that some of the dishes served at the Emperor's table were unfit to eat. One of the equerries remarked that the Ministers were fortunate not to be offered the Tsar's favourite food: cabbage soup and millet or 'grétcha' gruel.

All the various imperial households from St Petersburg down to Livadia in the Crimea were dumbfounded by the spate of economies ordered by the Emperor. Stewards' books, sent to Gatchina for his inspection, were returned full of terse marginalia in red ink. Table linen was not to be changed every day, soap and candles must not be thrown away until they were used up, lights were not to be left burning in empty rooms. The chief steward at one of the palaces was told that, with twenty people sitting down to a meal, there was no necessity to use one hundred eggs for an omelette.

Those seem rather cheese-paring details, but there followed many bigger economies, particularly in the administration field, and provincial governors were ordered to whittle down their entertainment expenditure. Alexander III was no Scrooge, but he knew better than most that the nation's finances had limped rather sadly since 1877, and he considered it his duty to show an example of thrift. 'Nobody knew better than he the value of a single copek', remembered Witte.

Having swept all his households with the economy broom, Alexander proceeded to cut down his own Civil List by eighteen million roubles a year. That measure was followed by a thorough reorganization of all the crown manors and lands so that by 1884 their revenues were more than doubled.

Those properties, known as 'oudély', were the fruit of the financial sagacity of Catherine the Great, who paid for their acquisition out of her Privy Purse in order to provide for the future needs of the dynasty. A great many of those 'oudély' were in the Crimea. Those lands provided the income of the entire Romanov family, greatly increased in numbers since the end of the eighteenth century. Nicholas I had had four sons, all of whom were married and had families. Grand-Duke Michael alone had six sons. Within another decade or two, as Alexander III saw it, the number of individual appanages would be doubled. He issued a Family Statute whereby only children and grandchildren of a sovereign were to bear the title of Grand-Duke and Grand-Duchess. All the others were to be known as Princes and Princesses with the title of 'Highness', and their allowances were proportionately diminished.*

Alexander's personal economies were no less stringent. He would wear his everyday clothes until they were past mending and in all likelihood he was the only Romanov not to scorn cobbled boots. What foreign relatives came to Gatchina were always taken aback by the spartan appointments of his private rooms. But he could also be generous. Once a minor civil servant, having been indicted for graft, petitioned the Emperor for clemency. Alexander would not come to a decision in a hurry. The wording of the petition seemed to trouble him. 'The man does not grovel or whine; odd that he should have fallen so low.' He ordered inquiries to be made. 'A wife, a mother, and eight children, and not a word about the family in the petition,' and, on learning what the clerk's salary was, the Tsar lost his temper. 'Such a pittance is an open invitation to thieving.' He reduced the man's sentence considerably since he did not feel he could grant a free pardon but he had the family provided for out of the Privy Purse, and he ordered an increase of salaries to untold thousands of small bureaucratic fry and tightened up penalties for graft.

'I have three enemies to fight at home,' he told his in-laws in Denmark, 'sedition, waste and peculation. Otherwise I am a man of peace.'

The Emperor's private creed consisted of three articles: orthodoxy, autocracy, and homogeneity – and it is within the scope of the latter that his reign appears at its darkest. Homogeneity might have answered with a Prince of Kiev in the tenth century. In Alexander's day it was an absurdity, and he chose to carry it to deplorable extremes.

He was Tsar of Siberia peopled by a multitude of tribes, Lord of the Caucasus, Grand-Duke of Finland, Tsar of Poland, Sovereign of the Baltic Provinces, Tsar of the Crimea, and of vast reaches of

* See Note at the end of the chapter.

Central Asia. His subjects spoke several hundred dialects. He had over five million Jews in his dominions. His people were Orthodox, Roman Catholic, Lutheran, Calvinist, Baptist, Methodist, Buddhist and Muslim. There were also numerous branches of home-bred nonconformity, to say nothing of various little-known beliefs adhered to by innumerable tribes in Siberia and elsewhere.

But the Emperor's watchword was 'Russia is for the Russians'. His knowledge of ethnology was too poor for him to realize that 'the pure Russian race' existed nowhere except in the imagination of a fanatic. But, since homogeneity was lacking in the Empire, he considered it his duty to enforce it.

It would be unfair to accuse Alexander III of having started anti-Semitism in Russia. It had been there long before. It would be equally untrue to deny that it was during his reign that anti-Semitism received a shameful measure of official approbation.

In broad terms the Jewish problem, as such, cannot be said to have existed in Russia before the Polish partitions. It is true that great numbers of Jews were settled in the western provinces of the Empire. They had always been disliked by their Gentile neighbours, but not until the second half of the eighteenth century was any legislation introduced to hamper their way of life and to penalize them for imaginary offences. The old Russian animosity had sprung from a peasant's attitude to anyone reluctant to work on the land. Furthermore, a nation of more than hazy views about economics and thrift mistrusted and hated a people, alien by blood and creed, who had a genius for winning a place in the sun, chiefly by hard work and sound domestic economy.

First glimpses of violent anti-Semitism became discernible in the nineteenth century, particularly under Nicholas I. With Alexander III, it grew rampant.

He had hated the Jews since his boyhood, when he had been greatly influenced by his tutor, Pobedonostzev. Come to manhood, Alexander was fond of repeating the cynical Russian adage, '*Zhid khretchény kak vor protchény*', i.e. 'a baptized Yid is like a forgiven thief.' The Holy Synod never tired of carrying on proselytism among Jews, Buddhists, Muslims and non-Orthodox Christians. The Emperor, duly subscribing to such policy, was inconsistent in dismissing Jewish conversions to Christianity as evidences of cowardice. 'You will never make them truly Orthodox,' he once said to a bishop. 'The Yiddish leaven is ineradicable.' Even in official documents he would sometimes write the contemptuous '*Zhid*' ('Yid') instead of '*Evréy*' ('Jew'). He firmly believed every calumny against them, and was convinced that a gigantic plot was being organized by international Jewry in order to undermine and finally to destroy the existing social pattern. When someone ventured to point out that such a plot was wholly imaginary, Alexander lost his temper and shouted:

'Imaginary? And look at our own country!'

He clung to the opinion unhappily held by a great many of his subjects that the Jews had been involved in his father's murder and that they continued to finance all the subversive 'cells' still in existence. It never occurred to him that the nihilism of the early sixties had had a Russian cradle. He blamed other governments for being blind to 'the peril', and was heard to call Queen Victoria 'an old fool' because of her regard for Disraeli.

The root of such a pathological attitude was neither racial nor political, nor even religious. To this author, at least, it seems to have been born of unconscious jealousy.

Himself an honourable and dedicated family man, the Emperor could not but deplore the low morality standards among his 'true-bred' Russians. In large sections of society, the seventh commandment was regarded as being as obsolete as their grandmother's gowns. In his own clan, divorce was still out of the question, but Alexander knew that some of his cousins and at least one of his brothers kept mistresses and made no secret of their '*affaires*'. He kept thundering at them, and they accepted his rebukes, but he could do no more. To deprive them of their Civil List would inevitably have led to a scandal he could not afford to face, since in public, at least, the Romanov honour must remain sacrosanct.

And there, to deepen his humiliation, were the five million Jews whose family life was not overshadowed by contempt for marriage vows, where kinship was cherished, and where parents held their children's respect. In the field of economics, the Emperor was doing his utmost to conquer fecklessness and to encourage thrift, and knew himself hampered by the happy-go-lucky, and in his eyes dishonest, attitude of true-bred Russians, some among whom were so brilliantly sketched in Tolstoy's *Anna Karenina*, men, who, owing more than a million, lived as though they did not owe a penny. But the Jews disliked running into debt and looked upon all squandering as a horror, and all too often came to the rescue of their improvident Gentile brethren.

And there was more than that.

A pious Orthodox and always jealous for the honour of the national Church, the Emperor was appalled by some of the reports reaching him about the country clergy. Numbers of village priests were ignorant, lazy, immoral and, themselves reduced to penury, lived mainly on their parishioners' offerings, the latter being anything but voluntary. Fees were extorted even for confession. And there were the Rabbis, most of them poor, all of them deeply learned and rigidly moral, and exercising an enviable influence over their flocks.

We cannot tell if the pogroms started within a few months after Alexander's accession had their origin in any official move since all such records would have been immediately destroyed. But it is beyond doubt that the climate which made those pogroms possible had been prepared by the administration. At Elizavetgrad, Kiev, Kharkov, Witebsk, Smolensk and in other towns Jewish quarters were attacked by mobs, and even women and children joined in the infamous chorus of '*Bey Zhidóv*' – 'beat up the Yids'. Shops were looted, houses burned down, many Jews killed, and savageries reminiscent of the day of the Tartars fell to the lot of womenfolk and children. A truly Christian superior of a Russian convent in Kiev opened her gates and gave sanctuary to some Jewish women and their babies. For that gesture of charity she received censure from the bishop. It was not a nun's business to interfere, he said, she should have left it to the appropriate authorities. All those towns were heavily policed, but in every case the police said that the mob 'had got beyond all control'.

Inquiry commissions were set up rather belatedly, but the dead could not be brought back to life, the compensation doled out by the Treasury was grievously inadequate, and it fell to the lot of the foreign Jewry to help their dispossessed kin in Russia.

In official utterances pogroms were deplored, though the ravages were always dwarfed. But the Emperor said to his Minister of the Interior, Count Ignatiev, as rabid an anti-Semite as himself: 'The Yids have brought it all upon themselves. They will batten on our people. Why, almost every "*Zhid*" is a usurer.'

The so-called Ignatiev Laws were published in 1882. They bore the Minister's name, but the Emperor and Pobedonostzev had done much of the work. The Pale of Settlement was defined most rigidly but, in large terms, the Ignatiev Laws covered far more ground than had ever been done under Alexander's predecessors. No Jew might hold the least important administrative post. The services and certain professions were closed to them. A Jew could practise as a solicitor but he was debarred from any progress up the juridical ladder. He could own no land. If he had a pawnshop, it must remain under constant police supervision. If he was engaged in any trade, he was not allowed to keep the Sabbath. He was forbidden to contract a marriage with a Christian unless he renounced his religion. No books were to be printed in Hebrew, and all Jewish schools were closed. The Rabbis alone were allowed to instruct children under certain conditions. Only in exceptional circumstances was a Jew permitted to leave the Pale of Settlement, but there were to be no Jewish butchers and bakers outside the Pale. He lost the right of appeal against any sentence of the courts, and it became very difficult for him to sue for monies owed to him by Christians. Finally, Jewish children could only attend such schools as were chosen for them by the authorities. Taxes decreed for the Jews became higher than those demanded of the Gentiles.

Let it be added that if the Ignatiev Laws had been submitted to a national plebiscite, they would have been approved by a sadly overwhelming majority.

The immediate consequence was an exodus of Jews from Alexander's Empire. They went to England and France, to Asia Minor and North Africa, and to the United States. The Russian administration put no obstacles in their way so long as their taxes, fines and other levies were paid. 'Let them carry their poison where they will,' said Alexander. 'Russia is for the Russians.'

At the same time he was carrying his chauvinist weapons into Finland, with no thought of the grievous legacy he was preparing for his son. Alexander III was the architect of the so-called 'Finnish problem' which would vex and disturb the last Romanov sovereign all through his reign.

Finland, for centuries wholly under the Swedish suzerainty and partly conquered by Peter the Great, entered the Russian Empire under Alexander I, whose Swedish campaign of 1807 had been undertaken at the suggestion of Napoleon, and 'The Blessed' did not feel particularly happy about its victorious outcome for himself. Nor did Russia, ashamed that her Tsar should have 'danced to Bonaparte's fiddle'. To quieten his own conscience and to please his people, Alexander I gave Finland an autonomy, a parliament and a free press not answerable to the Russian censors. Not even Nicholas's pig-headed policy interfered with the Finnish privileges. Parliament at Borgo carried on its business in Swedish and in Finnish, the local government continued its functions without being hampered by any directives from St Petersburg, and the Finnish Guards Regiment was one of the most loyal units in the Romanov army.

But such a pattern ran counter to Alexander III's conception of what his Empire should be, and many Finnish civic privileges were either thinned down or else done away with by one stroke of the imperial pen. Parliament was abolished, censorship introduced, and Russian made compulsory in all schools and colleges. Finally, an Orthodox cathedral was built in Helsingfors, the whole of the Grand-Duchy was 'raised' to the honour of an archepiscopal see, and an archbishop was sent to Helsingfors 'to represent the National Church' about which the Finnish masses had as clear an idea as about the surface of the moon. Alexander III, having planted seeds of future rebellions in the most law-abiding part of his dominions, turned his attention to the Baltic seaboard.

Here, his passion for Russification ran mad. The three provinces could have been compared with three geese laying golden eggs for the Empire. They enjoyed a certain measure of autonomy and their prosperity made Bismarck jealous in his day. The Treasury in St Petersburg never had to come to their aid. They were the dairy of European Russia. Their exports of timber, ore and fish were flourishing even during the periods when Russian export trade had little to boast about. Their ports were considered as jewels in the imperial diadem, and their past linked them to the proud days of the Hanseatic League.

But Alexander, swept on the wings of his Russomania, declared that 'the historic rights of the Baltic Provinces must yield to the necessities of the Russian state.' Soon afterwards the insidious canker of Russian bureaucracy crept into the hitherto healthy administration of the provinces. Taxes were raised and innumerable restrictions introduced to conform to the general pattern. In the past, experts, mainly from Germany and Sweden, had no difficulty in finding employment along the Baltic seaboard. Now no alien was allowed to accept a job of any kind. Somehow or other, the business rhythm slowed down, all the German officials who were permitted to retain their posts being put under Russian supervision. The result was a temporary chaos, particularly at the docks. The commercial side apart, the provinces were visited by a number of Russian missionaries, whose zeal, however, met with thin success.

All of it was all the more disappointing since the industrial development of Russia proper began to make gigantic strides ahead during the reign.

Having come to read serious history rather late in life, the Emperor never learned that his true-bred Russian was in reality an ethnological mongrel – Slav, Scandinavian, Greek, Tartar, to say nothing of other blood infusions. The parrot cry of 'Russia for the Russians' came rather oddly from a man who could claim no closer Russian relation than his great-great-great-grandmother, Anna, elder daughter of Peter the Great, herself but half a Russian by blood since her mother, Martha Skavronskaya, was a Livonian.

'The horrible sedition', as the Emperor called the anti-monarchist activity, had never really been uprooted all through the reign. By the mid-nineteenth century, a negative attitude to the throne had become part of a covenant accepted by an educated minority, the so-called intelligentsia, who rarely, if ever, translated that attitude into action. But away from their ranks, there was yet another minority, whose abstract ideas were undeniably excellent whilst they remained abstract. Once interpreted into action, they immediately shed their quality. But to that minority, action seemed as necessary as air, and they could not envisage 'progress' in any other terms than those of violence.

Political murders were vile and fruitless. Yet, for all the revulsion they produced, the homicidal pattern did not form the core of the crime to be laid at the door of the Social-Revolutionaries. The main indictment must be looked for elsewhere.

They were criminals because they were liars. They insisted that they were out to wrest liberty on behalf of the whole nation, whose real needs they had not begun to study. What they were offering was

an exchange of a worn-out autocracy for a new one, such an exchange
to be carried out at the cost of destroyed prosperity, mass bewilderment and many more lives than were ended at the hands of the
Emperor's hangmen. The Social-Revolutionaries spoke in the name
of the nation, and they spoke falsely: no single peasant had ever
been recruited into their ranks. Factory contingents and university
students listened to the 'red' propaganda and spread it in their turn,
but what were their numbers compared with the masses? The
gospel preached by the S-Rs was wholly alien to the national ethos.
A titanic change was necessary indeed, but its mere preliminaries
demanded years and years of preparation. The 'subversives' were
not trained to think in healthy terms of historical processes. They
were like amateur mountaineers, who, having climbed a steep hill
in the neighbourhood of their native village, decide that they are
fit to conquer the north face of the Eiger.

From some such viewpoint, Alexander III's ruthlessness is justified. His repressive measures unavoidably involved a great many
wholly innocent people. They hampered the way of normal enlightenment, muzzled the press, and deepened the bureaucratic canker,
but there was no alternative for the Emperor.

Yet the picture presented to the West by foreign correspondents
in Russia was wildly out of alignment with reality. It all but suggested
the autocrat spending all his time signing death-sentences, himself
crouching on all fours under a table, with a Social-Revolutionary,
bomb in hand, lurking behind every corner of the palace. Someone
even invented a pathetic story about Alexander kissing his English
relations in Copenhagen and saying, tears running down his cheeks:
'Good-bye, my dears. Now you go back to your happy English home,
and I must return to my Russian prison.' Prison indeed! Nowhere
did Alexander feel so utterly at ease as in his 'own very dear
Russia'. Abroad, the infrequency of his public appearances was
taken as an additional proof of his cowardice and the inability of the
police to protect him. It was true that Alexander did not often
appear in public, but that was due to an almost pathological reluctance to face publicity. It is true that Alexander III did not inherit
the courage shown by some of his predecessors, but he was no
craven coward.

There were also hair-raising stories about an army some 100,000
strong guarding the palace and the park at Gatchina. The Emperor's

home was indeed protected but never to the absurd extent of keeping the Gatchina station closed to anyone unconcerned with the business of court and government. Gatchina was not just palace and park. It was a township of some few thousand inhabitants, whose lives were not really overshadowed by the likelihood of a bomb left at the threshold.

Of course, Alexander's life was in constant danger, and he knew it. There were many unsuccessful attempts, many mass arrests, many sentences to Siberian exile, and a number of executions. Yet, however grossly mistaken he was in some of his policies, particularly in his rabid nationalism, one thing at least must be conceded to him: he thought, planned and acted in wide national terms. Personal safety, prestige and dignity were all engulfed within the office which, as he considered, was entrusted to him by his Maker.

Someone said of him that there were two things he kept most religiously: the seventh commandment and the peace of Europe. It should be added that, Denmark apart, Alexander III regarded Europe with a contempt not always disguised. He loathed Germany, mistrusted England, had little use for Austria, and his dalliance with France was rather a sham on one side and a farce on the other. Only once or twice in the thirteen years of his reign did the climate of peace grow tautened but on each occasion the danger was averted by timely arbitration. The Turkish problem, so thorny and immediate to all his predecessors, did not trouble Alexander III. The Black Sea Fleet, restored to its pre-1877 strength, was there for purely defensive purposes, as the Emperor declared in 1886, and his words held true until 1914. He decided to have Batum turned into a free port contrary to a clause in the Berlin Congress Treaty and promptly answered the British protest by pointing out that the treaty had already been violated by other signatories in the case of Bulgaria being united to Eastern Rumelia. No other Great Power echoed England's protest, and Alexander's action did not lead to any rupture of diplomatic relations with Britain.

When still a Grand-Duke, he used to say that war was a waste of time. As Emperor, he had even less time to waste. 'My household is so big, it demands every moment of the day,' he used to say. He was the first Romanov since Peter the Great to consider the industrial expansion of the Empire as a necessity. There was the building of many new railways, one linking the Caspian shores to Samarkand and another, the Great Siberian Railway, '*Velíky Sibírsky Put*', stretching for nearly seven thousand miles. A number of remarkable engineering enterprises came into shape during the reign, such as for instance the drainage of the Pinsk Marshes, an area of about the size of England. Several irrigation projects were started, and the earlier neglected matter of bridges up and down the countryside was taken in hand by the administration.

Above all else, Alexander left a beneficial imprint on the national finances, and he was wise enough to use the genius of a man like Witte in that field. The introduction of protective tariffs for home industries, the encouragement given to innumerable industrial enterprises from Novgorod to Vladivostok, the founding of Peasant Banks to steady and improve the peasants' economic status were all undertaken by the Emperor in the firm belief that Russia could and should be not merely solvent but wealthy. Such was his intention, realized some years before his premature death. Yet it remains part of Alexander's tragedy that, a nationalist to the last drop of his blood, he began, as it were, to pave the way towards a materialistic conception of life, so alien to the spirit of the nation. Russia, unbroken peace outside her borders, grew rich, her industries expanded, her natural wealth began yielding undreamt-of dividends, enormous private fortunes were made, even by artisans and peasants. Yet that influx of prosperity had the face of Janus: it enriched and it impoverished. On one side, it lifted the level of common amenities, widened the field of very necessary charitable activities, and brought much of the needed Western technology into the country. On the other, it sharpened the division not only between affluence and penury but between the former and a modest way of living, and by so doing added to the number of already existing social rifts. It also blunted spiritual perceptions and introduced an artificial standard of judging anyone's condition by his substance. Money ceased to be the means to an end and became the end for many and many, and great fortunes were made by some who had not been trained in wise spending and had no inborn instincts to guide them. Stories about merchants and 'jumped-up' technicians lighting their cigars with twenty-five-rouble notes were not particularly good for the national morale. When Alexander heard about a grain king who,

after his daughter's wedding, ordered the immediate destruction of
all crystal and porcelain bought for the banquet, the imperial comment was far more than sarcastic: 'I should make a law to penalize
such sinful extravagance.'

Being an autocrat, he might have introduced any law he pleased,
and it was a pity that he did not do so in that particular case.

Alexander III cannot be called the true representative of the dynasty.
He kept his marriage vows, deeply cared for his children, and had
regard, if not affection, for the rest of the numerous clan. Not a
breath of any scandal was ever associated with his name. Marie was
his wife, and they were each other's to have and to hold until death
parted them, and she was a fit consort for such a man. She never
ceased to influence him but that influence did not encroach upon
state matters. Husband and wife lived in closest harmony – and
had nothing in common between them. The Empress was not particularly thrifty; she loved fine clothes and good jewellery and the
glitter of great court occasions, which were worse than purgatory to
Alexander. The Empress detested walking, and would not even go
for a drive unless it were fine. He could not spend a day without
going on as long a wander as his scant leisure allowed, and rain and
sunshine made no difference to him. Marie's small and lovely hands
were not much good for anything except the occasional use of her
embroidery needle, and Alexander loved all manner of manual work
and was an expert in many handicrafts. She preferred her children
to be quiet. To Alexander, a quiet child was something out of
accord with nature, and he enjoyed romping about with his sons and
daughters. The Empress's ladies and maids were kept very busy. It
never occurred to the Emperor to ring for his valet to have his boots
pulled off. Finally, she loved the arts, and they said very little to him,
though he encouraged them out of his sense of duty. Yet all those
differences did not mar the perfect accord between them.

By the time the reign drew to its wholly unexpected close, the
Romanov clan had grown very numerous. Alexander's three uncles
were all married, and one of them, Grand-Duke Michael, had six
sons of his own. The Emperor had a crowd of cousins, nephews and
nieces. He had not much time to spare for them individually, but
he kept a vigilant eye on them. On certain occasions he invited them

all to a meal of a sumptuousness never seen on ordinary days. Then, easily slipping into a patriarch's role, Alexander would deliver something of a homily to add spice to the food.

'The nation's eyes are on us. We happen to be highly privileged because we belong to a dynasty. We must all do our duty and not shame our illustrious house by the least deviation from decent standards. If you cannot afford to pay for your wife's ruby brooch, then your wife must manage without a ruby brooch. If you fall in love, reflect on your responsibilities as husband and father. It is shameful for a Romanov to shame his marriage vows and to stay idle.'

There is no record left to tell us of the kinsmen's reactions to such sermons, but the facts speak clearly enough: there was certainly cohesion in the clan all through Alexander III's reign. Nor did he allow the menfolk to stay idle. No Grand-Duke could imagine that his regimental duties meant attendance at parades and mess banquets to the exclusion of all else. The Emperor did not permit himself to interfere with their use of leisure, except very occasionally. Once a nephew of his gambled away half his yearly allowance in one evening. A little later the young, man was summoned to Gatchina.

'I rather wanted to congratulate you,' said the Emperor. 'It is pleasant to know that one of my nephews is wholly clear of debt. . . .' And when the young Grand-Duke blushed scarlet, he exclaimed: 'What? Have you got any debts? To whom do you owe? And how much?' and when some details were given most reluctantly, Alexander drew himself up to his immense height and clenched his fists.

'My nephew? I wish you were not a Grand-Duke! It would be enough to make a hen laugh (*'kuram na smiekh*) if it were not tragic. You are a thief. The money you have gambled away did not belong to you but to your creditors. Now listen! I am not going to pay your debts because I feel sorry for you but because I am jealous for the family honour, and you shall swear by the cross here, in this room, that you will never touch cards again. Now out of my sight! Go for a long walk and when you come back, you will find the money – which is not yours,' added the Emperor.

The incident should close with a traditionally virtuous ending. That did not happen: Alexander died some time before the young man had gone beyond the wild oats stage, and he must have assured himself that an oath given out of fear could not be binding.

The Emperor's health was in full conformity with his giant's physique, but the catastrophe at Borki in 1888 when his train was derailed, and when he held up the caving-in roof of the coach to rescue his wife and some members of the household, was to cost him dear. He hated all manner of fuss, he held all doctors in contempt, and he assured his wife that he felt perfectly well. So he did, for a time. And then, at first quite imperceptibly, the titan's strength began ebbing away. His younger daughter, Grand-Duchess Olga, was the first to notice it when once, walking with her in the park at Gatchina, the Emperor changed colour, sat down on the grass, and murmured that when he felt 'better' he would go back to the palace. 'And you must not say anything to your mother,' he added, his face twitching as though he were in pain. His daughter obeyed him, but there followed other attacks, and the Empress insisted on summoning the court physician. In his turn, he asked for a consultant's opinion. The Emperor retorted that he felt 'perfectly fit' in between the attacks, but Marie won her way, and nephritis was diagnosed.

They decided that Alexander was strong enough for a journey to the south, and he came to the Crimea at the end of the summer of 1894. Adequate treatment, warm climate and rest somewhat restored him at first, but he had no illusions. With the coming of autumn, his condition worsened so sharply that all his Ministers were summoned to Livadia. In the morning of 1st November, the Emperor insisted on leaving his bed for a big armchair, and said to his wife: 'I believe it is coming. Don't worry about me. I am quite calm,' and she stayed by him. Later, his children and his heir's fiancée, Princess Alix of Hesse-Darmstadt, were summoned. The Emperor would not be carried back to bed, and Marie knelt by the chair. He smiled at her and murmured, 'I am not dead yet, but I know I have already met an angel. . . .' About two in the afternoon he died, his head pillowed on his wife's shoulder.

Unlovable in many ways, Alexander III yet possessed qualities denied to most of his predecessors. Such as he was, he remained himself, the least juggling with principles being utterly alien to him.

He never wore a mask or broke a promise. Not his own country only but the whole of Europe was poorer by his death. Whatever the mistakes and the unfortunate absurdities of his reign, he knew the worth of peace and the ghastly futility of war far better than most men of his generation and he was strong enough to make his policy accepted by others. He came to be known as the peacemaker Tsar (*Tsar Mirotvóretz*). His acceptance of peace was born of strength and not weakness.

NOTE

There were fifteen Grand-Dukes and ten Grand-Duchesses living in 1917. One Grand-Duke was living permanently in England. Seven escaped and seven were murdered by the Soviet government. Five of the Grand-Duchesses – Elizabeth, the Empress Alexandra's sister, and four daughters of the Emperor – were also murdered. Of the seven Grand-Dukes who escaped, two – Grand-Dukes Dimitry and Boris – were unmarried and one had no children. All seven were grandsons of sovereigns, Cyril, Boris, Andrew and Dimitry being grandsons of Alexander II, Alexander, Nicholas and Peter of Nicholas I.

There are no Russian Grand-Dukes living today. Grand Dukes Cyril and Peter each left a son, but both Prince Wladimir and Prince Roman, being great-grandsons of a sovereign, are debarred from the Grand-Ducal title by the Family Statute of Alexander III. The only other male Romanovs living today are the sons and grandsons of Grand-Duke Alexander and the only surviving son of Grand-Duke Constantine, Prince Gabriel.

The very last Grand-Duchess of Russia, Olga, younger daughter of Alexander III, died in Canada in 1961.

XII

The World They Left

Nicholas II, eldest son of the Emperor
Alexander III. Born in May 1868, succeeded
in November 1894, murdered in
July 1918

ON THE death of Alexander III, Clemenceau is supposed to have said: 'What is Nicholas II? Nobody knows, possibly not even himself.' Many foreign judgments on Russia and the Russians bordered on the fantastic. In this case, however, Clemenceau was not wrong. Not even his own countrymen knew what kind of person Nicholas was. One image of him contradicted another. People indulged in endless, all equally anxious, conjectures. There was some conventionally minted praise, based on little more than tittle-tattle from the back premises of great houses. There was a somewhat stronger current of contemptuous criticism stemming from the same source. Someone, having seen Nicholas's indifferent stare at a horse fallen down in a street of Gatchina, at once decided the heir was cruel to animals. Someone else, watching him stoop to pick up a humble worshipper's bag in the porch of Kazan Cathedral in St Petersburg, was convinced of Nicholas's kindness.

In the end, as everybody knows today, all the purely negative traits of the last Romanov sovereign had their colours so thickened that they came to overshadow all else in the man. The result was a daub of a portrait, and such a daub has been reproduced in many books and led many to form the impression that 1917 and all its terrible consequences should be laid at Nicholas's door. That judgment is nonsensical. At the lowest level, Nicholas was not big enough to give an impetus to a metamorphosis on a national scale. He certainly had his complexities but those were of a kind any ordinary man might possess. The root of Nicholas's tragedy did not lie either in himself or in his marriage. It stemmed from the accident of birth.

He was the only Romanov sovereign to have had a normal childhood set against an unshakeably normal background. Enough has been said about the family life of Alexander III and his Empress to see that the background was spared the ugly consequences of parental discord. None the less, affection on its own could not fill all the needs where an eldest son was concerned, and far too little was made of the future one day to fall to his lot. Nicholas's tutors were by no means mediocrities, but not one of them seems to have made the least effort to make their pupil overcome an excessive shyness, an almost morbid reserve, and a dangerous proneness to follow any counsel once it happened to accord with his personal need of the moment. Nor was anything done to fit the curriculum to the boy's abilities. The tutors were answerable to the Emperor alone and had to follow his wishes. In Alexander's opinion, mathematics and science were far more important than humanities, and that was a road Nicholas should never have had to tread. A different, wisely-balanced programme would have prepared his mind for the rudimentary knowledge of statesmanship. In the final reckoning, his own kind should have formed the centre of all his studies rather than mathematical formulae and the complicated problems of metallurgy.

Early grounded in French, English and German, Nicholas was taught neither Latin nor Greek. There was a certain amount of history, geography and political economy, and his tutors rather cautiously pronounced him to be 'studious but not brilliant', a somewhat disappointing judgment for the father. Their reports about the boy's character were equally cautious, if not non-committal. Nicholas was neither liar nor actor in his boyhood, but his reserve early enough formed a shell few could penetrate, and his surfaces were so many cryptographs.

His tutors failed sadly in at least one particular: they should have done far more to enlarge their pupil's vocabulary. All through his life Nicholas's diaries and letters would reflect an almost incredible poverty of language.

There was not much in common between the father and the son, though Nicholas came to share some of the Emperor's views, such as anti-Semitism and an indifference to foreign opinion. Fortunately he never came to echo the slogan that 'Russia was for the Russians'. Nor was there any affinity of manners between father and son: Alexander's ruggedness of speech and behaviour was wholly absent in Nicholas, whose gentleness and courtesy were remarked even by those who disliked him. The exaggerated shyness at court functions and other public occasions slipped off him once he found himself among his family and those who were 'sympathetic' to him. Such people, meeting Nicholas in an unlatticed mood, approved of him wholly. The disastrous famine of 1890-1 caused the American government to send a relief mission to Russia, and its head, Dr Talmage, met the heir several times. The subject of famine relief touched the Tsarevich very deeply. According to Dr Talmage, '. . . [he] is a most lovable young man, thoroughly cultured. . . . Neither Russians nor Europeans need fear anything from him in the way of antagonisms and asperities.' The same Witte who had little praise for Nicholas as emperor wrote enthusiastically about the heir's 'hard work' as Chairman of the Siberian Railway Committee summoned by the Emperor in 1890 in order to eliminate constructional delays. That particular activity fired Nicholas indeed. He examined all the reports most conscientiously, he consulted experts, he travelled about, greatly enlarging his acquaintance with the Empire one day to be his, and never missed a single meeting of the committee. Yet, at the very same time, the entries in his diary about the sittings of the Council of State speak of a boredom the heir to the throne should never have felt. There is no mention of him speaking at any of those sittings.

In the spring of 1894 he became engaged to Princess Alix of Hesse-Darmstadt. On his part, it had been a long, tedious and wellnigh desperate wooing, partly owing to her reluctance to enter the Orthodox Church and partly because of his parents' various objections. They had met Princess Alix in Russia during her visits to her elder sister, Elizabeth, married to Grand-Duke Serge, the Emperor's brother. Neither Alexander nor Marie had taken to Alix whom they thought 'gauche', and the Emperor was apprehensive of the possibly extended British influence if she married his son.

In April 1894, however, the last difficulties were overcome. They were all together at Coburg for the wedding of Princess Alix's brother, and that same evening Nicholas wrote in his diary: '. . . a heavenly, unforgettable day. . . . My betrothal with dear, beloved Alix . . . [have been] in a dream all day long. . . . A cold, grey day, but everything is bright in my heart. . . . We walked and talked . . . so peaceful & good to be with her . . . [All] is paradise. . . .'

In the following June Nicholas joined his fiancée at Windsor, a young man in good health, still treading 'the paths of paradise', a happiness he had all but despaired of having become his permanent sanctuary. One day he went to Westminster to hear a debate in the Commons, and T. P. O'Connor recorded his impressions of that visit.

'. . . there was something singular and even a little sinister and foreboding in the manner in which the Tsarevitch entered the Peers' Gallery. He was accompanied by a small group of gentlemen-in-waiting; they remained a little behind, giving him the opportunity to advance forward to the seats . . . reserved for Royalty. He seemed shy, uncertain, indecisive, looked back as if to get a hint, and altogether went to his place with much awkwardness. There was something suggestive of the lonely and perilous elevation to which he will . . . attain in this little scene – of all the solitude, desertion and uncertainty in the midst of millions of adoring subjects and thousands of servile courtiers. . . .'

A keenly observant eye caught at all the outward details and unerringly interpreted them. Who in the House could have imagined that they were looking at a young man but recently 're-born', to use Nicholas's own expression, who, by virtue of a love most amply returned, was walking 'in paradise'? But the House of Commons was not a drawing-room at Windsor Castle; Nicholas was 'on show' and that among an alien crowd, and he behaved in precisely the same way as he would have done at some public function in his own country, a behaviour which had led to so many reprimands from his parents. Uncertainty, timidity, reluctance – all were there.

None the less, the flowering of his love made Nicholas indeed feel 're-born' in more senses than one. His horror at the national distresses and his quality of compassion had been there before. Otherwise, his life had been carefree. His father still seemed at the height of his physical powers and the crown remained at a grateful distance from Nicholas who loved music, the theatre and dancing. Until his engagement, the diary is little more than a record of balls and banquets, hunting and shooting parties, his military duties

determined by parades and manoeuvres. Nothing – with the exception of his Siberian Committee work – made a single serious inroad
into that frothy existence.

But now he had won his Alix, in whose eyes all froth was unthinkable, who wanted 'all of him' and was herself 'wholly his', and
there were to be no reservations between them. Whatever would
come later, the girl from Darmstadt certainly succeeded in turning
a carefree imperial sprig into a young man with a clarified consciousness of his future responsibilities. She could not teach him the
business of governing but she certainly enlightened him about his
position. Their wedding was to take place in 1895; Alexander III
was then in his forty-ninth year. The girl from Darmstadt, brought
up in a climate of stern duty, saw the man she loved being given
many years to prepare himself for the heaviest burden in Europe.
'And I am resolved to help you in all things,' Alix kept assuring
Nicholas.

Between them, the young couple had built a wonderful house, its
foundations being love, mutual respect, a regard for duty, and an
ever deepening study of an autocrat's problems still many years
distant.

On a day in November 1894 that house lay in ruins, nothing but
their love for each other remaining of all the imagined splendours.
Nicholas II, aged twenty-six, was Emperor.

Even during his father's last days, it became obvious to Princess
Alix, hurriedly summoned to the Crimea, that Nicholas was wholly
disregarded. What orders he gave were not carried out. His uncles,
particularly Grand-Duke Wladimir, spoke to him in a manner
suggestive of a colonel addressing a subaltern. Princess Alix was
furious. 'Be firm,' she wrote hurriedly on a page of Nicholas's
diary. '. . . and make the doctors come to you . . . every day . . . see
that you are the first always to know. . . . Show your own mind and
don't let them forget who you are. . . .'

But Nicholas could not. He was terrified of his uncles. He was
very much under the influence of his mother, and she was the pivot
at the Palace of Livadia. He avoided his father's ministers. In his
fiancée's opinion, Nicholas crept and crawled where he should have
walked in pride. His days were necessarily crowded, and the only

refreshment for him lay in the moments he could spend with her. The doctors, the Ministers, the court, all knew there was no hope of Alexander's recovery, but his son and heir refused to believe it. He had two brothers. One was then dying of tuberculosis and the other was a mere boy. All the same, it would be no idle conjecture to say that, if left entirely to himself, with no fiancée to support and counsel him, Nicholas might have ceded his rights to Grand-Duke Michael, with the Dowager-Empress as Regent.

It did not happen. He married and was crowned, binding himself by an oath 'unto death'. He had no easy inheritance but, in Witte's words, 'in those early days the young Emperor carried in himself the seeds of the best that the human mind and heart can possess,' and that in spite of Nicholas's cold answer to the delegates from the Tver Zemstvo who waited on him one January day in 1895. He said that they were 'to put off all idle dreaming' in their minds. 'I want everybody to know that I hold to the principles of autocracy as firmly as my father did.' The words were spoken firmly enough, but did Nicholas understand what autocracy meant? He would issue one *ukaz* after another, and expect them to be obeyed, but their substance seldom stemmed from his independent judgment. Most conclusions he arrived at came from someone's remark on a given situation, a reaction in England or France, a trusted Minister's suggestion or, finally, his mother's opinion which in the early days weighed far more than that of the young Empress. Broadly speaking, Nicholas was never an autocrat in the true sense of the term.

Having inherited his father's foreign policy, he followed it, but with a difference: he meant to preserve peace but he had a feeling for France and a genuine love for England, which sprang mainly from his affection for his cousins, notably for the Duke of York. Witte had good grounds for his judgment. The young Emperor, however unprepared for his task, did not blunder or fumble at first. Peace of Europe was an essential to him, and he initiated The Hague Conference in 1899, and shaped his views in a clear and convincing manner so that his imperial cousin in Berlin was heard to ejaculate: 'Who would have thought that of Nicky? I quite imagined he would be just a figurehead!'

All the diplomats accredited to Nicholas's court were charmed by his courtesy, his readiness to listen, his concern with whatever they had to say. None of it was faked. He really listened, he was truly concerned, and the awkward gyves of his shyness seemed to have slipped off him.

Some of the home measures carried through at the beginning of the reign spoke of a fair future for the Empire – such as for instance, the Employers' Liability Act and the abolition of the iniquitous mutual tax responsibility whereby a village commune was held liable for all the dues owed by a defaulter.

The people heard of his married life. Three daughters were born to him between 1895 and 1900. They hoped that he would soon have a son. They thought poorly of his wife because of her cold reserve and her reluctance to make herself known, but she seemed a very good wife and mother, and in those days the young Empress did not interfere with any state matters. The Imperial family had left Gatchina for Tsarskoe Selo and Peterhof when they were not in St Petersburg, where they occupied the Winter Palace since the Dowager Empress lived on at the Anitchkov. But the cohesion of the clan was gone. There were unpleasant stories about some of the younger Grand-Dukes, their extravagances and rather wild 'parties'. There were rumours about the tension between the young Emperor and his uncles, particularly Grand-Duke Wladimir and Grand-Duke Serge. Little by little, family entertainment, such a feature of the former reign, began to thin down.

It was at the turn of the century that the Emperor's foreign policy took to zigzagging. Two rabid militarists, Bezobrazov and Ploeve, urged him 'to assert the honour of Russia in the Far East'. Just at that time the Boxer rebellion spread into Manchuria, a country hostile to Russia. Against the advice of most of his Ministers, Nicholas ordered Kuropatkin to occupy Manchuria, and Japan's protest was ignored. The situation grew more and more acute, with Russian troops staying in Manchuria long after the supposed *raison d'être* for their being there had ceased to exist. Finally, in January 1904 the Japanese attack on Port Arthur marked the beginning of a futile and most unpopular war. Defeat trailed after defeat until the Russian navy was annihilated at Tsushima in May 1905, with the Empire being exhausted by enemies within and without. His habitual lack of articulacy made Nicholas write woodenly-worded entries in his diary. That he was badly shaken could be proved by the witness of those who stood closest to him at the time and were not blind to either his defects or his qualities. But it is impossible to say if in 1905 Nicholas knew that he could not rule.

The five years gone before were chequered by political assassinations, recurrent strikes, mutinies in Finland, Poland, on board his ships at Cronstadt and in the Black Sea, and in the Baltic Provinces, to say nothing of frequent peasant revolts. A body of public opinion, wholly unconcerned with monarchical issues, was growing from month to month. And no clear directive came from the throne. Nicholas granted autonomy to universities and tightened the gendarme surveillance of their activities; he promised to restore the Finnish constitution and sent a man such as Bibikov as his Governor-General to Helsingfors. He declared there would be no war in the Far East and permitted hot-headed adventurers to compromise his utterances at every turn. And in the end he granted a constitution which satisfied nobody and summoned a Duma, without deleting the autocrat's title from his manifestos.

The country, aflame from north to south, was ready neither for a constitution nor for a Duma. All sense of history seemed to forsake those in responsible positions. They forgot that Rus, Muscovy and Russia had not thought creatively as a 'nation since the Mongol invasion at the beginning of the thirteenth century. The Great Khan of the Golden Horde, the Princes of Moscow, the Rurik Tsars and, finally the Romanovs, had all imposed their will upon the country in a way which could not be eliminated by one stroke of the pen. The unavoidable relegation of absolute authority had led to bureaucratic corruption. None the less, the authority had remained the unifying factor, the sovereign's person standing for a symbol.

That fact was understood by Nicholas, but he had not the strength to interpret it in the right way. In 1905, the chaos raging over his country seemed to engulf him in its fury, and his one urge was to escape from the ravages by signing a manifesto it was not in him to observe.

The right way would have been to by-pass the government, the bureaucracy and the military and to make a direct approach to the entire nation, a revolution challenging a revolution. It had been possible in the past. It would not have been impossible in 1905. The right way would have been not to hound 'the subversives' and to prohibit their literature, but to bring all of it into daylight, particularly in the heart of the country. And once such a direct approach had been made, Nicholas could have started on reforms, conscious that their meaning was clear to the nation. As things happened, the few and crippled 'concessions' granted in 1905 meant less than nothing to about seventy-five per cent of the population.

Such a direct approach asked for courage, and few among the Romanovs were endowed with it to a remarkable degree, though some of them learned how to go forward when they were afraid of the next step. Nicholas II was no coward in the crude sense of the word; naked violence saddened rather than terrified him, but he both feared and disliked the least 'innovation'. The most trivial departure from routine and tradition made him feel as though he were walking on marshy ground. He had imagined it possible to reconcile the irreconcilables, tradition and reform. So he fumbled, unable to see that the new spirit in the country could not be fought, if it were fought at all, with obsolete weapons. Yet, in the final reckoning, should he be blamed for being blind to the drifts it was not in him to understand? And, once crowned, he felt that he could not turn back, believing, as he did, that the oath was binding unto death.

But he should never have turned himself into a hermit at Tsarskoe Selo, thus losing touch with the nation. The stony imperial enclosure, a most undesirable legacy of the early Muscovite days, could not answer in the twentieth century. The walls should have been razed to the ground. Instead, they grew higher and thicker. The climate of 1917, its breaths already discernible at the end of the previous century, had a foundation given it in 1902.

Moreover, the slavish adherence to tradition served Nicholas very badly. To begin with, it forbade all easy, unstudied entertainment at court, all the ceremonial canons having been laid down in the days of Catherine the Great. In common with his predecessors, Alexander III had found informality, an essential for any normal existence, by accepting his subjects' invitations. With Nicholas II that healthy practice came to an end. The reasons were many: his own shyness, his wife's dislike of parties and her unpopularity in society, and the gigantic responsibilities falling on hosts and on police. Even at Tsarskoe Selo, where the Imperial family lived well-nigh permanently after 1902, daily life was hedged about with endless precautionary measures devised by the Okhrana – naturally with the

Emperor's approval. Even the brief railway journey to St Petersburg involved most complicated preparations, with the permanent way guarded from end to end by armed men of the Imperial Railway Regiment.

The common folk, '*prostóy národ*', were rigidly debarred from bridging the distance. The nobility had five palace balls during the season and a few other equally formal occasions to meet their Emperor and Empress, and that under conditions which served to increase rather than lessen the distance between the Throne and society. Even those widely-spaced entertainments ended with the fancy-dress ball during the 1903 season, the swan-song of imperial hospitality. Never again did the vast halls of the Winter Palace echo to the music of the great orchestra.

Yet there was so much for the people to learn about their sovereign. Nicholas's sincerity in trying to shoulder tasks far beyond his powers, his deep respect for national ways and customs and for all manner of manual work, his ideal family life and, finally, his deep capacity for compassion. However limited his vocabulary, Nicholas left moving enough entries in his diary about all the tragedies since 1902. But he stayed behind a high wall and nobody was allowed to look over it.

Some time in 1907 there was a luncheon for the boys and young men of the Imperial Naval College at the Winter Palace. The revolts at Cronstadt and Sebastopol were still fresh in the memory, and the Head of the College had good grounds to feel uneasy: quite a few of the young people were known to nurse 'pink' and 'red' ideas. Here is what one of those young men, himself no very ardent monarchist, had to say about that day. 'We were served in the Nicholas Hall after an inspection by the Minister. . . . We had no idea the Tsar was in St Petersburg. We had just sat down to a most magnificent spread when he came in unannounced. I dropped my napkin and my neighbour his fork. We all leapt to our feet. He told us to sit down and took his own place at one of the tables. We noticed that he ate very little and drank no wine. . . . Then he made the rounds of all the tables, telling us to remain seated even when he spoke to any of us. . . . Quite apart from his being a Tsar, we all felt that he was a warm-hearted, simple and hospitable man. . . . He spoke little and seemed to say so much, and he remembered names, too, of those who had fallen at Tsushima. . . . I do wish many more people could get to know him as he is . . . could have seen him just like that. . . . At the end there came such a homely detail: he told us to take all the fruit and the sweets to our "sisters" and "those others – you know what I mean. . . ." Never had I imagined the Tsar could be so simple. . . . I am sure nobody would hate him if they knew him. . . .'*

But who, except for a negligible minority had the opportunity of getting to know Nicholas, screened by police and a Cossack escort as he was? People certainly heard much about palace splendours, and they imagined the Emperor to be the wealthiest man in the land. In reality, he was far from rich.

The Russian financial year began on New Year's Day when well over two hundred million roubles were paid into the Tsar's Privy Purse, but only a very small part of it was allocated for his personal use. The entire Romanov clan shared in the revenues, and in the days of Nicholas II their numbers were great. Next came the up-keep of all the palaces in St Petersburg and its environs, Moscow and the Crimea. There were about twenty thousand men and women to find in uniform, board and wages. There were also generous presents at Christmas, Easter and on 6th December, the Emperor's feast-day. A big amount had to be paid annually into the so-called Imperial Dowries Fund. Three theatres in St Petersburg, two in Moscow, the Academy of Arts, four picture galleries and the Imperial Ballet School were all maintained at the sovereign's expense. Nicholas and his Empress between them had just under £40,000 a year, and not the whole of that was spent on themselves: their private charities were great and again the public knew nothing about them, except at second and even third hand. For all the starchiness of etiquette, the daily life at Tsarskoe Selo ran along a well-nigh bourgeois groove. Nicholas II was about as indifferent to food as his father had been. He was equally 'careful' in matters of wardrobe. Once, when on board his yacht *Standard*, he looked at the silk socks worn by an officer and laughed.

'Mine are cotton, and they do get darned sometimes. There is so much to do with the money – I can't afford luxuries.'

* The above quotation is from a letter of Cyril A. Almedingen, Imperial Navy, to his aunt, Hermione Poltoratzky, 13/26th September 1907.

Conventional morality, as it is known today, had been a dogma with Alexander III. In principle and in practice Nicholas followed his father's path. But the matrimonial vagaries among his kin proved to be a jungle the Emperor could not penetrate. All his efforts to make his relations accept what his father and himself considered as sanctities failed most pitifully. When Nicholas wrote about such matters to the Dowager Empress, his letters suggested a bewildered lamb facing a herd of obdurate rams. He liked to think he could be firm and it was humiliating to admit that, so far as his kin were concerned, his firmness had the quality of a melted jelly. Whenever his habitual self-control gave way to anger, they remained unperturbed. He took marriage seriously; he cared deeply for the honour of the dynasty, and such things meant less than a burnt-out candle to some of his relations. They said he was old-fashioned. They argued that fidelity in marriage was as obsolete as the Slavonic script in a modern book. Behind the Emperor's back, they were apt to laugh at the pattern followed at Tsarskoe Selo. 'Nicky has such narrow middle-class ideas,' they said.

One of the Emperor's uncles, Grand-Duke Alexis, the Lord High Admiral of the Russian Navy, neglected his duties and mostly lived abroad with his mistress. Another, Grand-Duke Paul, left a widower with two children in 1901, decided to marry a divorcée commoner, one Madame Pistelkors. In October 1902 Nicholas sent a despairing letter to his mother: 'As long ago as last spring I had a rather stern talk with Uncle Paul which ended by my warning him of all the consequences his proposed marriage would have for him. It had no effect. . . . How painful and distressing it all is and how ashamed one feels for the sake of our family before the world. What guarantee is there now that Cyril won't start the same thing tomorrow, and Boris and Sergey the day after ? . . . In the end, the whole colony of members of the Russian Imperial Family will be established in Paris with their semi-legitimate and illegitimate wives. God alone knows what times we are living in when undisguised selfishness stifles all feelings of conscience, duty, or even ordinary decency. . . .'

In 1902 Nicholas could not have known that such a letter was a bleak prophecy. Within a few years his first cousin, Grand-Duke Cyril, married the divorced wife of the Grand-Duke of Hesse-Darmstadt and was banished from the Empire. His brother Boris and Grand-Dukes Sergey and George lived quite openly with their mistresses, and society did not close its doors to all those '*chères amies*'. Still later, the Emperor's only surviving brother, Michael, took a twice-divorced commoner to wife. And there were other cousins whose behaviour was anything but commendable. The Emperor argued, 'stormed', threatened, and none of it meant anything to them. He would banish the offenders and then forgive them and recall them from exile, though no morganatic wives, still less mistresses, were ever received at Tsarskoe Selo.

'It is my fate always to fail, even in the family,' he once said to Madame Naryshkina, the Empress's senior lady-in-waiting when the news of Grand-Duke Michael's clandestine marriage abroad reached Tsarskoe Selo. 'He was once my heir. Should anything happen to my poor son, my brother ought to be my heir again. Such a woman could hardly be a Grand-Duchess, let alone Empress. For all I know, she may make him a good wife – I have nothing against her personally except those unfortunate divorces. My brother should never have forgotten that people like us don't belong to ourselves.'

Nicholas's birthday, 6th May, fell on the day when the Russian Church commemorates Job, and the idea that his own destinies were interwoven with the Patriarch's misfortunes came to the Emperor early enough. Little did he know that such thoughts were in sad accord with much of the dynastic past which he so stubbornly imagined to be full of splendours alone.

Neither in his letters nor in his diary did he ever complain of 'being misunderstood', or confess to a lack of ability to understand others. Both were there, and both helped to widen the gulf not only between himself and the nation but between him and those who served him. He failed to see the genius of Witte and mistrusted Stolypin, to give but two instances out of many. Nor did those standing closest to him always understand him. The abnormal reticence was all too often taken for cynical indifference. The admittedly thin vocabulary was interpreted as a hallmark of poor intelligence. In the end, many imagined him to be a marionette, opening and shutting his eyes at the bidding of another's will, and that other was his own wife.

That Alexandra had a great influence over her husband is a fact. His weakness, timidity and frequent spurts of vacillation were offset by her firmness and obduracy. Yet he did not always give in to her, and the fatal isolation of Tsarskoe was not wholly contrived by the

Empress. It began in 1902, years and years before the Empress became her husband's spokeswoman in political matters. Between 1902 and 1909, all the mutinies in the army, the navy and in the heart of the country, industrial unrest and so forth made the Emperor's counsellors say over and over again: 'Your Majesty, the safety and the well-being of the country depend on you. We can guard Tsarskoe Selo. We could not be responsible for the rest of your dominions. Sir, stay at Tsarskoe or Peterhof, go to Germany, Denmark or England, but we beg you not to attempt any journeys into the interior. It is not safe to appear among your own people. They have had such a lot of subversive propaganda. . . .'

Nicholas did not always listen to such persuasions. He went to Tambov, to Moscow, the Crimea and other places, and there were accidents none of which were accorded publicity at the time and none of which did him any hurt. The entire body of the Okhrana sighed in deep relief every time their sovereign was once again safely behind the high wall at Tsarskoe. But those journeys of Nicholas's gave the nation no chance of getting near him. Had he gone among his own people in the simple fashion of his predecessors and allowed them to look at him, no forbidding police cordon in between, it might well have led to the end of all mutinies on the land, which would have meant peace for the whole Empire since it stood and fell by the peasants. Only towards the end of the reign did two occasions prove how greatly Nicholas's untrammelled movements were valued by his people.

The first such was in 1913, a memorable year marking the tercentenary of the dynasty, and its celebrations included imperial visits to many provinces.

The splendours of the year began with a Te Deum at the Kazan Cathedral in St Petersburg. The Okhrana had been prepared for 'the very worst'. Their anxiety proved fruitless and their preparations futile. Crowds broke police and military cordons all along the way from the Winter Palace to the Nevsky Prospect. The hurrahs were deafening. The service at the cathedral was delayed because of the carriage being mobbed every few yards. The only ugly incidents to be recorded were the crowds' manhandling of the comparatively few who would not bare their heads. It fell on a winter's day and there had been a blizzard earlier in the morning, but the severity of the weather was not allowed to interfere with the crowds' resolve to see the Tsar.

The same enthusiasm swept over Moscow and all the other places visited by Nicholas and his family. Kokovtzev, his Prime Minister at the time, told the truth when he wrote in his memoirs: '. . . the Tsar's journey was in the nature of a family celebration. All concepts of state and government were pushed into the background . . . [People's] attitude suggested that the government stood as a barrier between [them] and their Tsar, whom they regarded with blind devotion as God's anointed. . . ' The Tsar's closest friends were persuaded that [he] could do anything by relying on the unbounded love and loyalty of his people. . . . The Ministers did not share that idea, nor did the Duma. . . .'

Of course they did not. By that time the monarchist element in the Duma and up and down the bureaucratic ranks had grown rather thin. Not so among the masses, whatever their opinion of the Empress. For one thing, the Rasputin affair, so damaging to the imperial prestige in other social strata, was considered by the common folk in quite a different light. It greatly pleased them to think that one of their own kind, a *mouzhik* and a layman at that, should have won the friendship of the Tsar and his wife. A bare three years later, in December 1916, the peasants would say: 'It is enough for one of our own kind to get near the throne for all those princes and counts to kill him out of jealousy.'

To Nicholas, all the events of the Tercentenary Year came like so many draughts of strong wine. Deep impressions stayed in the mind of a man whom his enemies considered as 'indifferent as a block of wood'. At Ipatiev Abbey near Kostroma Nicholas, unaware that he was to be the last Romanov, felt himself drawn very close to the first of the dynasty, Michael, elected by the nation in 1613.

The rewarding impressions of 1913 came to be confirmed in the following year when Russia entered the First World War and when for the last time the Tsar and his people stood shoulder to shoulder. Nobody who witnessed the scenes in both capitals and elsewhere could have doubted that the nation was held within a common dedication, with their sovereign for a leader. The initial successes of the Russian armies certainly enhanced the mood of resolute oneness. Grand-Duke Nicholas was in supreme command. The Empress disliked him and Rasputin urged his dismissal, but the Emperor would not hear of it and, very much against his wife's wishes, he would not allow Rasputin to leave his Siberian village.

But the fortunes of 'a war to end all wars' worsened sharply in the spring of 1915, particularly on the Galician front, and the idea of treason began seeping in. Crushing disasters at both fronts, growing chaos on the railways, increasing shortages, and deepening discontent led to strikes and mutinies all along the home front. In August 1915 Nicholas committed the greatest blunder of his reign by deciding to dismiss his cousin and to assume his office himself. The Ministers, led by Sazonov, were petrified and the country bewildered, but the Empress was triumphant, and her letters to Nicholas between August 1915 and December 1916 are those of an empowered Regent. She wrote to him at the end of August that she knew his 'sun was rising again'. Nicholas replied that he had signed his first Order to the Army 'with a rather shaky hand. . . .' But the change of Supreme Command was quickly followed by an advance into Galicia. '. . . a good omen,' Nicholas wrote to Alexandra, '. . . such a swift one, too. . . . Truly, God's blessing. . . .'

Yet the blessing was lamentably short-lived. Defeat after defeat fell to the Russian lot all along the front lines, and home affairs grew more and more tangled. Nicholas became weary of Rasputin's nominees to ministerial posts: 'you must agree that our Friend's ideas are sometimes odd . . . [Stürmer] cannot make up his mind to do what is necessary. . . . Complaints [come] from everywhere. . . . I cannot make out where the truth lies. . . .' And when presently the so-called ministerial leap-frog was coming to its peak, the Emperor wrote testily: '. . . [my head] is bursting with all these names. . . . Our Friend's opinions of people are sometimes very strange . . . one must be careful . . . all these changes are not good for the country.' A little later, in November 1916 he bluntly told his wife that Stürmer could not obviously overcome the difficulties. . . . 'Risky to have [Protopopov] at the Ministry of the Interior. . . . I beg you, do not drag our Friend into this. The responsibility is mine. . . .'

But Alexandra travelled down to the Imperial Headquarters and argued her case. Protopopov was appointed.

About a week before Christmas, Grand-Duke Paul, long since reconciled to his nephew, stayed with him at Moguilev. The Grand-Duke's wife, Princess Paley, remembered that her husband 'was struck by the Emperor's perfect serenity. . . . By that time he had heard the news from Petrograd. He did not speak of it but he had the air of a man released from a nightmare. . . .'

But the killing of Rasputin could never have stemmed the course of the national avalanche.

One day at the beginning of February 1917, the long since unused state apartments in the Alexander Palace at Tsarskoe Selo came to life again. All the porcelain stoves were lit, and the crystal chandeliers seemed like so many flaming flowers grown in a magic garden. Masses of flowers engayed the rooms – white lilac, violets, mimosa, iris, lilies of the valley and hyacinths; the Emperor and his wife were giving a dinner in honour of the British delegates, Lord Milner, Lord Revelstoke and Sir Henry Wilson. Being the *doyen* of the diplomatic corps, Sir George Buchanan sat to the right of the Empress who wore a cream silk gown embroidered in silver and blue, with diamonds in her hair and on her wrists.

He could not but notice that both host and hostess seemed tired and the young Grand-Duchesses were rather silent. But the delegates' business was not broached at table. The dinner was a purely social occasion, and Buchanan would long remember it as 'a friendly last meeting'. He would never see either the Emperor or his wife again.

The French ambassador had no such nostalgic memories of the evening. He preferred to find fault with the food. It was more or less a state dinner, but the guests were not offered any hors-d'oeuvres, savoury or dessert, and nothing but very ordinary Crimean wines were served. Paléologue recorded the menu in his memoirs: cream of barley soup, trout in aspic, roast veal, chicken with cucumber salad and tangerine ices. Accustomed to the lavish black market hospitality of Petrograd, Paléologue most likely did not know that Nicholas and Alexandra, mindful of sharp national privations, allowed themselves no luxuries of any kind. Meat at the palace was eaten twice a week, no more than three courses were served at dinner, butter and sugar were strictly rationed, and the great chandeliers in the private apartments remained unlit. The meal offered to the British delegation must have been a rare feast for the imperial family and members of their household.

And it was more than that. It proved the swan-song of the famous Romanov hospitality. Never again was the great dining-room filled with people fit to break bread at a sovereign's table, and never again were Nicholas and Alexandra to be host and hostess at such a gathering. Good-byes spoken in the crimson and silver-hung drawing-room belonged to an epochal moment, and for the last time a special train waited at the Tsarskoe Selo station to take the Tsar's guests back to Petrograd.

Within about ten days Nicholas left for Moguilev. Soon after his departure, the children sickened with measles. He wrote to his wife about them all going to the Crimea to convalesce. 'It won't be long till I return. . . . Terrible blizzards, working havoc on the railways. If trains don't start immediately, troops will starve in three to four days. This is terrible. . . .' The letter was followed by a brief telegram or two. Then all was silence.

Nicholas's entry in his diary about the abdication is very terse. 'This step must be taken to save Russia and to calm the troops.' Alone, unaided by anyone's counsel, he wrote his last Order to the army. Shulgin was to comment on it: 'How noble were those parting words. . . . One felt that the Emperor did love Russia indeed,' and so noble was that piece of writing that the government refused to let the troops hear it in case the simple and moving sentences were to reawaken their loyalty to the Crown. The Order was never read at all, but copies remained to afford some proof that the last Romanov was not quite a marionette, that he remained loyal to his allies to the end, and that his country's welfare meant far more to him than was alleged by his enemies.

A prisoner, a mere Colonel Romanov,* Nicholas reached Tsarskoe Selo and was reunited to his wife and children. The Tsarevich was very ill and at the time there would have been no question of their leaving Tsarskoe.

They were in March 1917. Certainly, at least, one tentative plan was made to get the entire family out of Russia. Nicholas recorded in his diary that he had been sorting out 'such things as I would need

---

* That rank was given him by the Emperor Alexander III. Nicholas bore it at the time of his father's death and he used to say that he could not very well promote himself to a general's rank.

in England'. But the plan came to nothing. For one thing, public opinion in Britain, moulded by the fantastic stories about the Empress's 'treason', was against their arrival. For another, the power of the provincial government ebbed from month to month, and Kerensky had to reckon with the hardening mood of the Soviet deputies.

A few members of the clan – Queen Olga of the Hellenes, Grand-Duke Paul, Princess Helen of Serbia, wife of Prince John, and Grand-Duke George – were in the neighbourhood of Tsarskoe, still unmolested, but no visitors were allowed at the Alexander Palace, though some news from the outside filtered in. When he heard of a successful attack on the south-western front, Nicholas put down in his diary: 'God be praised – I feel quite different today. . . . 'And in July 1917 he referred to the abortive Bolshevik attempt to seize power: '. . . it was all such a chaos . . . but luckily the troops remained loyal to the Government, and order is restored . . . [Kerensky] is a man in the right place. . . .'

But Kerensky knew he could not keep them at Tsarskoe much longer. A Soviet cell was already established at the palace and the Petrograd Soviet was beginning to clamour for the trial of 'Nicholas the Bloody'. In August they were sent to Siberia. The provincial government had about ten weeks left to them.

The family spent about eight months at Tobolsk, and the first stage was more or less comfortably cushioned, the worst physical hardship being lack of exercise, which fell heaviest on Nicholas, who was accustomed to long daily walks. But with the October Revolution, privations came in spate. Funds provided by the Kerensky government ceased to come. No credit could be expected in the shops, and what authorities there were at Tobolsk did not consider it necessary to provide for the prisoners' maintenance. There were alms smuggled in by nuns of a neighbouring convent, but stringent economies were introduced. The Empress's last letters speak of Nicholas's trousers 'all patched and darned' and his shoes being 'almost past cobbling'.

In the evening of 31st December 1917 the Emperor came to the bottom of the last page of his diary. 'After tea we all parted for the night without waiting for the New Year. Lord, my God, save Russia. . . .'

The guards at Tobolsk were perplexed. 'Doesn't he feel anything?' they asked one another. They could not tell. His unfailing courtesy defeated them. He followed the day's deadening routine as though it did not matter. He sawed logs for the stove. He gave lessons to his son. He read poetry to his wife. Whenever the soldiers spoke to him, he answered politely. He bore all the privations without complaint. A heavy smoker in his early days, Nicholas would spend whole days without a single cigarette and never mention it. His wife alone may have known what he felt through those months at Tobolsk.

It was neither indifference nor despair. Nicholas had come to the end of his road and he knew it, but the knowledge did not break him.

In the late spring of 1918 he, the Empress and their third daughter, Marie, were taken away from Tobolsk to Ekaterinburg. The very last authentic message about the family reached Madame Vyrubova in Petrograd late in 1918. It was sent by Grand-Duchess Olga. 'Papa and Mamma wrote on 23rd of April that the journey over the rough roads was terrible, [but] they are well. They live in three rooms and eat the same food as the soldiers. As soon as the little one [Grand-Duke Alexis] is well enough to be moved, we shall join them.'

The imperial family, their Doctor Botkin and four servants were all reunited at Ekaterinburg in May 1918. They were lodged at Ipatiev House and it was total imprisonment in the Tcheka fashion. Soldiers shared their meals served in a common bowl. There were no plates or forks. Soldiers wandered about the rooms. The family were forbidden to open the windows or to close the door of a very primitive lavatory. Their exercise in a small yard was limited to five minutes daily. Their drinking water was rationed, and the Tsarevich's medicines became more and more difficult to obtain. They had no communication with the outer world. On Sundays a priest was allowed to come and say mass, but they were forbidden to speak to him, and their guards stayed in the room the whole time.

After about three months, one hot night in July, they were woken by their head jailer, Commissar Yurovsky, ordered to dress, and led across the yard into a room in the basement. Alexis was too weak to walk and the Emperor carried his son in his arms.

The room was unfurnished, and Nicholas asked for two chairs for his wife and Alexis. They were brought in, and the family were left alone for a few minutes until Yurovsky, accompanied by ten Lettish soldiers, came into the room. Yurovsky stared hard at the

Emperor and said that the authorities knew about a plan to rescue the imperial family and 'therefore, Nikolai Alexandrovich, you are all going to be shot.'

Later evidence proved that Nicholas was the first to be murdered and that his last act on earth was to step forward to shield his wife. Her final gesture was a sign of the cross. In February 1613, at Ipatiev Abbey, near Kostroma in Central Russia, the first Romanov was hailed as a personified symbol of the nation's deliverance. In July 1918, at Ipatiev House in Ekaterinburg the last Romanov and his entire family were done to death in a manner which later shamed even their butchers. The Tsar's end alone received official mention and that at a later date. In the definitive edition of the imperial correspondence published recently in USSR no dates of death are given in the case of the Empress and the children. 'Alexandra Fedorovna, wife of Nikolai Romanov, born in 1872; Olga Nikolaevna, their eldest daughter, born in 1895 . . .' and so forth.

Nicholas was certainly weak, though on occasions he proved himself capable of surprising firmness. He stood committed to a hereditary pattern by him considered sacrosanct and he never grasped that the flux of history would sometimes carry far greater weight than tradition. His greatest faults lay in his mistrust of those who were really fit to serve him and their country, in the confidence too readily given to wrong-minded counsellors and, finally, in his clinging to half-way measures. Had Nicholas been born a commoner, he would never have made even an indifferent politician. Yet Fate called on him to be Tsar, an almost pathological fear of the burden deep in his heart.

His faults were many indeed, but he did not lack virtues, and to the forefront of them all stood his integrity. Very few people realize today that the war-weary Russia would have welcomed a truce in 1916, and the ending of hostilities would have made millions of his subjects bless his name. But to Nicholas honour meant more than an easily won popularity. To betray the Allies would have meant a slur he could not envisage. Yet he came to be betrayed – first of all by one of his own clan, his first cousin, Grand-Duke Cyril, who chose to declare for the provisional government in so public a manner as to create sorrow and confusion in the minds of many and many in Petrograd. Nicholas was betrayed by his nobility, some among whom, still unmolested in their great mansions, thought fit to give parties whilst their dethroned sovereign was prisoner at Tsarskoe Selo. He was betrayed by his stubborn belief that oaths he considered binding were respected by others, and his very inability to understand revolutionary processes was imputed to him as a fault when the complexities of the social and political needs of the Empire all through his reign would easily have defeated even a Peter the Great. Had the last Romanov married a different wife, had there been no wars, no Rasputin, no ministerial leap-frog, the underground movement in the Empire would have followed a course to it appointed. Alexander III would have continued the struggle and he might have been successful in the end. Nicholas II had about as much strength to face the storm as a poorly-rooted sapling in a November gale.

In the final reckoning, the hurricane failed to produce the eagerly promised metamorphosis. Liberty, lavishly mingled with licence, breathed through the nine months of the Kerensky government, and no longer. There exists a certain affinity between autocracy and dictatorship, but the similarity does not go very far. It was impossible openly to criticize the monarchy in the days of Tsarism. None the less, authority wielded in the monarch's name did not prevent anyone from making untrammelled cultural exchanges with the countries beyond the monarch's rule, and the Okhrana, however savagely persecuting all home-bred dissenters, paid due recognition to the international law.

Nicholas's shortcomings were many indeed, and they came to be blazoned in the four corners of the world, but even their aggregate does not sum up the man whose greatest misfortune lay in the accident of birth.

They may well be called an ill-fated dynasty, though not one of them was as obsessed by a sense of fate as their last representative. Yet the tapestry of the three centuries is not uniformly sombre. Varied splendours of pride, high effort and undeniable achievement have all woven their own threads into the tissue. They inherited a Muscovy well-nigh hidden behind the high wall of its futile separatedness. They moulded a Tsardom into an Empire, its voice and its policy reckoned with by the Western comity. And right through the three centuries, all the Romanov rulers with the exception of Peter II, who died too young, Ivan VI, deposed in his cradle, and the luckless Peter III, possessed one quality which enhanced the meaning of their coronation oath: they loved the country they governed however well or badly, and Nicholas's last Order to his armies was informed with the same spirit which came to life in the words of Catherine the Great: 'The most I could do for the country would be as nothing compared with the debt I owe to her.'

INDEX

INDEX

Date Due